D0563708

Love
Burning
in the Soul

PHIL 248.2209
H295

LOVE

BURNING

in the SOUL

THE STORY OF THE
CHRISTIAN MYSTICS, FROM
SAINT PAUL TO THOMAS MERTON

James Harpur

NEW SEEDS
BOSTON
2005

MAR

2006

New Seeds Books
An imprint of
Shambhala Publications, Inc.
Horticultural Hall
300 Massachusetts Avenue
Boston, Massachusetts 02115
www.newseeds-books.com

© 2005 James Harpur
All rights reserved. No part of this book may be reproduced in
any form or by any means, electronic or mechanical, including
photocopying, recording, or by any information storage and
retrieval system, without permission in writing from the publisher.

9 8 7 6 5 4 3 2 1

FIRST EDITION

Designed by Jonathan Sainsbury

Printed in the United States of America
∞ This edition is printed on acid-free paper that meets the
American National Standards Institute Z39.48 Standard.

Distributed in the United States by Random House, Inc.,
and in Canada by Random House of Canada Ltd

Library of Congress Cataloging-in-Publication Data
Harpur, James.
Love burning in the soul: the story of the Christian mystics, from
Saint Paul to Thomas Merton/James Harpur.—1st ed.
p.   cm.
Includes bibliographical references (p.   ).
ISBN 1-59030-112-9 (pbk.: alk. paper)
1. Mysticism—History.   2. Mysticism—Biography.   3. Mystics—
History.   4. Mystics—Biography.   I. Title.
BV5075.H36   2005
248.2'2'09—dc22
2005007663

CONTENTS

PREFACE

THIS BOOK IS INTENDED as a short introduction to the tradition of Christian mysticism over the last two thousand years. It is not aimed at theologians or other specialists but at those who have little or no knowledge of the subject matter and who wish to dip their toes into the vast ocean of mysticism. My modest hope is that readers might become sufficiently curious to read the writings of the mystics themselves, many of which are accessible and provide fascinating insights into the soul's journey toward God (the autobiography of Teresa of Ávila and the journals of Thomas Merton spring to mind). Or they might wish to turn to specialist secondary sources, such as the works of Evelyn Underhill or the volumes in Bernard McGinn's magisterial *Presence of God* series. The bibliography gives a selection of the works I have found most informative and engaging in the writing of this book.

The approach I have taken is a historical one. Anthologies of mystics are sometimes difficult to absorb, if only because mystics can often sound very much like one another. This is not only due to the fact that the experience of the presence of God is likely to be similar down the ages: mystics also consciously use in their writings images, symbols, and metaphors that they have borrowed from past authors in the same mystical tradition. So I have set the mystics in the context of their times and given brief outlines of their lives partly as a pragmatic strategy, a way of separating the mystics from each other and making them easier to remember. Thus, it was Catherine of Siena who helped to persuade Pope Gregory XI to move the papacy back to Rome from its "exile" in Avignon, whereas it was her namesake, Catherine of Genoa, who worked selflessly in a hospital alongside her husband. Gregory of Nyssa was a Cappadocian Father and the brother of Basil, founder of the monastic tradition in Eastern Christianity, whereas Gregory the Great was a Roman monk who became pope at a time when Rome was being threatened by the Lombards.

But context is principally important for showing how the light of mystical practice and experience was refracted into the colors of different cultures and mores. As Evelyn Underhill, a modern authority on mysticism, has written: "In reading the mystics . . . we must be careful not to cut them out of their backgrounds and try to judge them by spiritual standards alone. They are human beings immersed in the stream of human history; children of their own time, their own Church, as well as children of Eternal Love. Like other human beings, that is to say, they have their social and their individual aspects; and we shall not obtain a true idea of them unless both be kept in mind."[1]

I have therefore broken the book up into short chapters relating approximately to different historical or cultural epochs, which I have sometimes called by conventional terms such as "The Dark Ages" or "The Age of Enlightenment." Historians never tire of pointing out—and rightly so—that such terms are merely shorthand conveniences, used for the purposes of simplification and ordering. I should like to reiterate this view: history is a river without dams at regular intervals chopping up its flow. Otherwise it would be theoretically possible, as they say, to go to bed during the Middle Ages and wake up next morning in the Renaissance. So the brief historical introductions that preface each chapter are no more than simplified scene setters. They might be viewed as backdrops appearing as the curtain is raised on each new scene, before the players have made their entrances.

The players themselves, the Christian mystics, span two millennia, from the time of Christ to Thomas Merton and the Vietnam War era. I have concentrated on Western mystics but have included a chapter on the Orthodox tradition. It goes without saying that in an introductory work of this scope and size, much too much has had to be omitted, both in terms of the number of mystics and in the detail of the lives and teachings of those included. Nevertheless, it is my hope that I will have given enough of the flavor of the Christian mystical tradition to whet a greater appetite.

Even labors of love require support and encouragement, and I would like to thank Eveline, Grace, and Patrick for theirs. Also, many thanks to the staff of the Boole Library at University College, Cork, who have been of great assistance to me.

Love
Burning
in the Soul

INTRODUCTION

Who may ascend the hill of the Lord?
Who may stand in his holy place?
                                                    —Psalms 24:3

THERE IS MORE THAN ONE WAY of approaching, experiencing, and describing a reality. The astrophysicist and the astronaut, for example, will each have a different perspective of the moon. The astrophysicist might describe it in the following terms: "The Moon is a natural satellite of the Earth. . . . [Its] mean density is about 3.34 grams per cubic centimetre, close to the density of the Earth's mantle; but studies of rocks returned from the Moon's surface indicate that the Moon's interior composition is not the same as that of the Earth's mantle and that in the Moon there is only a very small (possibly no) core. Many of the rock samples retrieved from the large, dark, relatively smooth areas of the face of the Moon called the maria are best described as basalts, but they are uncharacteristic of any known terrestrial rock or meteorite. They are about the colour of graphite—charcoal gray."[1]

The lunar astronaut, however, is in a position to give a different order of description of the moon. James Irwin, the eighth man to land on the moon, in 1971, said after the experience: "I felt like I was an alien as I travelled through space. When I got on the moon, I felt at home. We had mountains on three sides and had the deep canyon to the west, a beautiful spot to camp. I felt in a way as Adam and Eve must have felt, as they were standing on the Earth and they realized that they were all alone. I talk about the moon as being a very holy place."[2]

The astrophysicist analyzes on the basis of empirical data, mathematics, and other scientific expertise. But the astronaut can describe what it *feels* like to be on the moon, to participate in it emotionally. Irwin calls his landing there a homecoming and conjures up the grandeur of the lunar topography, his allusion to Eden giving the place a primeval sacred quality. It should be stressed, however, that the two different perspectives are both valid and complementary: astrophysicists and astronauts together build a picture of the same reality, approaching it from different paths.

Similarly, theologians (who may be mystics as well) and mystics (who may be theologians) approach God in different ways. Theologians debate and write about such matters as the nature of God, or the relationship between God and Christ or God and humanity, trying to express subtleties of distinction in as precise a way as possible and building on a traditional corpus of writings. Mystics may do the same— for it is important to remember that until late medieval times the distinction between mystics and theologians was blurred, but what makes mystics unusual is that they claim to have had a direct, firsthand experience of God. Like astronauts, this gives them the authority to say what it feels like to know reality—which in their case is the ultimate reality: God.

At this point it is necessary to consider what exactly is meant by the terms *mystic* and *mysticism*, especially as they occur in the Christian tradition. In the same way that it is virtually impossible to define universal concepts such as *beauty* and *love* satisfactorily, it is extremely difficult to pin down mysticism in a way that does justice to all the experiences of those traditionally considered to be Christian mystics. The visionary, emotionally charged writings of the medieval English mystic Julian of Norwich, say, are very different from those of John of the Cross, with his rejection of visions and voices and emphasis on the soul's purgation on its way toward union with the divine. However, it can be safely said that the experience of mystics has usually revolved around a direct apprehension or awareness of God—an experience that goes beyond the rational faculty of the mind and self-willed activity. It can also be said that it is an experience that has often required devoted and disciplined preparation (for example, through prayer and ascetic practices) and that it admits of degrees of profundity, from relatively mild spiritual illumination to union with God, a conjoining in which the will of the mystic is obliterated, and which is often described as a spiritual marriage.

Modern commentators on mysticism have articulated their encapsulations of it along these lines. Evelyn Underhill said that mysticism "is the art of union with Reality" and that "the mystic is a person who has attained that union in a greater or lesser degree; or who aims at and believes in such attainment."[3] Bernard McGinn has said that mysticism is "the preparation for, the consciousness of, and the reaction to what can be described as the immediate or direct presence of God."[4] Joan M. Nuth says that mystical experience "involves an intense awareness of God's presence, accompanied by a knowledge and love of God that are recognized as extraordinary."[5]

As both McGinn and Nuth imply, the aftermath of the mystical experience is crucial to its definition: one of the traditional ways of distinguishing true from false mysticism has been to examine the fruits in question. Whereas false mysticism might result in a self-indulgent basking in spiritual delight, true mysticism has traditionally led to a profound transformation in the individual, who is blessed with a greater capacity for spiritual virtues, such as a heightened sense of compassion or greater humility or strength and energy in performing charitable works. Francis of Assisi was tireless in his preaching and ministry to the poor; Teresa of Ávila combined profound contemplative prayer with a reforming zeal that resulted in the creation of a new Carmelite order; Catherine of Genoa toiled away in her local municipal hospital.

Of course, there is bound to be a gray area as to who is or is not a mystic. For example, there is scholarly debate about the status of supernatural or suprasensual experiences such as visions, ecstasies, locutions (hearing what appears to be a divine voice), clairvoyance, and so on. Many mystics seem to have experienced these phenomena, but most have emphasized that they are ancillary and inessential to the direct awareness of the presence of God. Indeed, some mystics, such as John of the Cross, have been severely critical of suprasensual experiences, questioning their provenance. The general view is that the greater the pictorial content of a vision, the more the individual's personal experience and imagination is involved. For example, Paul's experience on the road to Damascus, when he saw a divine, literally blinding, light and heard the voice of Jesus, is often regarded as more of a vision and less of a mystical experience than the occasion when he was swept up in a visionless rapture—"caught up to the third heaven"—and he was unable to tell whether he was "in the body or apart from the body."[6] Clearly, much hinges on what the content of the vision or locution is and what effect, if any, it has on the life of the individual. The medieval German nun Hildegard of Bingen seems to have seen reality in a pictorial way denied to ordinary folk, but did she in her visions experience the presence of God?

Another area of debate concerns whether it is possible to be a mystic by writing about mysticism or contemplation without necessarily having had a "mystical experience." The question arises because there have been some persuasive mystical theologians (mystical theology being the science and study of the spiritual life), such as Meister Eckhart and Walter Hilton, who did not directly claim to have mystical experiences in the way that, say, Teresa of Ávila or Angela of Foligno did. Ultimately, it is impossible to assemble empirical evidence to "prove" whether someone has had a genuine mystical experience or not, and as Bernard McGinn has pointed out, it ends up being a fruitless exercise trying to sort out the experiential mystics from those who have only written about mysticism: "Theologically speaking, the issue is not, Was this person really a mystic because he or she claims to have had the experience I define as mystical? but, What is the significance of her or his writings, autobiographically mystical or not, in the history of Christian mysticism?"[7] In short, what matters in the end are the mystical texts themselves and the extent to which they shed light on the experience of becoming aware of the presence of God and its transformatory effect.

After this brief consideration of what is meant by *mystic* and *mysticism*, it should be noted that the use of *mystic* to describe someone who has had a direct experience of God did not come about until the later Middle Ages. Until that point, those whom we would now consider to be mystics were covered by the word *contemplatives*—which is used more or less synonymously with *mystics* in this book. (On a historical point, *mysticism* comes from the Greek *mysterion*, meaning something "secret" or "hidden," and it was originally used in the context of ancient pagan "mystery religions," such as those connected with Orpheus and Mithras. In the early Christian era, the adjective *mystikos* was first used in conjunction with reading the Bible and referred to the "hidden" meaning of the text, the deeper spiritual level of interpretation inspired by God. The word was also used to describe sacramental rites, especially the Eucharist, and also broadly came to mean "spiritual" or "sacred.")

Contemplatives, usually monks, were those whose lives revolved around the practice of contemplation, which had, and has, a technical sense. First of all, it is usually differentiated from meditation, which involves concentrating and reflecting upon a biblical passage or a sacred image or a mystery of the faith in order to gain a greater spiritual understanding or depth of feeling. Contemplation or contemplative prayer differs from meditation in that it is nondiscursive: it moves beyond the use of thought, words, and reflections to a point where the contemplative reaches a simple, loving attention on God. Contemplation is also divided into two types: "acquired contemplation" involves a degree of effort on the part of the individual, whereas "infused contemplation" comes as a result of divine grace. Those attracted to contemplative prayer naturally needed a certain amount of time and solitude in which to reach a direct communing with God, so it is not surprising that the great seedbeds of Christian contemplation or mysticism up to the Reformation were the monasteries.

It is one thing to have a mystical experience, but it is quite another to describe it, since by definition it occurs beyond the temporal in a realm where time and space, and the words used to describe the content of those dimensions, are no longer relevant. So mystics down the ages have had to resort to metaphors, similes, and symbols to convey the inexpressible. The medieval English mystic Richard Rolle talks about being "enflamed with the fire of Christ's love." Bernard of Clairvaux refers to the ingress of the divine softening his "hard and stony" heart and that when the feeling of euphoria disappeared it was as if a flame had been removed from a "bubbling pot." Catherine of Genoa says that the serenity the soul finds in God is like being "immersed in an ocean of utmost peace."

For some mystics the ineffability of the experience of God led to an approach that became as the negative, or "apophatic," way. This maintains that with God, about whom human concepts are ultimately inadequate, it is truer to express what he is not than what he is. So mystics in the apophatic tradition, such as Dionysius the Areopagite, Meister Eckhart, and Jan van Ruysbroeck, prefer to use terms such as "darkness," "nudity," "the void," and "the abyss" to convey the immeasurable and inexpressible divinity.

Many mystics not only described their encounters with the divine but went on to reflect upon, analyze, and write about their own and others' mystical experiences. This gave rise to mystical theology. One important development within this tradition was the idea that the soul's path to union with God had three parts to it. This tripartite journey, probably first formulated by Origen in the third century, became firmly established in the Middle Ages (and is referred to throughout this book). The three stages were called purgative, illuminative, and unitive. The first one, the purgative, involves the soul purifying itself by getting rid of bad habits and vices (such as gluttony and laziness) and cultivating Christian virtues, for example, patience and charity. In short, it represents the conversion from the worldly to the spiritual life. The second, illuminative, stage carries on from the first: the soul is further weaned from its attachment to the world and increasingly becomes illuminated by spiritual virtues. The last, unitive, stage involves the final process of being united with God.

It should be pointed out, however, that the three stages do not necessarily constitute a straightforward progression—for example, aspects of purgation and illumination can recur even during the unitive stage. Also, the Christian mystic's union with God is a union with a transcendent, personal being, not some impersonal cosmic principle (as epitomized by the Neoplatonic philosopher Plotinus's "flight of the alone to the Alone"). And for Christians, union with God always means that the distinction between creator and created is maintained—it is a union of wills and not a complete absorption and loss of identity on the part of the individual.

This book, then, is, properly speaking, an introduction to the written record of the mystics and mystical theologians of the last two thousand years. It combines descriptions of the mystics' experiences of encountering the presence of God with their reflections on the whole phenomenon of contemplation. It also attempts to put the voices of the mystics into the contexts of their individual and historical circumstances. Although mystical experiences have a timeless quality that transcends the boundaries of different ages, the way they are expressed and the theology that surrounds them are influenced by the currents of history. The systematization of the mystical path outlined by Bonaventure is as indicative of the medieval Scholastic period in which he lived as the reasonableness of the writings of William Law is of the Age of Enlightenment.

And if the way in which the mystics described the journey toward divine union was subject to time and place, so too was the way in which they prepared themselves for contemplation. For the fourteenth-century German mystic Henry (Heinrich) Suso, mortification consisted of several years of severe, self-inflicted physical pain. He wore a hair shirt and a close-fitting undergarment lined with brass nails, and he had a pair of leather gloves fitted with brass tacks, which "he used to put on at night, in order that if he should try while asleep to throw off the hair undergarment, or relieve himself from the gnawing of the vile insects, the tacks might then stick into his body."[8] More than three hundred years later, at the start of the Age of Enlightenment, the French mystic François Fénelon had a very different view of mortification: "We will find enough to mortify ourselves by entertaining contrary to our taste the people we cannot get rid of, and being tied down by all our real duties."[9]

It is difficult, however, to establish for certain what effect particular social or personal circumstances may or may not have had on the spirituality of different mystics. Is it significant that Catherine of Siena was born with a twin sister who died at birth (as some scholars have suggested)? That Julian of Norwich grew up at a time when the Black Death was raging over Europe (were her well-known words *"And all shall be well and shall be well, and all manner of things shall be well"* a mantra of self-reassurance rather than an expression of hope?)? And that John of the Cross, famous for his description of "the dark night of the soul," was incarcerated in the dark night of a prison by his fellow Carmelites?

It was undoubtedly significant that the medieval Beguine teacher and mystic Marguerite Porete lived at a time when irregular religious movements, especially those involving women, and writings and attitudes that challenged the authority of the church were being dealt with severely. If she had been born a few hundred years later, it is unlikely she would have been burned at the stake (in 1307). And in the Romantic age in Britain, it is not surprising that individuals with mystical temperaments (for example, the poet William Blake) would have preferred to remain outside the established church, for which *mysticism* was still associated with the pejorative term *enthusiasm*. Nor is it surprising that the modern French mystic Pierre Teilhard de Chardin developed his idea of spiritual evolution at a time when the theories of Charles Darwin (who died in 1882, the year after Teilhard was born) were very much in the air.

Love Burning in the Soul begins with New Testament times and the Gospel accounts of the mystical experiences of Christ, along with the writings of Paul and John, who laid the foundations of Christian mysticism. It describes how the church developed within the Roman Empire and how church fathers such as Clement of Alexandria and Origen had to formulate their view of God and the divine against a background of heretical Gnostic teachings and pagan Neoplatonism, which itself, especially through the teachings of Plotinus, had a far-reaching influence on successive generations of Christian mystics, from Augustine onward.

The Roman Empire became Christianized in the fourth century through Emperor Constantine the Great and his successors, and mysticism developed both in the eastern and western halves of the empire. In the East, the Cappadocian Father Gregory of Nyssa, who believed that the outer world was only "the garment and drapery of God," became renowned as the most mystical of the early Eastern Christians. Meanwhile, in the West, Augustine of Hippo in northern Africa, one of the giants of the church, emphasized the importance of self-knowledge in mysticism and the idea that man, or rather man's soul, is the image of God.

After the fall of the Western Roman Empire in the fifth century, most of western Europe entered the so-called Dark Ages. Meanwhile, in the Eastern church, Dionysius the Areopagite—the name attributed to someone who was probably a Syrian monk—wrote an enormously influential treatise that stressed the negative, or apophatic, way to God (he constantly uses phrases such as "divine darkness" to refer to the ineffability of God). In the West, Irish and British monks and missionaries kept the flame of faith burning both at home and on the European continent, and in the 800s the learned Irish philosopher and theologian John Scotus Erigena became a crucial link in transmitting early Christian mystical teachings to the later medieval world.

By the dawn of the new millennium, a new confidence was spreading throughout Christendom. This was manifested not only in the religiously inspired Crusades but also in the great flowering of medieval mysticism. The twelfth century was dominated by the figure of Bernard of Clairvaux, whose spirituality was based around the central place of love founded on humility. The following century saw the rise of the mendicant ("begging") orders, the Franciscan and Dominican friars, which produced a number of important mystics. Francis of Assisi's love of humanity and the natural world and his ideal of apostolic poverty set the tone for Franciscan spirituality, while Dominic's intellectual rigor and stress on learning fed the tradition of the Rhineland mystics, who included Meister Eckhart, Johannes Tauler, and Jan van Ruysbroeck.

Meanwhile, in the East, in the thirteenth and fourteenth centuries, a mystical practice known as hesychasm became extremely influential in the Orthodox Church, especially in monastic communities. Hesychasm, whose champions included Symeon the New Theologian (ca. 949) and Gregory Palamas (1296–1359), was centered on the meditative practice of prayer known as the Jesus prayer (involving the repetition of the phrase "Jesus Christ, Son of God, have mercy on me"). The aim was to reach a state of inner tranquillity that would be receptive to the ingress of divine grace.

Back in the West, the fourteenth century witnessed tremendous social and religious upheavals. At the beginning of the century, the papacy transferred itself from Rome to Avignon in the south of France, so beginning what was known as the Babylonian Exile, a period when popes were widely believed to be prey to the influence of French kings.

In the middle of the century, there came the Black Death, which wiped out one-third of Europe's population, followed by popular uprisings in France, England, and elsewhere. Toward the end of the century the papacy returned to Rome, but there then followed the Great Schism, when Christendom found itself having to choose between two popes, each claiming legitimacy. Yet against this background of death and division blossomed the great flowering of English mysticism through the likes of Richard Rolle, Walter Hilton, and Julian of Norwich. Meanwhile, on the Continent, Catherine of Siena and, in the fifteenth century, Catherine of Genoa, both combined mystical contemplation with an unstinting involvement in the affairs of the world.

The Reformation and the renewal of the Catholic Church, often called the Catholic Reformation, or Counter-Reformation, begins another era. It has been said that there are no Protestant mystics—because of the Protestants' suspicion of miracles, relics, the cult of the saints, and the supernatural in general. But Jacob Boehme, the son of a German Lutheran cobbler, was a major, if sometimes difficult, mystical writer. Central to Protestant mysticism is the goal of becoming aware of the inner light or the divine within, an idea that was important both to Boehme and later to the Englishman George Fox, founder of the Quakers.

The Counter-Reformation saw the appearance of Spain's greatest mystics, namely Teresa of Ávila (1515–1582) and John of the Cross (1542–1591), who together founded the Discalced (Barefoot) Carmelites. Teresa's importance lies in the fact that she gave precise descriptions of the mystic's way, from initial meditation to the so-called mystic marriage. John's mystical writings, some of them expressed in sensuous lyric poetry, include famous expositions of the soul's travails during what he called the "dark night of the senses" and the "dark night of the spirit."

The seventeenth century witnessed the increasing interest in and influence of science and empirical knowledge, a movement associated with names such as Francis Bacon, René Descartes, and Sir Isaac Newton. The same century saw a number of important French mystics, including Francis de Sales, Brother Lawrence—a monk who practiced contemplation while working in the monastic kitchen—and the

Quietists, Madame Guyon and François Fénelon. The Quietists believed that the will must be totally abandoned to God and that any mental activity that involved self-awareness hindered the desired state of perfection. This meant that they tended to reject or neglect traditional practices such as prayer and meditation, so it is not surprising that Quietists were soon accused of error and heresy and that the movement petered out by the start of the 1700s.

The Age of Enlightenment, in the eighteenth century, generally emphasized the place of reason and empiricism at the expense of the irrational and the mysterious, and the mysticism of this period broadly reflects the values of the time. The French Jesuit Jean-Pierre de Caussade and the English spiritual writer William Law were both temperate in their expression of the spiritual life, although no less profound or passionate. De Caussade has a particularly modern feel to his thought, especially with his emphasis on living in the present, the here and now, and on the importance of discovering God in even the most seemingly trivial, everyday things.

The reaction to the rationalism of the Enlightenment was manifested in the Romantic movement, which placed great stress on the imagination and feelings, and wild, uncultivated nature. This new sensibility, with its deeper appreciation of the inner life, was naturally more receptive to personal spirituality than that of the preceding age. Yet the spirit of mysticism seems to have been embraced more by poets and other artists than by the religious. This was certainly true in Britain, where William Blake and William Wordsworth were foremost among the poets who engaged with and explored the mysticism of nature.

The nineteenth and twentieth centuries have seen the churches of the West struggle in the face of a legion of societal changes and crises, such as industrialization, the increasing dominance of science and technology, secularization, world wars, as well as increasing competition from Eastern and other religious sects. Yet the candle of mysticism has been kept alight, notably through the French Jesuit Pierre Teilhard de Chardin and the American Trappist monk Thomas Merton. For Teilhard, who was a professional geologist and paleontologist, human beings are evolving spiritually toward a point he called "Omega," which he identified with Christ. Thomas Merton, like many a mystic before him, had a worldly and sensual life before his religious calling brought him to the monastery of Gethsemani in Kentucky. Merton not only had a deep appreciation of the mystical tradition but married it in his writings with his own acute psychological insights. His involvement in the contemporary civil rights and antiwar movements also showed that mystical thought, even in the largely urbanized and relatively frenetic countries of the West, is still able to cast its sage, calming, and timeless shadow.

1

New Testament Times

I no longer live, but Christ lives in me.
—St. Paul

T HERE WOULD BE NO TRADITION of Christian mysticism without Jesus Christ (*christ* is the Greek form of the Hebrew *messiah*, meaning "anointed one"), whose followers believed and believe that he was the Son of God and that he was executed by order of the Roman governor, Pontius Pilate, rose from the dead, and ascended into heaven. Christians hold that by following Jesus's teachings, with their emphasis on selfless love and compassion, and the example of his life, which includes the darkness of Calvary as much as the glory of the Resurrection, they can reach salvation.

But if Jesus is the cornerstone of Christian mysticism, it is a matter of debate how much he himself was a mystic, at least in the popular conception, established in medieval times, of someone devoted to ascetic practices and contemplative prayer. In the Gospel accounts of Matthew, Mark, and Luke (known as the synoptic Gospels because they share a similar point of view), Jesus is portrayed during his mission more as a spiritual and ethical teacher and a healer than as a contemplative expounding a mystical theology. In the Gospel of John (known as the fourth Gospel) there is indeed a greater emphasis on Jesus's spiritual and mystical thoughts, especially in the Farewell Discourses (chapters 14–17), so called because they mark Jesus's final teaching to his disciples before his death. The problem here is that many scholars believe that John's Gospel records not so much the actual words of Jesus as the reflections and meditations written by the author (traditionally identified with John the apostle but more likely to have been a later Christian perhaps living in Asia Minor) inspired by Jesus's teachings. Scholars therefore refer to "Johannine spirituality" (which also draws on the three New Testament letters attributed to John), and this constitutes the main repository of New Testament mysticism along with what emerges from the life and teachings of Paul, who is in fact often referred to as the first Christian mystic.

The New Testament world was one dominated both territorially and culturally by the Roman Empire. By the time Augustus, the first emperor, died in A.D. 14, Roman-controlled lands stretched from the Atlantic Ocean to the Black Sea, from Egypt to the Rhine, and consisted of more than thirty provinces. The relatively stable conditions the Romans brought extended eastward to Asia Minor and Syria. Only Judea proved the exception in the region. The Jews had come under direct Roman jurisdiction in A.D. 6, and despite certain concessions (for example, exemption from military service), their religious and nationalist zeal was sorely tested by their pagan and often corrupt and tactless governors. The embers of resentment were constantly being fanned, and in A.D. 66 the fire flared into the great rebellion. Four years later, after bitter fighting, the Romans put an end to it, destroying Jerusalem in the process.

Although the Romans could be ruthless, they were also generally tolerant of other peoples' traditions and culture so long as these did not threaten Roman security. This tendency is especially visible in the Roman attitude toward religion. The last centuries B.C. saw an influx into Rome of religious cults from abroad. By this time Rome's traditional state religion, centered on gods such as Jupiter and Mars, was failing to satisfy the needs of many of its citizens, who seem to have found it too cold and impersonal, devoid of an inner spirituality. What they sought was a more intimate and emotional style of worship—one that entailed greater personal involvement. Into this spiritual vacuum came a host of exotic cults and "mystery religions" from Greece and the Middle East. They included those of Dionysus, Orpheus, Cybele (the Great Mother), Isis and Osiris, and Mithras.

Unfortunately, knowledge about these religions is relatively scarce, mainly because their adherents were bound to secrecy. Although they had their own particular sets of rituals and beliefs, they did share some common features, for example, worship of a savior deity, initiatory rites, private gatherings of members, shared sacramental meals, and the promise of personal salvation and life after death. Unsurprisingly, when Christianity began to spread, there were many pagans who viewed it as just another mystery religion, and indeed Paul and later Clement of Alexandria are examples of Christians who used the language of the mysteries in their writings. Yet there were crucial differences. Christianity was not exclusive: unlike most of the mystery religions, it welcomed not only men but women into its ranks. Also, most important, Christianity stressed that its founder was not a mythical deity such as Cybele or Dionysus but a flesh-and-blood historical person.

Jesus

That historical person was Jesus of Nazareth, who was born in about 6 B.C. during the reign of Herod the Great. Concerning Jesus's early life in the town of Nazareth in Galilee, the Gospels have little to say. He would have lived with his parents and siblings, gradually learning his father's, Joseph's, trade of carpentry and attending the local synagogue. There is no mention of his training to be a rabbi, as Paul did, but Jesus was respected for his profound grasp of the Jewish Law. Even at the age of twelve, during a visit to Jerusalem, he was able to question and answer experts of the Law with an understanding that amazed all who witnessed it (Luke 2:46–47). Apart from this glimpse of Jesus's childhood, a curtain is drawn over his early years. When the Gospels relate the next phase of his life, he is an adult, ready to be baptized by his cousin John the Baptist and to begin his mission of teaching and healing.

Central to Jesus's place in the Christian mystical tradition is the Incarnation: for believers, the dimension of God, creator of the world, and the dimension of man, his creation, intersected in the person of Jesus, in whom was realized the perfect manifestation of God's eternal nature. For many later Christians—for example, Athanasius—the extraordinary reality that God had become man inspired the mystical thought that man could become God, or like God. Christ was the door to God: "No-one knows the Son except the Father, and no-one knows the Father except the Son and those to whom the Son chooses to reveal him" (Matt. 11:27).

But to what extent did Jesus himself show mystical leanings during his life? Certainly he seems to have been constantly aware of the presence of God, whom he referred to intimately as "Father." He exhibited various supernatural powers—healing, exorcism, clairvoyance, and prophecy—that have often been associated with mysticism (but do not in themselves guarantee communion with the divine). And there were two major events in his life that have been interpreted as profound mystical experiences: his baptism and, later in his mission, his "transfiguration" on a mountain in the north of Palestine.

According to the Gospels, Jesus's baptism marked the start of his mission to the people of Palestine and confirmed his status as the Christ or Messiah. Matthew's description (3:13–17) of how it occurred is decidedly low-key: "Then Jesus came from Galilee to the Jordan to be baptized by John." Meeting Jesus face-to-face for the first recorded time, John was initially taken aback that Jesus sought to be baptized by him, but Jesus persuaded him to carry out the ritual. Matthew says that as Jesus emerged from the water, he saw the heavens open and the "Spirit of God" descend upon him in the form of a dove. At the same time, a voice from heaven spoke the words: "This is my Son, whom I love; with him I am well pleased." In this way Jesus's destiny as the Christ was confirmed: the sign of the dove—which was a traditional symbol of peace and, for the Jewish rabbis, of the nation of Israel itself—along with that of the heavenly voice confirmed his messianic status (in Mark and Luke, the voice actually says "You are my Son," implying a personal revelation to Jesus rather than, as in Matthew, a public pronouncement aimed at bystanders). It is impossible to say how closely the Gospel narratives record what actually happened, yet it is fair to surmise that Jesus did have a profound mystical experience that inaugurated his ministry, analogous to the call of the prophets Isaiah and Ezekiel in the Old Testament.

The synoptics' accounts of Jesus's transfiguration, suffused as they are with a sense of a glorious light, give a more dramatic indication of a mystical experience. The event occurred after Jesus had led Peter, James, and John up an unnamed mountain in Galilee, traditionally identified as Mount Tabor. At a certain point, as the disciples gazed in rapture, Jesus was "transfigured": according to Matthew, "His face shone like the sun, and his clothes became as white as the light" (17:2). Then suddenly the great Old Testament figures of Moses and Elijah appeared and talked with him. Peter responded to this vision of splendor by telling Jesus that he would be willing to build "three shelters" for them. But the words had no sooner left Peter's lips when a divine voice from a cloud declared, echoing the words at Jesus's baptism: "This is my Son, whom I love; with him I am well pleased. Listen to him!" (Matt. 17:5). After the voice had spoken, the disciples looked again toward the three figures but saw only Jesus, standing by himself.

Jesus's transfiguration came at a significant point in his ministry. Shortly before it occurred he had asked his disciples who they thought he was. In a moment of inspiration, Peter uttered that he was the "Christ, the Son of the living God" (Matt. 16:16). Now, high up on a mountain, Jesus gave three of his closest disciples visual confirmation of his messianic status, which Peter had correctly intuited. Appearing with Jesus on the mountain were Moses, Israel's great lawgiver, and Elijah, preeminent among the prophets. Together they represented the Law and the Prophets, which Jesus had previously said he would bring to perfection (Matt. 5:17). Furthermore, in Jesus's time, many Jews believed that at the advent of the messianic age, Moses, Elijah, and other great figures of their past would appear (Luke 13:28; Mal. 3:23). So the Gospel writers wanted to emphasize that by their very presence, Moses and Elijah were pointing to the fact that Jesus was the Christ.

The scene ends with God's voice speaking from a cloud—itself a traditional symbol of God's presence (Exod. 16:10; Ezek. 1:4). If there was any doubt that Jesus was more than equal to Moses and Elijah,

God dispelled it by pronouncing Jesus his "Son, whom I love." As the Messiah, Jesus had incorporated and gone beyond the Old Testament Law and Prophets. His closest disciples had received confirmation of this through witnessing his transfiguration into light, a potent image that recurs throughout the history of mysticism, particularly in the Orthodox tradition, which emphasizes the place of Christ glorified. Also, in the Middle Ages, the Greek monk and mystic Gregory of Palamas drew an important distinction between God's "essence," which could not be known by mortals, and his "energies," which could be known through grace, and he cited the dazzling light of Jesus's body on Mount Tabor as an example of the divine energies.

Apart from these two initiatory spiritual experiences, Jesus is also reported to have sustained his mission with periods of solitary prayer— probably the most fundamental requirement of mystical practices. Luke says that he "often withdrew to lonely places and prayed" (5:16) and that on one occasion "Jesus went out to a mountainside to pray, and spent the night praying to God" (6:12). The other synoptic Gospels also give instances: "After he had dismissed them, he went up on a mountainside by himself to pray" (Matt. 14:23); "Very early in the morning, while it was still dark, Jesus got up, left the house and went off to a solitary place, where he prayed" (Mark 1:35). It is not surprising that his followers became intrigued by his example: "One day Jesus was praying in a certain place. When he finished, one of his disciples said to him, 'Lord, teach us to pray'" (Luke 11:1).

In short, the impression the Gospels give is of someone who, like the later mystics, ensured that he had the requisite solitude and quiet to engage in intense personal prayer, which gave him the spiritual energy to help him fulfill his ministry of teaching and healing. It is salutary to be reminded that, following the example of Jesus, the great mystics did combine profound states of prayer with dynamic action, the one sustaining the other. Francis of Assisi ministering to the poor, Meister Eckhart running Dominican institutions, Teresa of Ávila founding new convents, Teilhard de Chardin digging up prehistoric fossils in China—these and others lived and worked in the world not at the expense of their inner spiritual lives but made more dynamic by them.

Paul

St. Paul never met Jesus during the latter's time on earth. But Paul's letters are infused with an acute sense of their author's knowing or experiencing a mystical communion with Christ "exalted" (that is, resurrected from the dead and sitting at the right hand of God). He also came to formulate the idea of the mystical body of Christ, that is, the church, in which the faithful participated: "The body is a unit, though it is made up of many parts; and though all its parts are many, they form one body" (1 Cor. 12:12).

Paul was born in about A.D. 10 and grew up in the city of Tarsus in the Roman province of Cilicia in what is now southern Turkey. At some point in his youth he went to Jerusalem to study at the academy of the renowned rabbi Gamaliel. He later became a Pharisee, and he himself says that he was a rigorous practitioner of the Jewish Law (Gal. 1). At first he was a zealous persecutor of the nascent Christian church, but after his conversion on the road to Damascus, he became a fervent Christian and embarked on three arduous missionary journeys to spread his vision of the way of Christ to the people of the Greco-Roman world.

Despite verbal insults, beatings, stonings, and imprisonment, Paul made his missions a great success: he founded churches—some of which he would later encourage with his letters—and made many converts among the Jews and Gentiles he met. When he finally told the Christian leaders in Jerusalem of his travels, "they praised God" (Acts 21:20). That he was successful in his evangelizing is shown by the fact that when in A.D. 70 the Romans captured and destroyed Jerusalem, and with it the local church, there were enough Christian communities elsewhere in the empire to enable the faith to weather the storm and continue to expand.

During his life Paul experienced mystical, visionary, and ecstatic states. His most celebrated vision, and the one that affected the course of Christianity, inaugurated his conversion to the faith. Paul had set out from Jerusalem with some companions on the road that led north to Damascus in the Roman province of Syria. His purpose was to arrest the Christians of Damascus. As he neared his destination, however, "a light from heaven flashed around him." Paul fell to the ground and heard the voice of Jesus asking why he was persecuting him (Acts 9:3–5). Jesus then told him to get up and continue his journey to Damascus and await further instructions there. But Paul now found that he was blind and had to be led to the city. For the next three days he remained sightless. Then a disciple named Ananias, who had been told by God to seek out Paul, came and blessed him: straightaway, "something like scales" fell from Paul's eyes and he regained his sight. He was then baptized into the church.

Paul's conversion is described by Luke, the author of Acts, on three occasions (Acts 9, 22, and 26), and Paul himself refers to it in two of his letters (Gal. 1 and 1 Cor. 15). Luke suggests that Paul's experience was not purely subjective by stating that his companions also saw the brilliant light and fell to the ground (Acts 22:9 and 26:14). Although Luke says that Paul only heard but did not see Jesus, Paul himself wrote that God "revealed his Son in me" (Gal. 1:16), and he equates in importance the post-Resurrection appearances of Jesus to his disciples with what happened to himself (1 Cor. 15:7–8).

Whether or not Paul's conversion experience was, strictly speaking, visionary rather than mystical,[1] he does appear to have had another, completely nonsensuous mystical experience, which he found difficult to relate in words. He mentions it in 2 Corinthians 12:2–4, where he refers to himself in the third person: "I know a man in Christ who fourteen years ago was caught up to the third heaven. Whether it was in the body or out of the body or apart from the body I do not know—God knows. And I know that this man—whether in the body or apart from the body I do not know, but God knows—was caught up to Paradise. He heard inexpressible things, things that man is not permitted to tell." For many later Christians, this ineffable rapture made Paul "the archetypal mystic."[2] Paul also experienced other ecstatic states. Once while praying at the Temple in Jerusalem, he "fell into a trance and saw the Lord speaking" (Acts 22:17); he also had the gift of ecstatic utterance, or "speaking in tongues" (1 Cor. 14:18), and of receiving prophetic visions.

Paul's claim, therefore, is that his experience of Christ did not come indirectly from hearsay and anecdotes but directly as a living spiritual reality. It is this powerful sense of immediacy that gives his letters their persuasive urgency: he writes not as a theologian picking over dry facts but as someone who is in personal communion with Christ. In Galatians 2:20, for example, he says "I have been crucified with Christ and *I no longer live, but Christ lives in me*" (author's emphasis). Becoming like Christ is the goal of the spiritual journey, and it involves identification with Christ's passion and death before eternal life can be gained. Paul also refers to the "Spirit of Christ"—which he seems to use interchangeably with the "Spirit" and the "Spirit of God" (Rom. 8:9)—as the divine vitalizing power that makes us "sons of God" (Rom. 8:14), and he repeatedly uses the phrase "in Christ" to express union with him. (It is this emphasis that has been called "Christ-mysticism"—that is, the idea that people can become united with the transcendent God through the mediation of Christ.)

Paul's mystical instinct was not that of a solitary seeking to be removed from his fellow human beings in order to pursue God, and he warns against the self-indulgent use of spiritual gifts ("But in the church I would rather speak five intelligible words to instruct others than ten thousand words in a tongue" [1 Cor. 14:19]). The gifts of the spirit are to be laid at the service of the church as a whole. Paul stresses the corporate nature of the church and thinks of it as a mystical union whose different members, by participating in the same spirit, make up the one body. There can be no division, and members must share each other's sufferings and joys. No one is excluded from membership, and it is the natural outcome of participating in Christ, of being filled with the spirit of Christ, that external differences are negated: "There is neither Jew nor Greek, slave nor free, male nor female, for you are all one in Christ Jesus" (Gal. 3:28).

John

The Christ-mysticism found in Paul's letters, which were probably written between about A.D. 50 and 60 and form the earliest part of the New Testament, finds a different expression in John's Gospel, the latest of the four Gospel accounts (it is thought to date to about the end of the first century) and the one considered to be the most "spiritual." John attempts to convey to his readers the way in which they can be saved by Jesus Christ through the power of the spirit, and in doing so he attempts to convey the essential nature and role of Jesus in terms of different concepts and images, for example, the Word, light, true vine, and bread of life.

The first chapter of the Gospel introduces Jesus as "the Word" (*logos* in Greek), an idea that carried resonances for both Greek and Jewish readers. For Greeks, *logos* not only had the everyday sense of a word spoken but also meant "reason" and referred to the underlying principle that ordered the universe. In the Jewish tradition, the Word had come to represent the creative power of God—and even God himself. Philo of Alexandria, a Jewish thinker who was a contemporary of both Jesus and Paul, drew on both of these lines of thought in his interpretation of the Word, as did John, who went further by saying that the Word was actually made incarnate in Jesus of Nazareth. John then says that Jesus was the "light of men" and "the true light that gives light to every man," that is, a source of spiritual illumination enabling those who welcomed and believed in him to become "children of God."

Light is an important element in John (he often contrasts it with the darkness of spiritual benightedness or ignorance), and it occurs repeatedly throughout the history of Christian mysticism as the expression of divine reality. So too is the Holy Spirit, to which John, like Paul, attributes an inner spiritual transformatory power (it was the Spirit, of course, that had come as "tongues of fire" to the apostles on the day of the Pentecost, as recounted in Acts 2, enabling them to speak languages they had not learned). In John's account of Jesus's discourse with Nicodemus, a Pharisee who had come to talk to him at night, Jesus makes it clear that people must be born again "of water and the Spirit" (3:5) if they are to enter the "kingdom of God." Later, during his encounter at the well of Jacob with a Samaritan woman, he declares unequivocally that "God is spirit, and his worshippers must worship in spirit and in truth" (4:24). John's motifs of light and spirit were to recur frequently as symbols of the divine throughout the subsequent Christian mystical tradition. To take just one example, the English mystic William Law, writing more than a millennium and a half after John's time, declared: "Seek for Him in thy heart, and thou wilt never seek in vain, for there He dwells, there is the seat of His Light and Holy Spirit."[3]

John's mysticism reveals itself most fully in the Farewell Discourses, during which Jesus explains to his disciples the close relationship between himself, humanity, and God, whom he refers to as the Father. He makes clear his own intimate relationship with God the Father by saying that only through himself can the Father be known: "I am the way and the truth and the life. No-one comes to the Father except through me" (14:6). The human dependency on Christ for attaining the life of the spirit, and the sense of corporate unity engendered by becoming a member of the church, are brought out by the image of the vine and the branches (15:1–17). The vine occurs in the Old Testament as an image of Israel (for example, Psalms 80:8–16: "You brought a vine out of Egypt . . ."), but here John has Jesus referring to himself as the "true vine," the true Israel, and using the image to convey the mystical communion in him without which spiritual death must follow: "I am the vine; you are the branches. If a man remains in me and I in him, he will bear much fruit; apart from me you can do nothing" (15:5).

The strong sense of a mutually interpenetrating union of God, Christ, and believers comes out in Jesus's final prayer, in chapter 17. "I have given them the glory that you gave me, that they may be one as we are one: I in them and you in me" (17:22–23). There can be no closer relationship than Jesus and the Father's, and this is the model for the relationship between members of the faithful, which is sustained by Jesus abiding in them, just as the Father abides in him. In essence this is the Christian mystic's goal: a union with God, through the power of Christ, which also brings about a living relationship with the mystic's fellow human beings. It is a relationship grounded in a love that is again based on reciprocity: "He who loves me will be loved by my Father, and I too will love him and show myself to him" (14:21). For Evelyn Underhill this indwelling love was central to John's spirituality—it is the power through which we come to grasp ultimate realities: "His was that piercing vision which discovered that the Spirit of Love is one with the Spirit of Truth, and that only those who love will ever understand. It was this which definitely established the essentially mystic character of Christian faith."[4]

2

THE EARLY CHURCH

*The more a man loves, the more deeply does he
penetrate into God.*
—Clement of Alexandria

F ROM THE TIME OF THE APOSTLES to the reign of Constantine the Great in the early fourth century, Christianity spread steadily throughout the Roman Empire, particularly in towns and cities, gaining converts from all levels of society. At first the Christian way of life was at odds with the pagan culture in which it existed. The faithful were exhorted to live soberly, dress simply, and refrain from attending gladiatorial shows and serving in the army. More significantly, they refused to sacrifice to the Roman gods or participate in the cult of the deified emperor, even nominally. They kept to themselves and worshiped together in private houses. Inevitably, they came to be seen as outsiders, "atheists" (because they rejected the gods), and even, in the phrase of the Roman historian Tacitus, "haters of the human race," and there were rumors that they indulged in wild orgies, incest, and cannibalism (probably a misunderstanding of the Eucharist).

There was little systematic state persecution of Christians until the third century, notably in 250 by Decius, followed by Diocletian in 303, but they were always vulnerable to the whims of local governors and mobs, especially when a calamity prompted the search for a scapegoat (the church father Tertullian [ca.160–ca. 225] noted ironically that "if the Tiber rises too high or the Nile sinks too low, the cry is 'The Christians to the lion'"). Emperor Nero had set an ominous precedent when he blamed and executed Christians for starting the great fire of Rome in A.D. 64. But for Christians, martyrdom had the reward of a place in heaven among the blessed, and many actively sought it, provoking the authorities to achieve their end. Although many lives were lost in martyrdom, many more were attracted to the Christian cause. As Tertullian pointed out, the blood of the martyrs is seed: the heroic way in which men and women met their deaths impressed onlookers and promoted the faith. There were other reasons why pagans converted. Most evidently, perhaps, was the way Christians helped each other. Widows and orphans were cared for, prisoners visited, burials arranged for the poor, travelers given hospitality, and food made available during famines and war. "See how these Christians love each other!" exclaimed one pagan, according to Tertullian.[1]

As the church grew and established an organization based around local communities led by bishops, it also began to define its doctrine and establish its scriptures. One of the pressures to do so came from the threat of Gnosticism, a hybrid spiritual movement that became prominent in the second century. Gnosticism (from the Greek *gnosis*, "knowledge") was an eclectic movement mixing theological and philosophical ideas drawn from Judaism, Christianity, and Greek and Persian thought, mixed up with astrology, myth, and magic. In its Christian, and predominant, form, it stressed the central place of gnosis, or revealed knowledge, in bringing about salvation. Orthodox Christianity also recognized the place of revealed knowledge but viewed it more as something that had been given to the apostles and transmitted by the church to the faithful than as something directly receivable by the individual.[2]

Gnostics also distinguished between a supreme, transcendent, unknowable god and a lesser creator god, or demiurge, who had made the imperfect world, the human race, and matter. They were dualists, pitting spirit against matter, mind against body, light against dark, and they had a pessimistic view of the world, believing matter to be inherently evil. However, they did think some people could be saved by a gnosis that enabled them to liberate the divine spark within themselves from its prison of flesh so that it could return to its heavenly home. Most Gnostics considered Christ to be a redeemer figure, but they denied the Incarnation: how could the pure spirit of Christ have inhabited corrupt flesh? Gnostics believed Christ had merely assumed the appearance of a human being and therefore did not really die on the cross.

In a world of intellectual change and confusion, Gnosticism, with its esoteric timbre and bewildering variety of beliefs, proved attractive to many. For orthodox Christians, the silver lining to the Gnostic cloud was that in combating it they were forced to define and articulate their faith; for example, Christians came to believe that the soul, although capable of becoming divine, was not inherently so, as the Gnostics thought. One of the first Christian thinkers to enter the lists against Gnosticism was Clement of Alexandria, a city where the movement had put down strong roots. Clement also strove to make Christianity respectable to cultured pagans who doubted its intellectual sophistication; and he was important in mystical theology for bringing a Platonic vision to the Christian spiritual tradition. Following in the same mystical tradition was Origen, reckoned to be the greatest theologian before the age of Constantine. Origen also happened to share the same Alexandrian teacher as the greatest pagan thinker of the time, the Neoplatonic philosopher Plotinus, whose mystical system of reality influenced the Christian contemplative tradition down the centuries.

Clement of Alexandria

Clement of Alexandria, the first Christian writer to use the word *mystical* in his works, is important for the way that he blends Christian theology with the philosophical tradition of Plato, with its stress on the reality of a spiritual realm, the transcendence of God or the One, and the soul's ascent and union with it. As would be the case with Plotinus and subsequent mystics, such as Dionysius the Areopagite, who drew on the Neoplatonist tradition, Clement emphasizes the mystery and ineffableness of God: What can be said, he asks, of something that is "neither genus, nor difference, nor species, nor individual, nor number"? He admits that in practice we do in fact use terms to describe God, such as the One, the Good, Father, and Creator, but these are really crutches for the mind: nothing can be predicated of him, for to do so would be to limit the illimitable. Our understanding of him, the great Unknown, must depend on divine grace and "the world alone that proceeds from him."[3] Clement also stresses the importance to the spiritual lives of the Christians of "true gnosis," or revealed knowledge—as opposed to the false knowledge of the Gnostics, and he was important for developing the notion of "divinization," an influential idea summed up in the affirmation that God became man so that people could learn how to become like God. For Clement, the soul, although not originally divine, was capable of becoming divine.

Not much is known about Clement's life. He was born in the middle of the second century, probably in Athens, and was evidently well educated in the pagan classics. At some stage he embraced Christianity and set out abroad to find a suitable teacher. His travels took him to Italy, Palestine, Syria, and elsewhere, but to no avail. If the Chinese saying "When the pupil is ready, the master will come" is correct, Clement was ready by the time he reached Alexandria in Egypt—where he found the right man: Pantaenus, probably a Sicilian, and a pagan convert who had become a Christian teacher.

Alexandria at this time was one of the great cultural centers of the Roman Empire, the home of a famous university, and a meeting place of people from many different ethnic and cultural backgrounds. In its liberal intellectual ethos, pagan Platonists could argue about the nature of God with Jews, and Christians could debate the importance of faith with Gnostics. It was in this tolerant atmosphere that a Christian catechetical school came into being during the second century. Its aim was to teach theology to Christians, but interested pagans were also allowed to attend certain lectures. Pantaenus was the first known head of the school, and Clement, his pupil, succeeded him in 190, remaining at his post until 202, when a persecution in the city during the reign of Emperor Severus compelled him to flee. What happened to him next is obscure, but at some stage he seems to have arrived in Caesarea in Cappadocia (in modern Turkey), where he probably ended his days.

Clement wrote three principal works: *Exhortation to Conversion* (*Protrepticus*), an apologia for the faith and an attack on pagan worship; *The Tutor* (*Paedagogus*), a practical guide to Christian life and ethics; and, the most important, the unfinished *Miscellanies* (*Stromateis*), a work he compared to a field full of wildflowers because it was written in a consciously random, unsystematic way, engaging its readers more by poetic glimpses and variety than by a solid, methodical approach.

Clement's great challenge was to address himself to the needs of different groups in Alexandria. There were many Christians who had received little or no education and found pagan philosophy obscure and, since they associated it with the Gnostic heretics, suspect. Schooled in the classics himself, Clement was convinced that many a valuable truth could be found in pagan philosophy and poetry and that rejecting them wholesale was counterproductive. Instead he tried to make them at least palatable to his skeptical brethren by insisting that Plato had in fact received his inspiration from reading Moses and the prophets.

Conversely, Clement also wanted to make Christianity attractive to potential pagan converts and to show them that Christianity was not just for the underprivileged of society but capable of sophisticated thought and expression. He was aware that many pagans were disdainful of the literary style of the scriptures, so he peppered his own writings with hundreds of allusions to classical authors; he also summarized Jesus's Sermon on the Mount in a manner the pagan intelligentsia would find congenial.

Clement also attempted to show that far from underpinning Gnosticism, classical philosophy could be used to undermine it. Yet although he attacked Gnostic ideas, he did emphasize the need in the spiritual life for true gnosis, which was not, however, a prerequisite for salvation. Whereas for the Gnostics gnosis was a "skill in the manipulation of words and ideas in order to find a safe path through the cosmic maze,"[4] for Clement true gnosis was set firmly within church orthodoxy and was not just a matter of the intellect: "He who would enter the shrine must be pure, and purity is to think holy things.... The more a man loves, the more deeply does he penetrate into God."[5] Gnosis makes possible the vision of God, the highest human attainment (he refers to the divine vision more than eighty times in his writings).[6] Clement does not ignore the importance of faith, by which we confess the existence of and worship God, but he maintains that "faith is perfected" by knowledge, which comes through the grace of God to those who have prepared themselves. And in the same way that knowledge is added to those who already have faith, so love is added to knowledge, and "the worth of love beams forth from light to light."[7]

Lying at the heart of the soul's mystical ascent to God, this knowledge or gnosis purifies and transforms us, transporting the soul to be with what is sacred and divine, as its own nature is. Knowledge, with its innate light, carries us along the mystical path: "It removes [the soul] to what is akin to the soul, divine and holy, and by its own light conveys man through the mystic stages of advancement; till it restores the pure in heart to the crowning place of rest; teaching to gaze on God, face to face, with knowledge and comprehension."[8]

Origen

In 203 the Christian catechetical school in Alexandria, which had been left rudderless by the departure of Clement during the Severan persecution, was taken over by Origen, who was then only eighteen years old. Origen was more critical of the pagan classical writers than Clement, but he followed his master in trying to reconcile the best of Greek thought with Christian teaching, especially as found in the holy scriptures, and he, too, championed the faith against its Gnostic and pagan enemies. As a biblical commentator, theologian, preacher, and letter writer, he was enormously prolific and wrote literally hundreds of works, although relatively little has survived. After his death, some of his views, as passed down by his supporters, proved to be controversial, if not in error, for example, his idea that no one is ultimately barred from salvation, including the devil himself. But he was immensely influential on subsequent generations, including in the following century the Cappadocian Fathers—Basil the Great, Gregory of Nazianzus, and Gregory of Nyssa—who called him the prince of Christian learning.

Origen's importance to mysticism lies in his Platonist-Christian vision of the one, transcendent God; the essentially spiritual nature of the true reality; and the idea of the soul's return or ascent to God.[9] The soul, he says, is in existence before it inhabits its human body, and it will continue to exist after the death of its corporeal vehicle. When this happens, the soul faces the consequences of its sins and is purged by fire, which is not simply a divine punishment but a necessary, albeit painful, means of purification. Origen is also important for his personal asceticism (influential in monastic spirituality) and the essentially Christian view that prayer, in the fullness of its experience, provides the means for the soul to ascend to contemplate God.

Most of what we know about Origen was written by the early church historian Eusebius (ca. 260–ca. 340) in book 6 of his celebrated *Ecclesiastical History*. Origen was born in about 185, probably in Alexandria, and brought up as a Christian by his parents. In 202, while he was in his teenage years, he suffered a personal tragedy when his father, Leonides, was thrown into prison, then put to death during the persecution of Emperor Severus. The young Origen tried to join his father in his fate, but his resourceful mother is said to have prevented him by the expedient of hiding his clothes. With his father dead, Origen supported his mother and six younger brothers by teaching, and he was also helped financially by a local woman of means. After he took over the catechetical school in the absence of Clement, he was able to devote himself to teaching, reading the Bible, and studying pagan philosophy, receiving instruction from Ammonius Saccas, the teacher of Plotinus. All the while he adopted an ascetic lifestyle, praying, fasting, and keeping vigils. He is even said by Eusebius to have taken literally Matthew 19:12 (the verse that alludes to "those who have made themselves eunuchs for the sake of the kingdom of heaven") and castrated himself, although in a later commentary on the verse he decried taking a literal approach to it.

Origen continued to reside in Alexandria, writing his works, especially his gargantuan commentary on the Bible, until 230. In that year he was ordained a priest while staying in Caesarea in Palestine, an event that his local bishop of Alexandria, Demetrius, saw as a breach of his authority, to which he responded by banishing Origen. So Origen settled in Caesarea, where he founded a Christian school that quickly gained a reputation for excellence. For the next twenty years he continued to preach and write prolifically, occasionally making trips abroad to Greece and Arabia. In 250, now in his sixties, he fell victim to the persecution instituted by Emperor Decius and was imprisoned and tortured. Although he survived the immediate ordeal, the experience eventually took its toll, and he died in about 254.

Perhaps the most important contribution Origen made to Christian mysticism was his biblical exegesis, which he saw as a wholehearted spiritual endeavor, not just a scholarly pursuit, along with his view that the Bible had different strata of meaning and could be interpreted at a literal, a moral, and—the one he favored most—an allegorical level. For Origen, the Bible was a divinely inspired work, primarily a depository of spiritual truths, and its value as a historical record was less significant. This approach, that the biblical stories led to a deeper spiritual meaning, was in line with his belief in the Platonic notion that the things of the material world pointed toward an invisible, mystical realm accessible only to a spiritual elite by their ascent to Christ and God. This view, that the highest realms of spirituality were open only to the few, held the danger of creating a two-tier system in the church comprising a select group set over the community of believers as a whole.[10]

Origen's allegorical method is best known from his highly influential commentary on the Song of Songs in the Old Testament, a method that would later be developed by such greats of Christian mysticism as Bernard of Clairvaux, Teresa of Ávila, and John of the Cross. Origen interpreted the relationship between the lovers in this sensual book (it begins, "Let him kiss me with the kisses of his mouth") primarily in terms of the love between the Logos, or Christ, and the individual soul—Jews had traditionally viewed the relationship as being between God and Israel. For Origen, the soul's love for Christ, despite the sensual language, is intellectual, resulting in the soul's illumination. Another influential concept Origen explores in his commentary on the Song is the idea of the "senses of the soul," which are counterparts to the five bodily senses (so, the reference at the start of the Song to receiving a physical kiss actually refers, he thought, to the soul receiving the wisdom of the Logos). Together, the spiritual senses give the soul the sensitivity to "tune in" to God's will.

Origen was also influential in formulating the idea that the soul's journey to God had three progressive stages, which he characterized as practice of the virtues, natural contemplation of the world and a realization that it is essentially ephemeral, and contemplation of God. This threefold division would later be developed by Gregory of Nyssa and Dionysius the Areopagite, the latter terming the stages purgative, illuminative, and unitive, the form in which they became famous in the later Middle Ages.

Another mystical theme Origen helped to establish was the superiority of the contemplative life over the active life (though both must work in tandem). He found support for this in Luke 10:38–42, the occasion when Jesus visits the sisters Mary and Martha (representing for Origen the ideals of contemplation and action, respectively) and defends Mary's "inaction" in the face of Martha's criticism. Some of Origen's insightful thoughts on contemplation can be found in his short treatise *On Prayer*, in which he talks about the mystical transference of the "eyes of the mind" from the objects of the sensible world to the contemplation of God alone—those eyes will then reflect the glory of God and be transformed into that divine splendor.[11] For Origen, prayer, properly speaking, is not just a matter of directing a petition or supplication or thanksgiving to God but should be a way of life. At the heart of prayer is the practice of the commandments and virtues, so that it consists of a continuous round of holy actions, thoughts, and words. The life of the saint then becomes one extended ceaseless prayer.[12]

Plotinus

Origen's teacher Ammonius Saccas was also the master of Plotinus, one of the great philosophers and mystics of history. Although Plotinus was not a Christian, it has been said that "no single man outside the Bible has exerted, directly or indirectly, so great an influence as Plotinus on the thought of Christian mystics."[13] Drawing on the works of Plato as well as later Platonic thinkers, Plotinus constructed a hierarchical system of reality that had a sort of circular rhythm to it: on the one hand, God, the ineffable, undifferentiated One, flowed out, or emanated, down through intermediary levels to the universe and matter; on the other, individual souls sought to ascend and return to their divine home and unite with the One. His works, which are known as the *Enneads* (from the Greek for "nine," because they were arranged by

Plotinus's pupil Porphyry into six groups of nine sections), deeply influenced Augustine and Dionysius the Areopagite and through them the Christian mystics of the Middle Ages. Plotinus himself experienced mystical ecstasies on a number of occasions, when he was lifted out of his body "into himself" and had the sense of "becoming external to all other things," witnessing a wonderful beauty and feeling that he was united with the divine, before eventually descending again to normal consciousness.

According to Porphyry, Plotinus was born in about 205—he was probably an Egyptian with a Greek cultural background—and studied in Alexandria for eleven years. In 242 he apparently joined the military expedition led by the Roman emperor Gordian III against the Persians, although it is unclear in what capacity he went. He later moved to Rome, where he established himself as a teacher of philosophy, attracting pupils of different ethnic backgrounds and gender, with many of them drawn from among the intelligentsia, including politicians and doctors. He also became friendly with Emperor Gallienus (r. 253–268), through whom he hoped to fulfill his ambition to found a city in Campania near Naples that would be run according to the ideals of Plato (it was to be called Platonopolis), but his plans were never realized.

Plotinus taught in Rome for twenty-five years, living through a period of political turmoil. During this time he gained a reputation for being gentle, kindly, good-humored, and an inspiring teacher; Porphyry said that when he spoke "his intellect lit up even his face."[14] He was greatly respected by one and all and was frequently entrusted with the care of orphaned children, a role he seems to have relished. Just before his death, suffering from a serious illness, he retired to Campania, where he passed away in 270. With his last words he declared that he was trying to return the divine in himself to the divine in the all, which succinctly articulates his aspiration for mankind.

In the *Enneads*, Plotinus sets out his vision of reality, which consists of three descending levels or stages (often called hypostases), which are distinct from one another but also interpenetrating. At the top is the One, or the Good, sometimes referred to as God, although it is not a personal deity like the Christian God. The One is the first principle and is prior to all things that exist, and it is that to which all things aspire to reach. It is so transcendent that it is beyond all categories.

Nothing at all can be predicated it, not even terms such as *being, essence,* or *life.* Nor can it be described in words or thought of or understood in any way.

From the One comes the second hypostasis, known as Mind, or Intelligence (some refer to it by the original Greek word, *nous*). Unlike the conscious act of creation of the Christian God, the One produces Mind through a timeless emanation or flowing out, not through choice but because, Plotinus says, something good will naturally engender a reality that is less than itself. Plotinus compares this process of emanation to the way that a fire produces heat or the sun creates light.

So the One produces Mind, the second level of reality, and Mind is the timeless and spaceless realm of the archetypes, that is, the Forms, or Ideas, of Plato. (For Plato, reality was divided into the material, sensible world of everyday objects and the immaterial, intelligible realm accessed by intellectual contemplation and consisting of the unchanging models, or Forms, of things, for example Beauty and Love. That which exists in the material world is only a copy or a shadow of a divine original in the realm of Forms. So a person's love for another is merely a copy of the Form of Love.) In Plotinus's scheme, the Forms exist in Mind individually, but each one also contains all the others in a system of mutual interpenetration.

From Mind there emanates the third and last hypostasis, Soul, which acts as a link between our everyday world and the suprasensible realm above it. (It might be added here that it was relatively easy for Christian Platonists to associate Plotinus's triad of One, Mind, and Soul with the Trinity of Father, Logos [Son], and Spirit.) Soul has two aspects: the higher one still participates in the realm of Mind, while the lower creates the things of our world—based on the archetypal models that it contemplates in Mind—and gives life and order to everything. Soul not only exists as a universal realm, or as the World Soul, but is also present, in whole, in all forms of life, including, of course, human beings. And just as the World Soul has a higher and lower aspect, so too does the human soul: the higher part can be united with Mind, which shines in and illumines it, whereas the lower part is conformed to sense perception and the external world.

At the furthest point from the One there is matter, which is described as nonbeing. While the One is the manifestation of the highest reality, matter is the embodiment of the lowest and is accounted evil, or rather, the deprivation of good. Although the soul can partake of the divine, it can also, through the encroachment of matter, which subjects the will, become subservient to the body and estranged from its higher nature: trapped in flesh, the soul forgets its true self and God. Yet Plotinus does not say that the material world is evil in itself (unlike the Gnostics, whose ideas he attacked): rather, it was created by Soul from immutable models and is full of beautiful things, which lead us to look beyond them to their divine causes and origins.

So the true vocation of the individual soul is to break free from the chains of flesh and rise to the realm of Mind and thence to God, the Good. The soul must practice detachment, leaving behind its attraction to physical beauty in the realization that it is merely a trace or shadow of something greater, and it must become purified of the corporeal accretions it has gained in the world. Plotinus likens this process to a sculptor of a statue who chips away and polishes a block of stone until he creates a beautiful face. So must we labor at our own inner statues, chiseling and honing, until the divine "splendor of virtue" shines out.[15] Through contemplation the soul can ascend to Mind and achieve union with it, a prelude to union with the One.

Drawing on his personal experience of union, Plotinus famously describes it as the "flight of the alone to the Alone."[16] He says that the One is always before us but that we do not fix our gaze on it because we are too distracted—like members of a choir who do not look at their conductor for direction: when they do, they are able to sing with great beauty. If we do receive a glimpse of the divine light, the temptation is to question whether it came from within or without, whereas all we can really say is that we saw it and now we do not. We cannot chase such an experience but only prepare ourselves for it and wait calmly, as we would wait for the sun to rise above the horizon. There is no quick shortcut to union; the cardinal virtues must be observed, and we must be patient in our contemplation. If we do so we might reach the state in which the observer is one with the observed; there is no movement, passion, and desire; mental activity, including self-consciousness, is in abeyance; and the soul, now "filled with God," resides in stillness and tranquillity, having become restfulness itself.[17]

3

THE CHRISTIAN EMPIRE

Try to make your intellect deaf and dumb during
prayer; you will then be able to pray.
                                        —Evagrius Ponticus

AFTER THE ROMAN GENERAL Constantine became emperor
of the Western Roman Empire in 312 (and the Eastern in 324),
the status of the church changed dramatically. It is said that
before his decisive battle against his rival Maxentius, Constantine was
encouraged by a vision of the cross; after his victory he showed his
gratitude to the Christian God by making the faith the most favored
in the empire. Clergy were excused taxes and municipal duties, the
church was legally allowed to inherit property, financial penalties for
celibacy were repealed, and Sunday was recognized as a holiday. The
emperor ensured funds were made available for building churches,
and in 330 he founded his new eastern capital of Constantinople on
the Bosporus with Christian ceremonies. He himself got involved in
church affairs, presiding over the Council of Nicaea in 325. (The coun-

cil condemned the Arian heresy, the view put forward by an Alexandrian presbyter named Arius that Jesus Christ was created by God the Father from nothing and was therefore a creature subject to change and not truly divine—against the orthodox view that Christ was both fully human and fully divine. The controversy rumbled on for most of the century until Arianism was finally vanquished at the Council of Constantinople in 381.)

After Constantine's death in 337, his successors continued to support the church—except for Emperor Julian the Apostate (r. 361–363), who tried in vain to reestablish paganism as the state religion. By the end of the fourth century, Emperor Theodosius I had made heresies punishable offenses and had banned pagan sacrifices and destroyed temples, effectively making the empire an orthodox Christian state (although pockets of paganism did continue to survive). But even as the church became part of the establishment, enjoying its newfound status, many Christians rejected life in the world, with all its material distractions, and journeyed to desert places in Egypt and Syria to pursue ascetic lives dedicated to God. Thus started the monastic tradition that over the centuries became a great breeding ground of Christian mystics. The impulse behind the desert movement has been characterized as a desire for "white martyrdom," a dying to the world at a time when "red martyrdom"—death at the hands of the imperial authorities—was no longer an issue in the new Constantinian dispensation.[1] The modern theologian Karl Barth called it "a highly responsible and effective protest and opposition to the world, and not least to a worldly Church."[2]

Best known of these first monks (the word *monk* derives from the Greek for "alone") was Anthony of Egypt (ca. 251–ca. 356), who lived as a hermit on a mountain in Egypt, eventually attracting other solitaries to the area. In 305 he formed these hermits into a loosely knit group that was obedient to a rule but maintained the eremitical (hermitlike) life. A few years later, a contemporary of Anthony's named Pachomius is said to have started the cenobitical (common) tradition of monasticism (based around a communal life) in about 320 near Thebes in Egypt. Pachomius founded a number of monasteries in the area for men and women and instituted a common rule for them. His cenobitical model was favored by Basil of Caesarea, one of the Cappadocian Fathers (along with his brother Gregory of Nyssa and Gregory of Nazianzus), who introduced it into the Eastern Roman Empire in the latter half of the fourth century.

The cenobitical form of monasticism also reached the West through the likes of John Cassian, a Scythian who had been a disciple of a hermit and mystic named Evagrius Ponticus, who lived in a desert in Egypt. Cassian brought his desert experience to southern Gaul (France), where he founded two monasteries near Marseilles in about 415. By this time the cracks in the Roman Empire were beginning to widen; Rome itself had been sacked by the Visigoths in 410, an almost unimaginable event to contemporaries. It prompted the greatest theologian of the age, Augustine, to begin writing his magnum opus, *The City of God*, as an attempt to defend Christianity against its pagan enemies, who attributed the demise of the Eternal City to Christianity's usurpation of pagan worship.

Gregory of Nyssa

During the fourth century, the region of Cappadocia in what is now modern Turkey produced three outstanding churchmen, Basil the Great, his younger brother Gregory of Nyssa, and their friend Gregory of Nazianzus. Of the three, Basil was probably the most significant figure, for his work in establishing communal monasticism in Eastern Christendom, while his brother Gregory of Nyssa was the most mystical. Born in the mid to late 330s in Caesarea in Cappadocia, Gregory of Nyssa at first resisted a career in the church, married, and became a teacher of rhetoric. But he was eventually drawn into the ecclesiastical fold, and in 371 his brother Basil appointed him, against his will, bishop of Nyssa, a small town on the river Halys about ten miles from Caesarea. Eight years later, after Basil's death, Gregory took up the baton of leadership of the church in the East. In 381 he played a significant role at the Council of Constantinople, which the emperor Theodosius I had convened to end Arianism and establish orthodoxy for good. Not much is known of Gregory's subsequent life, except that it was one of prayer, contemplation, preaching, and writing. He died in about 395.

Gregory's thoughts on mysticism are found in various works, including *On Virginity, Commentary on the Song of Songs,* and *Life of*

Moses (in which Moses's ascent to God on Mount Sinai typifies the soul's climb to divine reality—Gregory may have been the first to use this image of spiritual ascent, which was later brought to fulfillment by Dante). He shows his debt to the Platonist tradition in *On Virginity*, his earliest work, in which he states that to reach the goal of absolute beauty—the desired end of Platonists—it is necessary to become detached from the things of this world, such as the desire for money, honor, and fame, and transient sensual pleasures.[3] All of these must be left behind as the soul rises on its spiritual quest. Our "powers of loving" must be cleansed from their attraction to base things, and as the soul ascends higher, it will come to realize the glory that exists above the heavens. It will become as beautiful and radiant as the Beauty and Light it has reached. Gregory then compares this process of spiritual illumination to the phenomenon of shooting stars. He refers to the contemporary theory that the gleams of light produced by shooting stars are caused by air around the earth being forced upward by blasts and irrupting into the ether (the upper regions of the sky), where it changes into the ether's luminous light. In a similar way the mind, under pressure from the spirit, enters the "true Purity" and takes on a radiant form. Gregory also compares illumination to a mirror or smooth expanse of water that can reflect light and shine when shone upon, but only if the surface is unstained and perfect: in other words, the soul must be pure and spotless if it is to be filled with and reflect back the divine light.[4]

Gregory eventually grew away from Platonism, as shown by his emphasis on the central place of feeling in the spiritual life and his stress that an unbridgeable divide separates the uncreated realm of the Trinity from the created world.[5] Therefore the soul, which is part of the created order—whereas for Platonists it was divine—cannot cross over into the uncreated sphere. Yet although the soul cannot know God directly, it can approach him, unknowable though he is, through the incarnate Christ.

Like Origen, Gregory sees the spiritual progress of the soul in three, sometimes overlapping, stages. In his eleventh homily on the Song of Songs, Gregory describes how the soul progresses through light, cloud, and darkness. The first stage (light) corresponds to the enlightenment that comes when our benighted views of God have been corrected. The second (cloud) involves a groping through the sensible world toward the realm of the invisible. The last (darkness) comes when the soul has progressed to the "secret chamber of divine darkness" and, with sense perception and reason now irrelevant, it can contemplate the divine mystery. As he says elsewhere: "The true vision and the true knowledge of what we seek consists precisely in not seeing, in an awareness that our goal transcends all knowledge and is everywhere cut off from us by the darkness of incomprehensibility."[6]

Gregory's speculation on the "divine darkness" and the incomprehensible nature of God is what is called negative theology, which, as we shall see, was more fully developed by Dionysius the Areopagite. In a similar "negative" way, Gregory described the soul's ascent to God as a never-ending journey—a correlative to the fact that God himself is boundless. This reaching out, or *epektasis*, for God is fulfilled only with a further desire to reach him. It is as if when having enjoyed the satisfaction of climbing to the top of a hill, we then see there is a higher peak beyond, which inspires us to continue our journey, until we see there is yet another higher peak, and so on ad infinitum.

Evagrius Ponticus

One of the profoundest students of the Cappadocian Fathers was Evagrius Ponticus, a hermit, sage, and spiritual writer who was "one of the first who made contemplative prayer the essence of monastic life and thus linked the forces of monasticism and mysticism in a powerful way."[7] For Evagrius, prayer in its highest form means contemplation of the Holy Trinity, a blessed state of being, devoid of mental images, that can occur only after the soul has been purified.[8] He was eloquent on mystical prayer, as his treatise *On Prayer* demonstrates, with aphoristic utterances such as "Try to make your intellect deaf and dumb during prayer; you will then be able to pray" and, "If you patiently accept what comes, you will always pray with joy."[9] He also made a contribution to negative theology with his idea of "infinite ignorance," which has echoes of Gregory of Nyssa's *epektasis*: whereas lack of knowledge of the created world is rectifiable by natural contemplation, ignorance of the immeasurably mysterious Holy Trinity must be infinite. In a similar vein, souls that reach the unitive state are para-doxically "always satisfied in their insatiability."[10]

Evagrius was born in Cappadocia in about 345. He was ordained a lector, or reader, by Basil the Great, then a deacon by Gregory of Nazianzus. In 381 Evagrius moved to Constantinople, where he relished the city's intellectual atmosphere. But the entanglements of a love affair and an admonitory vision persuaded him to leave the metropolis of temptations for the more spiritual climate of Jerusalem. In 383 he embraced the eremitical life in the deserts of Egypt, first in Nitria, then Kellia. He lived as a solitary for sixteen years, until his death in 399, gaining a reputation for his asceticism and practical and speculative wisdom. However, his Origenist views on the preexistence of the soul and the idea of *apokatastasis*—that all things are finally restored in Christ at the end of time, so that even the devil will be saved—were eventually condemned at the Second Council of Constantinople in 553. His works were written in short, terse, gnomic chapters, a form that lends itself to meditation.

Influenced by Origen, Evagrius believed that reality consisted of three stages (Evagrius is keen on tripartite divisions).[11] In the first, God created spiritual beings known as *logikoi*, who were originally united with the Holy Trinity but then fell from their beatific state through "negligence." The only unfallen *logikos* was Christ, and it is through him that the second creation was brought about. In this second stage, the *logikoi* became one of three entities, depending on their share of negligence: angelic beings, humans, and demons. Each *logikos* has a soul made up of three parts—a rational principle, desire, and a disposition toward anger, with the rational principle predominating in angels, desire in humans, and anger in demons.

In the third and final stage, souls return to God on a journey that also has three parts to it.[12] The first part, *praktike*, or "active life," involves in effect combating temptation and controlling the passions to arrive at a state of *apatheia*, a term that plays an important part in Evagrius's spirituality and does not mean "apathy" but rather a state of imperturbable peacefulness. In the second part, *physike*, or "natural contemplation," the soul begins to gaze on the created world's underlying principles, which exist in God. In this way it comes to comprehend

the workings of demonic powers and so is able to progress to the fulfillment of *apatheia*.

The third part is *theologia*, which is contemplation of God as the
Holy Trinity, a unitive state in which the soul experiences no sense of
separation from the object of its knowledge. Now it practices what
Evagrius refers to as "true prayer," although it is more correct to say
that this is not something you do so much as something you are:
prayer is not so much a mental act—"For prayer means the shedding
of thoughts"[13]—as a way of being.

Augustine of Hippo

At about the time that Gregory of Nyssa died and Evagrius was in the
last years of his sojourn in the Egyptian wilderness, over in the west a
younger contemporary of theirs named Augustine was appointed bishop of Hippo Regius in northern Africa. He was to become one of the
greatest of Christian churchmen and was later recognized as a doctor
of the church (a title reserved for the most eminent, holy, and influential theologians). Augustine was a thinker, preacher, polemicist, and
biblical commentator whose writings have had an incalculable effect
on the history of the church. His best-known works are the *Confessions*—one of the great spiritual autobiographies, candidly describing
his personal life and search for truth up to the point of his conversion
to the Christian faith—and *The City of God*.

Augustine's place in the roll call of Christian mystics is still a matter of debate. He did not set out a systematic treatment of mystical theology in the manner of later medieval mystics, but then he lived at a
time when there was no differentiation between mystical and dogmatic
theology. It was Augustine's conviction that it was part of our nature to
be restless until we find God, and that contemplation begins in this life
but is perfected in the next: "Our hearts find no peace until they rest in
you."[14] His high estimation of the contemplative life and his thoughts on
the soul's ascent to God can be found in a number of works in his vast
corpus—more than 500 sermons, some 200 letters, and 113 books have
survived; and it seems from passages in the *Confessions* that he himself
enjoyed mystical experiences.

A key element in Augustine's spirituality is the idea that man, or rather man's soul, is the image of God, and since God consists of the Holy Trinity, this will also be the form of the divine image in man. Self-knowledge—another important aspect in Augustine's mysticism—makes the individual realize the need to reform, through divine grace, this interior image of God, which has been deformed by sin. This can be achieved by the mediation of Christ. Through the Incarnation, whereby Christ partook of mortality, it is possible for man to partake of divinity.

Termed the "prince of mystics" by the modern Benedictine scholar Cuthbert Butler, Augustine was born in 354 in the Roman provincial town of Tagaste in what is now Algeria. His father, Patrick, was a pagan and his mother, Monica, a devout Christian, who brought him up in the faith. At the age of about seventeen Augustine went off to Carthage (in modern Tunisia) to study rhetoric at the university there. Living a somewhat dissipated lifestyle, he fathered an illegitimate son and was drawn toward Manichaeism (a dualistic religion positing a cosmic conflict between the forces of good and evil, light and darkness), which was to dominate his spiritual life for almost a decade.

Augustine stayed in Carthage almost continuously until 383, when he moved to Rome to set up a school of rhetoric. A year later he accepted a professorship in Milan. By this time he was disenchanted with his Manichaeism and was becoming attracted to the teachings of the Neoplatonists. He also fell under the spell of Milan's charismatic bishop, Ambrose, whose sermons Augustine admired both for their content and for their elegant style. In 386 he was finally converted to Christianity and in the following year baptized by Ambrose. Shortly after this he returned to Africa and set up a quasi-monastic community in his home town of Tagaste.

Augustine's secluded life in Tagaste was to last only a few years. In 391 he was visiting the town of Hippo Regius on the coast when the townspeople pressed him, against his will, into becoming a priest. Augustine accepted ordination, and by 396 he had become bishop of Hippo, a position he held for the next thirty-four years, until his death. Apart from his considerable pastoral work as bishop, Augustine wrote his great works of theology and philosophy, his biblical exegeses, and his polemics against those groups who threatened the unity and doctrine of the church, namely the Donatists, Manichaeans, and Pelagians.

In 413 he began his gargantuan *City of God*, which he continued writing until 426. Two years later the barbarian Vandals invaded northern Africa and by May 430 were laying siege to Hippo. Four months after that, Augustine died and was spared witnessing the fall of the city in the following year.

Although Augustine's mysticism has a pronounced intellectual element, he stressed that love for one's neighbor was a precondition for loving God,[15] and his descriptions of personal mystical experiences in the *Confessions* have infectious warmth and enthusiasm. In book 7, for example, he describes an experience he had in Milan in 386 after reading some Platonist works. He withdrew into himself and saw with the "eye of my soul" the unchangeable light, which lay above his soul not "as oil is above water" nor as "heaven is above earth" but "above to my soul, because It made me; and I below It, because I was made by It." From an almost scientific musing on the nature of the light, the passage becomes increasingly affective or imbued with emotion, as Augustine conveys the excitement of his spiritual insight: "He that knows the Truth, knows what that Light is; and he that knows It, knows eternity. Love knoweth it. O Truth Who art Eternity! and Love Who art Truth! and Eternity Who art Love! Thou art my God, to Thee do I sigh night and day. Thee when I first knew, Thou liftedst me up, that I might see there was what I might see, and that I was not yet such as to see. And Thou didst beat back the weakness of my sight, streaming forth Thy beams of light upon me most strongly, and I trembled with love and awe."[16]

This pattern of withdrawal from the world, turning inward, and seeing a revelatory light bears the stamp of Plotinus.[17] But though influenced by the Neoplatonist, Augustine differed from him crucially in his view of God, divine grace, and man's need for mediation. For Plotinus, the One is impersonal, and the soul, being inherently divine, is always able to ascend to it. For Augustine, God is personal (as one modern scholar has said, "Plotinus never *gossiped* with the One, as Augustine gossips in the *Confessions*"[18]); the soul is fallen and sinful and must rely for its ascent on the intervention of God through the incarnate Christ.

Perhaps the best and most quoted example of Augustine's personal encounters with the divine is the occasion in the *Confessions* when at the port of Ostia in Italy he shared with his mother, Monica— not long before her death in 387—a rapturous ascent of the spirit to the realm of ultimate truth. They were having a philosophical discussion when, Augustine says, "we rose up with a more ardent affection toward [God] and by degrees passed through all material things, even through heaven from where the sun and moon and stars shine upon the earth; yes, we were soaring higher yet, by inward musing and discourse, and marvelling at Your works; and we came to our own minds, and went beyond them, that we might arrive at that region of never-failing plenty, where You feed Israel forever with the food of truth. . . . And while we were discoursing and yearning for her, we for a moment touched on her with the whole effort of our heart; and we sighed, and there we left bound the first fruits of the spirit; and returned to verbal communication, where the spoken word has beginning and end."[19] Again, the experience has a Neoplatonist feel to it, reminiscent of the idea of the soul's return to its divine home. Yet, as the modern scholar Andrew Louth has pointed out, unlike Plotinus's "flight of the alone to the Alone," Augustine's rapture is personal but not solitary and bears witness to that aspect of his thought that stresses the "social nature of final beatitude."[20]

One important aspect of Augustine's mystical thought that exerted a great influence on the Middle Ages was his analysis of visions. In book 12 of his treatise *Literal Commentary on Genesis*, he considers the nature of Paul's ecstatic experience, referred to in 2 Corinthians 12:2–4, when he was "caught up to the third heaven," unsure whether he was "in the body or apart from the body." Augustine goes on to categorize visions into three types: corporeal, spiritual (or imaginary), and intellectual. He illustrates these with an example. If we read a sentence that tells us to love our neighbor, our eyes see the physical words on the page as corporeal vision; our spirit or imagination then pictures our neighbor, although he or she is not present before us; and our intellectual vision can "see" the idea of love without the need of images—it, therefore, has the purest vision, the one that results in true knowledge. Spiritual/imaginary visions are not so pure and require divine help to distinguish them from ordinary dreams or the delirium of the sick.[21]

With regard to ecstasy, Augustine says that in this state the mind is withdrawn from sense experience. The person's eyes are open but sights and sounds cannot be seen or heard: the attention of the mind is directed either to the images of a spiritual vision or to the imageless things of an intellectual vision. The soul is "withdrawn from the senses more than is usual in sleep, but less than in death."[22] The highest form of ecstasy is that in which an intellectual vision occurs—as happened to Paul—when, in the words of the modern scholar Frank Tobin, "the soul is freed from carnality and confronts the intellectual object more intensely. . . . The light which enables the soul to see intellectually is God himself."[23]

Elsewhere, Augustine sets out his thoughts on contemplation in his commentary on Psalms 41 and his treatise *On the Greatness of the Soul*. In the latter, Augustine gives a systematic treatment of the soul's ascent to the divine, enumerating seven stages in the soul's operations, the last four of which correspond to what would become the three traditional divisions of the mystical quest into purgation, illumination, and union. In the first three stages the soul is said to be the principle of life, sensation, and intelligence. In the fourth and fifth the soul is purged and reformed before, in the sixth, it proceeds to the threshold of contemplation. The seventh and last stage is contemplation itself, through which the soul is able to gaze on truth.[24]

In his commentary on Psalms 41 he makes it clear that the starting point of mystical experience is eradicating personal vices, such as greed and sensuality, hatred and spite. He also outlines how the soul rises to the heights of the divine but then has to return to the realm of mortality and impermanence. More specifically, he describes the light of God as a "light that shall never be darkened," a light that may be seen only by the inward eye, if it has been prepared in the right way. The mind itself, which is subject to change, seeks God, or ultimate truth, which is immutable, but its attempt to find God in material things and in itself is fruitless. God's dwelling place is "above" the soul and is said to be full of angelic music, which "the ears of the heart" can hear as a mysterious and sweet melody—if it has not been drowned out by the sounds of the world. But although we may for a brief moment hear the sound of angelic music and glimpse the unchangeable God, the human condition is such that we must fall back from the heights of divine experience to our everyday condition, with its sorrows, and be filled again with worldly cares and an awareness of our separation from that place of delight.[25]

4

THE DARK AGES

*The whole world, gathered as it were under one
ray of the sun, was brought before his eyes.*
—Gregory the Great on a vision of Benedict of Nursia

W HY THE WESTERN ROMAN EMPIRE "declined" and "fell," to use the traditional terms, unable to resist the incursions of barbarian tribes in the fifth century, is still much debated. Economic problems, societal weaknesses, and poor morale in the army (to which many barbarian soldiers had been recruited) all contributed. There was also a widespread, debilitating political ineptitude characterized by what the historian Peter Brown has called "amateurism, the victory of vested interests, [and] narrow horizons."[1] In any case, the beneficiaries of this situation were Germanic tribes such as the Goths, Franks, and Vandals who, pressured by the westward movement of central Asian peoples, sporadically crossed the imperial borders to little resistance. In 476 the last Western Roman emperor, Romulus Augustulus, was deposed, and by the early sixth century Germanic tribes had carved out kingdoms within the empire. However, the early Middle Ages, often called the Dark Ages (from about the end of the fifth century to the eleventh century), was not without chinks of light. Although infrastructure, communications, and learning generally declined, barbarian elites did adopt and preserve some of the ways and customs of the conquered, and many were already Christians, albeit mostly of the heretical Arian variety. The exception was in Gaul, where Clovis, king of the Franks, was converted to orthodox Catholicism in 496.

The church in the West still retained a dominant role in this new society, centered on the papacy. Strengthened by Pope Leo I (d. 461), the see of Rome became widely regarded as the supreme authority in the Western church during the dynamic leadership of Gregory I, the Great (590–604), the father of the medieval papacy. At a local level, bishops continued to nurture their communities, and new monasteries were founded that became self-sustaining havens of spirituality and scholarship. Monasticism in the West was consolidated by the Italian monk Benedict of Nursia (ca. 480–547) and his monastic Rule, which emphasized a balanced regime of prayer, study, and manual work. By the ninth century most monasteries in Europe would be following the Benedictine model. Perhaps the most spectacular example of early monastic growth occurred in Ireland, where, the century after the mission of Saint Patrick (ca. 390–ca. 460), monasteries were established at Bangor, Derry, Clonard, Clonmacnoise, and elsewhere. From them a stream of pious and learned Irish monks, such as Columba and Columban—with their English counterparts not far behind—made tracks to various parts of Europe to reinvigorate the faith, convert pagans, and found new monasteries.

By the 700s, the impetus of the Irish missions faltered as the Continental church became better organized, especially during the reign of the Frankish king Charlemagne, who was crowned Holy Roman Emperor by Pope Leo III in 800. Charlemagne tightened ecclesiastical discipline and unified liturgical practices. He also stimulated learning, standardized laws, and expanded the Carolingian empire. Yet it was during Charlemagne's generally enlightened reign and his revival of culture and scholarship that western Europe began to suffer from the depredations of the Vikings and, later, Muslim pirates in the Mediterranean and the Magyars from the Asian steppes. Only in the later tenth century was relative peace restored.

Although the Western Roman Empire had succumbed to the barbarian tide, the Eastern empire (which became known as the Byzantine Empire) survived for another thousand years until its fall to the Ottoman Turks in 1453. Its capital, Constantinople, gained in prestige from being the home of the sole Roman emperor; and the city's bishop, the patriarch, acquired a status that was second only to that of the pope. During the sixth century, Byzantine armies invaded Africa, Spain, and northern Italy to reclaim imperial territory, with some, albeit temporary, success.

In the seventh century, however, the map of the eastern Mediterranean and the security of the empire changed permanently with the rise of Islam. Founded by the prophet Muhammad, who died in 632, the Muslim faith fanned out from Arabia, with its armies quickly conquering Persia, Palestine, Syria, and parts of Asia Minor in the East, and the coastal lands of northern Africa in the West. In 711 a Muslim Arab and Berber army invaded and conquered most of Spain, its advance into France checked in 732 at the battle of Poitiers. Constantinople itself remained unvanquished, but from now on its perennial concern would be with survival rather than expansion.

Dionysius the Areopagite

The most significant—and mysterious—mystical writer of the early Middle Ages was arguably a man who called himself Dionysius the Areopagite. For Christians used to conceiving of God in terms of love, light, goodness, and the like, Dionysius is like a gust of cold wind. For Dionysius is the best-known exponent of what is known as negative (apophatic) theology. This approach to God is usually compared with affirmative (cataphatic) theology, by which God is given positive attributes that are normally used to describe humans (for example, "wise"), but extended to an infinite degree. So God is Wise or Just or Good, and so on. Negative theology takes a different approach. It maintains that it is truer to speak of what God is *not* than what he is. This is because God as the ultimate mystery exists beyond our understanding and so beyond all possible concepts or words. In short, nothing at all may be predicated of him. So in his *Mystical Theology*, Dionysius constantly resorts to symbolic or metaphorical language to refer to the ineffable divine—"darkness" being a favorite term. He refers, for example, to the "ray of divine darkness," "the darkness where lives the one which is beyond all things," and the "darkness which is beyond light."

Yet for one who lays such stress on the ultimate inadequacy of thought and language to describe the divine, Dionysius can still illuminate with words and images. For example, prayer is compared to the act of grabbing a shining cord hanging down from heaven to this world. As we tug at it, with our hands pulling alternately, we think we are drawing it down, but in fact we are being raised to the divine light. Or it is like being on a ship and pulling on ropes that are tied to a rock to anchor the vessel: whereas we think we are drawing the rock toward our ship, we are in fact moving toward the rock.[2]

For centuries Dionysius the Areopagite was presumed to be the man whom Paul converted when he was preaching in Athens, as recorded in Acts 17:16–34. In the late nineteenth century, however, scholars showed that the Areopagite's writings were written much later than New Testament times. The consensus is that the author—commonly referred to as Pseudo-Dionysius—was in fact a Christian Syrian monk living in about 500 who adopted the name of Dionysius to give his writings authority, a practice that was common in the ancient world. Not much else is know about him apart from what can be inferred from his works. These show that he was indebted to Neoplatonic thought as well as to thinkers such as Gregory of Nyssa and Philo of Alexandria, and of course the scriptures. It is strangely fitting that the author who stressed the mystery and darkness of God should himself be shrouded in darkness. Yet his influence has been profound and crystal clear. Many important later mystics, such as Eckhart, Ruysbroeck, and John of the Cross, have dipped their pens into Dionysius's inkhorn of divine darkness, and his *Mystical Theology*, translated into Middle English by the anonymous author of *The Cloud of Unknowing*, was said by a medieval chronicler to have "run across England like deer."

As well as the short *Mystical Theology*, Dionysius wrote three longer treatises: *The Divine Names*, *The Celestial Hierarchy*, and *The Ecclesiastical Hierarchy*. In these latter three works, Dionysius actually adopts an affirmative approach to God, for the affirmation and negation of God are really two sides of the same coin. Although it is, correctly speaking, false to speak of God as being Good, Just, and so on—because God is essentially unknowable—we may do so unstrictly because he is the cause of goodness or justice in the world.

Dionysius was also concerned, as the Neoplatonists were, with how God, who is beyond everything we know, can be connected with the world in any meaningful way. Taking his cue from the later Neoplatonist Proclus, Dionysius addresses this problem by asserting that reality consists of different gradations of beings in the form of threefold hierarchies (as for Evagrius Ponticus, triads loom large in Dionysius's thinking). At the peak is the triad of the Holy Trinity; below it is the celestial hierarchy of three groups of three orders of angels (seraphim, cherubim, and thrones, followed by dominations, virtues, and powers, then principalities, archangels, and angels). Then comes the terrestrial hierarchy, with another three groups of three orders: the first rank are not people but sacramental rites (Eucharist, baptism, and anointing with oil); the second are bishops, priests, and deacons; and the third are monks, baptized Christians, and catechumens.

Dionysius's scheme follows the Neoplatonic pattern of a procession from the One followed by a return to the source (which for Christians begins with spiritual truths found in the symbolic reality of the liturgy and the Bible). But there is a significant difference between the Neoplatonic system and Dionysius's model: "The Neoplatonic 'One' proceeds into multiplicity and participation as a matter of course; but the Dionysian God *desires* to share himself."[3] Dionysius also saw this graduated order not so much as a ladder of progression, with each group striving to move up a rung, but as a way in which each stratum could fulfill its spiritual potential proper to its place in the grand scheme, thereby becoming assimilated to God.

Yet for all his speculation on the affirmative approach to God and the use of symbols, it is Dionysius's apophaticism, set out in his short but highly influential *Mystical Theology*, for which he is best known. By ridding ourselves of ultimately futile attempts to describe God through his attributes, we draw nearer to the truth about his ineffable nature. Dionysius himself expresses this idea through the image (used by Plotinus) of a sculptor who must chip away at his block of marble before he is able to reveal, as it were, the statue hidden within.[4]

Dionysius advises that the senses and intellectual activity should be left behind and that with the understanding made quiet, we should strain toward union with God, who is beyond all being and understanding. By renouncing the self and all the things of the world, it is possible to be drawn upward to the "ray of divine darkness" that surpasses all existence.[5] He compares the mystic's journey to Moses's ascent of Mount Sinai in the book of Exodus 19–20. For Dionysius, as for Gregory of Nyssa, Moses represents the soul questing for God, and he uses the Moses story to illustrate the three stages in the soul's journey to God: the names he coined for these stages—purification, or purgation; illumination; and union—would become the classic formulation for later medieval mystics. First of all, Moses has to undergo purification before he hears the trumpet blast and sees flashes of lightning; he ascends the mountain but sees not God, who is invisible, but "the place where he dwells" (the stage of illumination). In a similar way, a person who perceives the "most high and divine things" must realize that these are merely symbolic of the God who transcends them. They may signify the divine presence "upon the heights of his holy places," but the divine presence then breaks away and plunges the "true initiate" into the darkness of unknowing (the stage of union). In this darkness, with the stilling of his rational mind, he is united to the unknowable God, and "by a rejection of knowledge he possesses a knowledge that exceeds his understanding."[6]

Dionysius ends the *Mystical Theology* with a list of what can be said, or rather what cannot be said, about God. Like his imaginary sculptor, he patiently chips away the excrescences that hinder the vision of ultimate reality and ends up with a triumphant affirmation of negation:

> Once more, ascending yet higher we maintain that It is not soul, or mind, or endowed with the faculty of imagination, conjecture, reason, or understanding; nor is It any act of reason or understanding; nor can It be described by the reason or perceived by the understanding, since It is not number, or order, or greatness, or littleness. . . . Nor is It one, nor is It unity, nor is It Godhead or Goodness; nor is It a Spirit, as we understand the term, since It is not Sonship

or Fatherhood; nor is It any other thing such as eye or any other being can have knowledge of.[7]

Pope Gregory the Great

Pope Gregory I, the Great, did not have the flair for speculative theology that Dionysius had, but he was nevertheless a highly influential figure in the history of Christian mysticism, especially in his role as one of the principal conduits through which patristic spirituality passed to the later Middle Ages and by his emphasis on the importance of monastic life in contemplation. For Gregory the life of contemplation was always an ideal, and he harbored regrets that his public duties prevented him from enjoying it. He was elected pope in 590 at a time when Rome's existence was being threatened by the barbarian Lombards, and its citizens were dying of plague and hunger. Gregory's heroic efforts in bringing relief to the suffering and organizing the affairs of church and state, as well as promoting monasticism and missions and writing numerous influential spiritual works, made him one of the greatest of popes and the father of the medieval papacy. Although he never wrote a systematic treatise on mysticism, his works, influenced by Dionysius and Augustine in particular, reveal a rich vein of thought about the subject: "The flame of Platonic mysticism, which had passed from Plotinus to Augustine, flared up again in the sermons of Gregory."[8]

Gregory was born in Rome in about 540 to a patrician family who owned a palatial residence on the city's Caelian Hill as well as extensive estates in Sicily. In about 573 he was appointed prefect of the city, the highest civic position Rome could offer. But within a year or so he stepped down from this position and embraced the life of a monk. In Rome he converted his family home into the monastery of Saint Andrew, which he joined, while in Sicily he established six more monastic communities on his ancestral estates. His time in the cloister, however, was soon curtailed by Pope Pelagius II, who in 579 dispatched Gregory to Constantinople to be his ambassador at the court of the Byzantine emperor (who was governing Italy through a representative known as the exarch, based in Ravenna). Gregory stayed there for about six years before returning to Rome, where he became abbot of Saint Andrew's.

His life of contemplation abruptly came to a halt in 590 with the death of Pope Pelagius: Gregory was the overwhelming choice of the clergy and people of Rome to become the new pope, much to his personal distress, since he realized his monastic days had been irretrievably snatched away from him. Gregory's appointment came at a time of crisis. Apart from the threat of the Lombards, Rome was still feeling the effects of the destructive floods the year before. Buildings and granaries had been swept away, and famine and plague were taking their toll. Gregory set about tackling the various problems with skill and energy. He personally conducted negotiations with the Lombards; he spent vast amounts of church funds on relieving the plight of the sick and suffering; he reaffirmed the authority of the papacy both in the East and the West; and he strengthened the churches of Italy, Spain, and France and sent missionaries to England. For fourteen years he devoted himself to the spiritual and practical welfare of his flock, organizing, preaching, and writing commentaries and letters, of which more than 850 survive. All this was achieved despite poor health (possibly the result of constant fasting), which left him weak and in pain. He died in 604 and was canonized immediately by popular acclaim.

Gregory's thoughts on contemplation and mysticism have to be gleaned from a variety of works, including his *Dialogues, Homilies on Ezekiel, Pastoral Rule,* and *Moralia on Job.* He himself seems to have had three personal mystical experiences, for example, when, one time in his monastery, his mind "rose above all that was transitory, and, though still in the body, went out in contemplation beyond the bars of flesh."[9] Gregory makes it clear that contemplation requires self-discipline, asceticism, and practicing the virtues of faith, hope, and charity. An attitude of humility is also crucial, as is the study of the scriptures. However, although all our efforts are necessary, they are not enough in themselves to bring about successful contemplation, which is ultimately a gift from God, an act of his loving-kindness.

Furthermore, the contemplative must have love, which is "an engine of the soul" (or "machine of the mind"), which draws the individual away from the distractions of the world.[10] The mind must rid itself of images and sense impressions before it starts the process of recollection, which involves gathering in scattered thoughts and turning inward to ascend to contemplation proper. This turning away from the world is crucial: "But you cannot recollect yourself unless you have learned to lock out the ghosts of images of earthly and heavenly things from the mind's eyes."[11] He refers to the "sweetness" of mystical experience and how it reveals spiritual truths and the baseness of earthly things.[12]

Gregory also speaks of the mind narrowing itself so that it might be enlarged, that is, keeping tightly focused on heavenly things and discarding temporal concerns in the hope that it may be filled with spiritual amplitude.[13] This idea of the soul's being expanded comes out in one of his anecdotes about Benedict of Nursia, the father of Western monasticism. One night when Benedict was praying to God at the window of a tower, he looked out and saw that the darkness had been scattered by a celestial light that was brighter than daylight. Then "the whole world, gathered as it were under one ray of the sun, was brought before his eyes."[14] Gregory explains that the soul who sees the light of God, no matter how little, expands within to the extent that everything created, even the world itself, seems to shrink. In a similar vein, he uses the image of light streaming through "slanting" or "splayed" windows, which are narrow on the outside but wide on the inside, to convey the idea that our minds, although receiving a small glimpse of the divine light, are greatly enlarged within.[15] The divine light is a recurrent image in Gregory's description of mystical experience (although Bernard McGinn has pointed out that beneath this affirmative approach there is also a strain of negative theology in Gregory's thought, for example, that the limited human spirit cannot comprehend the unlimited spirit of God). He talks, for instance, of the mind overcoming its own dark ignorance and momentarily glimpsing boundless or unencompassed light before returning to its former self and the travails of everyday life.[16] And he refers to the boundless light being seen as a beam of sun pouring through a chink, an image that suggests we cannot see the sun directly, that is, God himself. The full vision of God—which was enjoyed by Adam before the fall—can be partially restored to the individual through Christ but only fully enjoyed after death. Gregory maintains (not always consistently) that in this life "the mist of corruption darkens us from the incorruptible light"[17]—a reflection of Gregory's acknowledgment of the fallen world of sin and of human suffering.

John Scotus Erigena

For several centuries after the time of Gregory the Great, the flame of mysticism in the West burned low, tended almost solely in the monasteries. It did flare up, however, in the person of the ninth-century Irishman John Scotus Erigena (or Eriugena), who is generally regarded as the one brilliant star in the intellectual firmament of the time. Influenced by Dionysius the Areopagite and the Greek monk and theologian Maximus the Confessor (ca. 580–662), John made translations from the works of both men and was an important link in transmitting their spiritual thought to the later Middle Ages. He himself was a philosopher and theologian whose speculative, sometimes difficult, works in the Neoplatonic and Dionysian traditions tried to reconcile mystical pagan philosophy with the Christian revelation.

John Scotus Erigena was born in the early 800s somewhere in Ireland. His name actually means "John the Irishman" (Ireland was known as Scotia in the early Middle Ages) "from Ireland" (Erigena). Very little is known about his life. At some point it seems he decided to seek his fortune abroad, and in about 845 he ended up in west Francia (the area that later became France) at the court of Charles the Bald, the grandson of Charlemagne. Charles appointed him head of his prestigious palace school, and in the following years, John taught and wrote, translating Dionysius (whose works had been presented to Charles by the Byzantine emperor) and Maximus the Confessor, and producing commentaries, homilies, and even poems. He died in about 877, probably in France, although a later tradition says he retired to England during the reign of Alfred the Great. In later centuries the church authorities came to believe that some of his ideas were in error—for example, by straying too close to pantheism—and they were condemned in 1210 and 1225. Modern scholars, however, tend to emphasize John's originality of thought and the depth of his learning—certainly his knowledge of Greek was a rarity in the West at the time.

John's greatest work was *On the Division of Nature*, with *nature* referring not just to the created world but to the whole of reality, including God. Imbued with Neoplatonic mysticism, the book was written during the 860s and takes the form of a dialogue between a master and a student. In it John considers the relationship between the ineffable God and creation and the way in which all things flow out from God before returning to him. John divides his grand scheme of nature into four parts: (1) that which creates and is not created, (2) that which creates and is created, (3) that which is created but does not create, and (4) that which neither creates nor is created.

The first division (that which creates and is not created) is God. He is the transcendent source of everything and exists beyond all categories. John describes him as being beyond human reason and as a "nothingness" and says that the correlative of his being infinite and incomprehensible is that he is unknowable even to himself. Yet John knew from the scriptures that God had appeared to people indirectly, so he made use of the idea of theophany, the manifestation on earth of the divine, notably seen in the case of the incarnate Christ. Yet in a way all parts of nature are theophanies inasmuch as everything partakes of the divine, the ultimate source of all being. So for John, the whole of creation is really "a graduated revelation of God."[18]

John's second division of nature (that which creates and is created) consists of the divine archetypes, or Platonic Ideas. God manifests himself timelessly as the Logos, or Word, which mediates between himself, the One, and the multiplicity of creation. And it is the Logos that contains or is the totality of the Platonic Ideas. The Ideas—for example Goodness, Power, and Wisdom—are created by God and constitute the patterns of the things of the visible universe, which they create in an eternal process through the power of the Holy Spirit.

The third division (that which is created but does not create) therefore consists of the phenomena of the universe, the created visible things, including man, brought forth by the Ideas as genera, species, and individuals. The created world, engendered by the Logos, is a manifestation of God and subsists in him.

John's fourth division (that which neither creates nor is created) is also God. But it is not God as creator but God in his aspect as the goal to which all things aspire to return. It is the nature of the cosmic cycle that it begins with God proceeding from himself and ends with all things returning to him, their source. Christ, the incarnate Word, is the means by which we journey back to God. And for the Christian elect, the final stage of the return is union with the divine. Employing images used by Maximus the Confessor, John says that the soul is united with

God "as air is wholly illuminated by light, and the whole lump of iron is liquefied by the whole of the fire" (these comparisons would be frequently repeated in later medieval times).[19] But John did not envisage a complete merging of identity between God and the human soul, for God ultimately remains beyond all comprehension, known only through theophanies.

So in John's Christianized Neoplatonic vision, God stands at the beginning, as uncreated creator, and at the end of a process of creation that culminates with all things, not only man but also the rest of nature, returning to him. "Everything," as the modern scholar Gordon Leff notes, "is a participation in God's nature as expressed in creation; it is like the rays of light which reflect the sun. Because all creatures both derive from God as principle, and move toward Him as end, the whole of nature is a movement powered by love of God."[20]

5

THE AGE OF THE CRUSADES

There was no movement of his by which I could
know his coming; none of my senses showed me
that he had flooded the depths of my being.
—Bernard of Clairvaux

A T THE START OF THE ELEVENTH CENTURY, the Burgundian historian Radulfus Glaber, commenting on the optimistic spirit of the new millennium in Europe, declared that the continent was clothing itself in "a white cloak of churches." Yet the Western church at this time was actually suffering from a weak papacy and widespread abuse, including simony and clerical marriage. Matters began to improve, however, with the election of the reforming popes Leo IX in 1049 and Gregory VII in 1073, the latter famously clashing with the Holy Roman Emperor, Henry IV, over whether the church or the state should make high-ranking clerical appointments (a struggle known as the investiture contest). The controversy continued until the

Concordat of Worms in 1122, when a compromise solution helped to defuse, but not eradicate, the tension between pope and emperor.

The eleventh-century impulse for church reform also manifested itself in the monasteries. Western monasticism had suffered during the troubled times of the Viking age, but in the early tenth century there were green shoots of recovery, particularly through the influential Benedictine abbey at Cluny in Burgundy, founded in 910. By the eleventh century, many monastic houses had become large institutions with great estates, as well as patrons of art and centers of scholarship: as wealth and worldliness inevitably crept into them, a countermovement of reforming orders arose, seeking to return to the putative simplicity of the apostolic era, with a greater emphasis on poverty and discipline. Such an order was the Augustinian canons, who came into being in about the middle of the eleventh century, when small groups of clergy in southern France, northern Italy, and other parts of Europe formed themselves into communities dedicated to lives of poverty, celibacy, and obedience. In time they adopted the Rule of Saint Augustine, although this was modified locally. Some Augustinians were strict, stressing discipline, manual labor, and abstinence; others followed a more relaxed rule and became more involved in the world, running schools and hospitals. One of the best-known Augustinian establishments was the Abbey of Saint-Victor at Paris, founded in 1113, which produced a number of illustrious scholars and mystics, including the Scottish-born Richard of Saint-Victor.

The most significant reforming order at this time, however, was the Cistercians. The White Monks (so called for the color of their habits) were founded in 1098 by Abbot Robert of Molesme at Cîteaux (Cistercium in Latin) and sought to live their lives according to a more strict and primitive version of Saint Benedict's Rule. In their quest for austerity, the Cistercians built their monasteries in wild, remote locations, often on the frontiers of civilization, where they would cultivate large tracts of land, with the considerable help of *conversi*, or lay brothers; they emphasized the place of manual labor, strict diet, and silence, and their churches were grand but plain. Through good organization and inspiring leadership, notably by Abbots Stephen Harding (d.1134) and Bernard of Clairvaux (1090–1153), the Cistercian houses expanded rapidly, with more than five hundred houses founded by the end of the 1100s.

Something of the pioneer spirit and aggressive confidence of the Cistercians can also be discerned in the impulse behind the Crusades. The first of these great military expeditions—which exhibited the piety and fervor of pilgrimage—occurred after the Seljuk Turks took control of Palestine, the Holy Land, in the late 1000s. Rallied by Pope Urban II, a huge army of Christian knights, foot soldiers, and hangers-on set out to recapture Jerusalem, which they took in 1099. Over the next two centuries the crusaders managed to maintain a fortified presence in Palestine, sporadically bolstered by a number of further Crusades (the first four being the most important), whose success was limited at best. By the end of the 1200s, however, the crusading movement had more or less fizzled out, and the last crusader stronghold of Acre fell to the Muslims in 1291.

Apart from the Crusades and monastic renewal, the twelfth century also saw the growth of Scholasticism, a method or approach to theology that emphasized the need for a systematic investigation of religious mysteries and the reconciliation of apparent contradictions in the scriptures. The main intellectual tools of the Scholastics were logic—which would be refined by an influx of Aristotle's work in new translations—and formal debates. Although traditional theologians were alarmed by this new approach, the Scholastics did not aim to undermine faith but to support it by reason and to map out an all-embracing view of truth. And the enthusiasm for system and order embraced by the Scholastics percolated through to spiritual writers of the time.

Bernard of Clairvaux

The most influential churchman of the twelfth century was probably Bernard of Clairvaux, a Cistercian monk, theologian, scholar, mystic, charismatic speaker, and tireless traveler who wrote, preached, and dispensed wisdom and warnings to kings, popes, and nobles alike. His personality and eloquence were so powerful that it is said that "mothers hid their sons, wives their husbands, companions their friends"[1] in case they were led away pied piper–like by his persuasive witness to the faith. His reputation for profound spirituality was canonized by Dante in *Paradiso* (canto 31), in which Bernard takes over from Beatrice as Dante's guide and directs the poet's gaze to the glory of the Virgin Mary. As a monk, Bernard did not shelter inside the cloister, nor did he flinch from weighing in when he thought he could make a difference to the affairs of the world. Despite the demands of the active life, Bernard was still able to practice contemplation and write passionately about it, albeit unsystematically, especially in his sermons on the Song of Songs. Indeed, it was his strongly held view that the active and contemplative lives are complementary—through contemplation the soul becomes zealous in its desire to serve God.

Bernard was born in 1090 of a noble Burgundian family and joined the Cistercian abbey at Cîteaux near Dijon when he was twenty-two years old. Three years later he left and established in a nearby Burgundian valley a Cistercian house that was named Clairvaux and with which he was associated for the rest of his life. There he maintained a severe, ascetic regime—detrimental to his own health—that attracted many new disciples, including his brothers and widowed father. Eventually the numbers proved too many for the monastery, so monks were sent off to found new houses (more than sixty were established directly from Clairvaux during Bernard's life).

Over the years, Bernard gained a reputation for honesty, piety, forcefulness, energy, and intolerance of corruption. He placed his considerable spiritual weight and rhetorical skill behind Innocent II in his struggle with Anacletus II for the throne of Saint Peter, and in 1140, at a church council in Sens, he presented the case against the controversial thinker and theologian Peter Abelard, who had been accused of heretical teachings. Six years later he again used his eloquence to devastating effect, when he preached the Second Crusade, galvanizing the French king and German emperor to launch an enormous expedition to reclaim the Holy Land for the faith. The crusade proved a dismal failure, however, and Bernard's reputation suffered as a result. In his last years he continued to involve himself in the affairs of the world, although his morale was hit by the death of a number of friends, especially Pope Eugenius III, who had been his disciple. He himself died on August 20, 1153, at the age of sixty-three.

Bernard's mysticism emphasizes the supreme place of love, which is founded on humility.[2] In his short but influential treatise *On Loving God*, he outlines humanity's progressive journey from selfish to spiritual love, stating that there are four degrees of love. First there is a person's basic, selfish love for himself. Our human nature is such that we are frail, enslaved to the flesh, and cannot love anything beyond ourselves. The second degree occurs when we realize that we cannot exist by ourselves. God sends us trials and tribulations, and through them we turn to him for help. In this way, we come to love God not for his sake but for ours. Then when we have learned to honor and pray to God and to read the scriptures, we come to the third state, loving God for himself and not merely as a benefactor. The fourth degree, the love of self for the sake of God, is a state of blessed union in which happiness lies in acting in perfect conformity with the will of God—Bernard doubts whether it is possible to reach such a degree in this life, except, perhaps, for a fleeting moment, and he admits that he himself has not attained it.

Bernard's words on love and contemplation were based to some extent on personal experience. Although by later standards he was not particularly forthcoming about his experience of mystical states, he does describe the effect of perceiving God as one of peacefulness: "The tranquil God tranquillizes all things, and to behold him is to rest."[3] He also speaks of frequent visits by Christ as the divine Word, who would enter his soul mysteriously: "There was no movement of his by which I could know his coming; none of my senses showed me that he had flooded the depths of my being."[4] Yet the Word could be known by the way he roused his "sleeping soul" and softened his "hard and stony" heart with an accompanying warmth. The withdrawal of the Word was equally mysterious: suddenly the sense of graceful euphoria would disappear, as if the flame had been removed from a "bubbling pot," leaving the soul deflated until the next visit.

Bernard's thoughts about the contemplative life are mostly scattered within his eighty-six sermons on the Song of Songs, which freely employ the biblical book's use of erotic imagery. Interpreting the Song allegorically, Bernard associates the bride primarily with the church or sometimes with the individual soul. The bridegroom is Jesus Christ (when the church is the bride) or the divine Word (when the soul is the bride). The Holy Spirit is represented by the kiss given by the bridegroom to the bride at the start of the Song. The idea that the union of the Song's two lovers symbolizes the "spiritual marriage" of the soul with the divine Word had been used centuries before by Origen, and Gregory the Great had interpreted the lovers as Christ and the church, but in Bernard's work the spiritual marriage found its supreme formulation, continuing a tradition that later flowered in the writings of Jan Ruysbroeck, Teresa of Ávila, and others.

Bernard states that the contemplative life is open to everyone but is most likely to be fulfilled in the confines of the cloister. He also thought of the soul's journey to God as having three parts, along similar lines to the stages that Dionysius the Areopagite and others had formulated: purgation, illumination, and union. The mystic quest can only begin once the soul has conquered everyday vices such as anger and envy and is practicing virtues such as humility, justice, and gentleness, as well as good works.[5] The soul must then recollect itself (gather together its thoughts on God) and become detached from the sensory world.

Bernard also distinguishes between two types or ways of contemplation further along the mystic path: that of the heart and that of the intellect. The first way, which he favored, is to do with warmth of devotion and how the contemplative feels inside—in his sermons on the Song of Songs he talks about the soul's being embraced and how it is made to glow or has the sensation of a "sweetness" of love pouring into it. But Bernard did not ignore the vital contribution of knowledge and the intellect in the contemplative life. If the individual has been purified of sin, there may follow a sudden and extraordinary enlargement of the mind and a sense of the intellect's being illumined by an inpouring of light, enabling it to grasp the true meaning of the scriptures and sacred mysteries.[6] But such moments of sweetness in the heart and inner mental expansion are brief, and they are inevitably followed by the heightened pain of returning to the everyday world of suffering, the spiritual dryness that John of the Cross would be so eloquent about.

Bernard describes the union of the soul with God in *On Loving God* as deification.[7] This occurs when the will has been totally purified and is conformed with the will of God: it is, he says, as if a drop of water had blended with wine, taking on its taste and color, or, using imagery employed by John Scotus Erigena, he likens it to an iron that is glowing with fire or air that has become the sunlight to which it has been exposed. But Bernard did not believe in a loss of identity between God and the soul, for the two are not of the same substance or nature. Rather, they are conjoined as one spirit (Bernard was fond of quoting 1 Corinthians 6.17: "But he who unites himself with the Lord is one with him in spirit"). In any case, such a union is reserved for the afterlife. In this life, Bernard suggests, the soul cannot see God face-to-face but dreams of him, as it were, in contemplation, able to see him only indirectly "through a mirror and in an enigma."[8] Our experience of God in this life can only be brief, and though this is more satisfying than any other earthly delight, it leaves us wanting more. Yet even in the afterlife, the soul continues to engage in a perpetual round of seeking and finding God—similar to the endless reaching out, or *epektasis*, of Gregory of Nyssa—"a searching never satisfied, yet without any restlessness . . . that eternal, inexplicable longing that knows no dissatisfaction and want."[9]

Richard of Saint-Victor

During the twelfth century the Abbey of Saint-Victor in Paris, an Augustinian house of canons, was home to a number of distinguished theologians, mystics, and scholars and wielded great influence throughout France and beyond. Its two most important figures at this time were Hugh (ca. 1096–1141) and, a generation later, Richard, a Scot by birth, who eventually became prior of the abbey. It was Richard who showed the greater mystical bent, building on the work that Hugh had begun. Not much is known about Richard's life. His birth date is unknown, and he died in 1173. Unlike Bernard, who combined monastic duties with affairs of the world, Richard's life seems to have been devoted almost entirely to the cloister and his theological and mystical works, among the most important of which were his studies on contemplation, particularly the *Benjamin Minor* and *Benjamin Major* and *The Four Degrees of Passionate Love*. Richard, in tune with the Scholastic zeitgeist, was a great systematizer, one who is important and influential for bringing orderliness to the experience of contemplation, presenting it in terms of different stages and qualities.

In the *Benjamin Minor* Richard uses the figures of the Hebrew patriarch Jacob and his family to represent the various stages that are required to prepare the soul for contemplation, which climaxes when "human reason succumbs to what it beholds of the divine light when it is lifted above itself and rapt in ecstasy."[10] Richard elaborated his thoughts on contemplation in the *Benjamin Major* (also called *The Mystical Ark*, referring to the Ark of the Covenant), a five-part work that influenced Dante. In it, Richard states that there are six stages through which the soul ascends until it finally "rejoices and dances when from the irradiation of the divine light it learns and considers those things which all human reason cries out."[11]

Richard also says that there are three qualities or modes of contemplation that the mind can attain.[12] The mind's vision can be "enlarged" through its own efforts; it can be elevated with the help of divine illumination and perceive things beyond the normal sphere of consciousness; and it can experience ecstasy, or "alienation of the mind," during which it loses its sense of self and time and gazes on divine truth without hindrance. With his love of analysis, Richard also states that this last, ecstatic experience has three, in the modern Anglican churchman Dean Inge's phrase, "predisposing conditions": first there is devotion, which Richard pictures in terms of the heat of love transforming the mind into smoke rising to God; then wonder, which Richard compares to the way a vessel of water receives sunlight and becomes so joined with it that when the water is still or expands, the light follows suit; and finally, exultation, joy, which points to "a new note of ecstatic rejoicing that was to find increasing favor among the mystics of the Middle Ages."[13]

Richard's thoughts on contemplation and his love of order are also shown in his short but influential treatise *The Four Degrees of Passionate Love*, written shortly before his death.[14] Richard sets out the different levels the soul can reach on the contemplative path. In the first degree, through meditation, the soul is visited by God and experiences a delicious sensation that is "sweeter than honey." Yet although it can feel God's presence, it cannot see God's form, which is still shrouded in darkness. The soul's desire for God is inflamed, and now, with much more effort on its part, it enters the second degree of love, receiving a vision of the divine light so powerful that it can neither forget it nor be distracted from it.

In the third degree, the soul is so caught up in the divine light that it loses all sense of itself and is filled with the glory of God. Those who have come this far abandon their desires and resign their will to God—their actions are now wholly determined by God's will. The soul is ready to be shaped, just as molten metal is shaped into different forms by molds.

The fourth and highest degree requires the soul to put on the humility of Christ, who, although divine, became a humble servant, obedient to God, even though it entailed the Crucifixion. So, having been glorified in the third degree, the soul must now "empty itself" and like Christ become a servant and return to the world to help its neighbors out of compassion.

Hildegard of Bingen

Contemporary with Bernard and Richard, but very different from them both, was the extraordinary Hildegard of Bingen. A medieval Renaissance woman, Hildegard was a visionary nun who corresponded with kings, emperors, and popes, a poet who composed songs and a play set to music, and a writer who wrote books not only on theology but also about the medicinal properties of plants and human physiology. A complex woman who was humble yet authoritative, diffident yet willful, she was widely recognized as a holy person during her lifetime, and although she was never officially canonized, she was, and is, commonly referred to as Saint Hildegard. But she was, perhaps, first and foremost a mystical seer, whose strange visions, recorded in her *Scivias* and other works, continue to puzzle and enchant. She writes about what she calls the illumination of "the shadow of the living light" and about seeing within it the "living light" itself, which made all her woes and sadness evaporate, so that she felt "like a simple maiden rather than an old woman."[15] This idea of a dynamic, divine life force also comes across in her concept of *viriditas*, which literally means "greenness," but with the added sense of fertility, of a life-giving, creative energy.

The "Sibyl of the Rhine" was born in 1098 into a noble German family in the Rhineland in western Germany, the tenth child of the family. From an early age she suffered from poor health, and she was aware of receiving visions from the age of three. When she was eight years old, her parents entrusted her to the care of a nun named Jutta, who lived as a recluse beside the Benedictine abbey at Disibodenberg in the diocese of Speyer. Hildegard received from Jutta a basic education, learning enough Latin to be able to read the Psalter and other texts. Over the years, as Jutta attracted more followers, a small community obedient to the Rule of Saint Benedict grew up around her. By the time Jutta died in 1136, Hildegard, now thirty-eight years old, was ready to step into her shoes as abbess of what was now a double monastery, that is, one for both men and women.

About five years later Hildegard began to write her visionary books, after a dramatic mystical experience: she saw a brilliant fiery light shining from the opened heavens and felt it permeate her brain and ignite a flame within her chest, "not like a burning, but like a warming flame, as the sun warms everything its rays touch."[16] This celestial light illuminated her understanding of the holy scriptures; at the same time she also felt a divine call to write down the content of her visions, which she eventually showed to a monk named Volmar, her friend and confessor. The latter had no doubt about their divine provenance and was to provide support and encouragement to Hildegard until his death in 1173. Over time, Hildegard also sought and gained endorsement for visions from various church authorities, including Bernard of Clairvaux. "This meant that, once her prophetic gift had been officially acknowledged as genuine . . . her utterances were almost beyond challenge."[17] So, with church endorsement, Hildegard set to work over the following decades, writing her visionary works.

Before long, Hildegard's fame as a wise and holy person who could work miracle cures and perform exorcisms spread, and increasing numbers of women came to join her convent until, in 1147, Hildegard decided to found a new establishment at Rupertsberg, which lies across the Rhine opposite the town of Bingen. Nearly twenty years later she established a second, smaller convent at nearby Eibingen. For the rest of her life Hildegard supervised her nuns, wrote her books, and met and corresponded with people of all ranks of society—nearly four hundred of her letters survive—including the likes of Henry II of

England and Emperor Conrad III. Also, despite constant poor health and advancing age, she managed to travel throughout Germany and beyond, preaching the word of God, advocating church reforms, and attracting crowds wherever she went. She died in September 1179.

One interesting aspect of Hildegard's visions is that she emphasizes that they came to her via the eyes of the soul when she was fully awake and alert and able to see with her physical eyes at the same time. She describes her soul as ascending "to the heights of the firmament" and spreading itself out "among various peoples . . . in far away regions." And she describes an illuminating light that is brighter than a "sun-struck cloud" and in it "the scriptures, the virtues, and certain works of men" are reflected as water reflects the sun or moon."[18]

Hildegard typically experienced her visions in the form of luminous images, their spiritual significance usually being explained to her by a divine voice. She sees figures that represent institutions and principles, such as the church and love. Ecclesia (church) is dressed in pure white silk with a gem-studded cloak and onyx sandals; her clothing, though, is torn and muddied because of the sinful behavior of her priests. Heavenly Love has a cloak brighter than starlight and bears a sapphire image of a human being on her chest, and she embraces the sun and the moon.[19]

The fruits of her visions are best known from her trilogy of visionary works, *Scivias, The Book of Life's Merits,* and *The Book of Divine Works.* The best known of these, *Scivias* (short for *Scito vias Domini,* "Know the ways of the Lord"), took ten years to complete and is more prophetic than mystical, closer in tone to the book of Revelation than, say, the treatises of Bernard or Richard. The book is grandiose in its themes, covering the whole of creation, from Lucifer's fall to redemption through Christ and the day of Judgment. Arresting symbols and images abound; for example, Lucifer and his angels are depicted as shooting stars that are turned to cinders as they fall, and salvation is described as an edifice built on God's mountain, with the building's walls, cornerstones, and proportions having various allegorical meanings. There are frequent moments of great beauty, as in her description of the Trinity, which gives a good idea of the intensity of Hildegard's visions: "Then I saw a most splendid light, and in that light, the whole of which burnt in a most beautiful, shining fire, was the figure of a man of a sapphire colour, and that most splendid light poured over the whole of that shining fire."[20] The book ends with songs in praise of the Virgin Mary, angels, and saints, and a short morality play about the pilgrimage of the soul to heaven.

Despite Hildegard's intimacy with vision and prophecy, there is still debate among scholars as to whether she should be counted as a genuine mystic.[21] It is clear that she was a visionary, but it is a question of whether or not in her visions she experienced the presence of God, the core of mysticism, and also whether her writings shed light on the practice of contemplation. Certainly some of her descriptions of her ecstasies suggest that she did encounter the divine directly, such as the "fiery light" that entered her and illuminated her understanding of the scriptures, but her theological works are more prophetic than mystical. She is really sui generis, a seer whose mystical inclinations informed her writings, her musical compositions, and her holistic vision of the cosmos.

6

FRANCISCANS

This whole world is pregnant with God!
—Angela of Foligno

THE RISE OF THE FRANCISCANS and their fellow friars—and sometimes rivals—the Dominicans in the early thirteenth century was partly due to the genius of their founders and partly because they were suited to the social conditions of the age. The friars added impetus to the reform movement inside the church at a time when the more recent monastic orders, such as the Cistercians and Augustinian canons, were losing their initial zeal. The friars were very much associated with universities and towns, and it has been said that "without the towns the friars would never have come into existence; without the universities they would never have become great."[1] The growth and revival of towns began from the eleventh century onward, after the end of the Viking age. Political stability, the revival of trade, and improvement in food production all contributed to urban prosperity. Some towns, such as Cologne and Milan, were ancient foundations that now experienced a new lease on life. Some places grew up around castles or monasteries, or a holy shrine—Santiago de Compostela in northern Spain developed from being an important pilgrimage center. Other towns prospered from being centers of trade and manufacturing, such as the Flemish cloth towns of Ghent and Bruges.

The friars needed the towns because they were mendicant, or "begging," orders who relied on charity to live. For the Franciscans, poverty was the central plank in their philosophy. Their founder, Francis of Assisi, distrusted the newfound mercantile prosperity he saw around him and held up as an ideal the spiritual wealth of owning nothing. But inspirational exemplar though he was, Francis's organizational skills left something to be desired, and after his death his ever-expanding order had to come to terms with how to survive. Begging for alms was feasible in the countryside only for small groups of mendicants. For large numbers a greater population density was needed, and towns supplied the answer. Whereas Cistercians had built at the frontiers of the known world, Franciscans, and Dominicans, sought out sites in the very center of towns. There they set up houses of, say, twenty friars, who would receive alms and bequests for performing services such as burials and preaching the word of God to a populace often disenchanted by their local clergy. Needless to say the latter often viewed the friars with suspicion and hostility, aggrieved that these zealous newcomers were often criticizing them explicitly or implicitly and competing with them for charitable gifts.

The friars were also active in the new universities. Until the twelfth century, the schools attached to cathedrals and monasteries had been the providers of education. But in the late twelfth and early thirteenth centuries, groups of professional teachers in certain cities and towns formed themselves into guilds or corporations (*universitas* is the late Latin for a guild or society of men) and taught small bands of students, who, if they stayed the course and paid the fees, came away with degrees, valid throughout the Continent, that also gave them license to lecture. Universities often specialized in subjects: Bologna was renowned for law, Paris for theology, a subject that Oxford also gained a reputation for. The friars needed training from theologians not only to preach and act as confessors but also to win the argument against heretics. Also, those who joined the mendicant orders were supported while they studied at universities in a way that others, reliant on family wealth, private patronage, or a church benefice, were not. So it is not surprising that many of the greatest theologians of the medieval period, including Albertus Magnus, Thomas Aquinas, Bonaventure, and William of Ockham, were either Dominicans or Franciscans.

Both orders expanded throughout the thirteenth century, and by the start of the next there were about fourteen hundred Franciscan houses and twenty-eight thousand friars spread across Europe.[2] Inevitably, the increase in numbers put a strain on the Franciscans' commitment to absolute poverty. Although they were allowed to use buildings, books, and other necessities that were kept in trust by custodians, a split occurred between the majority (the Conventuals), who wanted to adapt to changing times and requirements and to relax the rule of poverty, and a smaller group (the Spirituals), who insisted on maintaining the purity of their founder's vision. In the end the Spirituals' hard-line adherence to poverty was condemned as heretical by Pope John XXII in 1322.

Francis of Assisi

Francis of Assisi, with his heartfelt and demonstrable love for his fellow human beings and the natural world, and his unrelenting emphasis on humility, poverty, and charity, is generally regarded as the saints' saint, the one individual who has come closest to Christ's example of how to live one's life on earth. The spiritual path Francis took was not outwardly predictable from his somewhat dissipated youth. By the end of his days, however, his followers were fanning out over Europe, spreading his ideals and injecting a new warmth and vitality into church practices. His life combined action and prayer, the one sustaining the other; his mysticism is evident not so much in what he wrote as how he lived, with his graceful and intuitive love of the world around him. His awareness of the presence of God in nature and everyday life was profound (his mystical disposition toward creation was formally recognized in modern times by Pope John Paul II, who declared Francis patron of ecology in 1980), and he also received more-specific spiritual experiences, as when he heard Christ speak to him from a crucifix and when, later on in his life, he received the stigmata, the five wounds of Christ.

Francis was born in the Umbrian town of Assisi in 1181 or 1182. His father was a wealthy cloth merchant, who must have hoped his son would follow in his footsteps. But Francis was guided in his career, his biographers tell us, by a divine voice. It was this that told him in a dream, after he had set out south to embark on the career of a soldier, to return to Assisi, reinforcing what was in fact a growing commitment to the spiritual life. There were other fateful moments strengthening his newfound direction, the most profound of which occurring when he was praying before a crucifix in the small Church of Saint Damian near Assisi. Suddenly he heard God speak to him with the words "Go and repair my house because it is falling into ruin." Taking the words literally, Francis sold some of his father's cloth and gave the proceeds to the priest of Saint Damian's. His father was enraged, but Francis had taken the plunge: he renounced his inheritance and embraced a life of absolute poverty, helping those in need and toiling by himself to restore Saint Damian's as well as another local church, Saint Mary of the Angels, at a place called the Portiuncula.

In 1208 his spiritual destiny was seemingly sealed when, while attending Mass, he heard a reading from Matthew 10:7–10 in which Christ exhorts his disciples to go out into the world and preach the Gospel and heal the sick, adopting a life of absolute material poverty. Francis heard the words as a personal summons and immediately began to put them into action. Soon he was joined by a small number of followers, inspired by his example, and in this way the Friars Minor, or Little Friars, came into being. In 1210 Francis and his companions received the approval of Pope Innocent III, and in the following year they made their headquarters at the Portiuncula, where they built their wattle-and-daub huts. As the brothers went off into the countryside to preach the word of God, sleeping rough and working alongside the lowest in society, the movement grew in reputation and numbers. Among the new recruits was a young, well-to-do Assisi woman named Clare, who ran away from home to join Francis. Struck by her religious enthusiasm, Francis founded in 1212 the Poor Clares for women who wished to follow the Franciscan ideals (although they differed from the friars in being an enclosed order), appointing Clare as its head.

In the following years, Francis's evangelical zeal prompted him to take his message abroad. Two expeditions to Syria and Morocco to convert the Muslims had to be aborted through shipwreck and illness, respectively. But in 1219 he arrived in Damietta in Egypt, during the Fifth Crusade, and managed to preach before the Egyptian sultan, Malik-al-Kamal, who politely listened to this brave spiritual warrior before returning him to the Christian camp. On his eventual return to Italy, Francis was confronted with various problems concerning his brethren. In short, the movement had grown so quickly that its commitment to simplicity and poverty was under threat. Consequently, at a grand assembly of about five thousand friars at the Portiuncula in 1221, Francis decided it was time for him to step aside and let someone else take over the increasing administrative responsibilities the order was in need of.

During his last years he continued his life of preaching and praying, and he also drew up a new rule for the order. In 1224 he received the most profound mystical experience of his life, when his imitation of Christ would be acknowledged by the marks of Christ's crucified body on his own flesh. While praying during Lent on Mount La Verna, a local mountain in the Apennines, Francis saw "a Seraph having six wings, flaming and resplendent, coming down from the heights of heaven" with the figure of Christ's crucified body between its wings.[3] The vision left Francis with a "wondrous glow" in his heart, but he also found that he bore the stigmata, the five marks of Christ's wounds, on his hands and feet and the right side of his body (the scars of these were noticed on his body after his death). For Francis's followers the stigmata, which can be seen as a type of union with God, were confirmation that Francis had imitated the life of Christ to the very last—that he had the "seal of the living God." However, by this time Francis's health, damaged by years of toil, asceticism, and illness, was beginning to deteriorate. He lived on for another two years, but eventually died at the Portiuncula on October 3, 1226, at the age of forty-four. He was canonized two years later.

Although Francis's life was guided by spiritual experiences, he did not write systematically about contemplation; indeed, it has been said that "the heart of Franciscan spirituality seems to be caught up in the mystery of the human person of Francis."[4] It is necessary to go to the saint's life and deeds, his wholehearted commitment to poverty and identification with the lepers, the poor, and the outcasts of society to find his deep spirituality. That he felt God was everywhere, revealed in his glorious revelation, comes out in the many stories told about Francis's love for nature, including the well-known occasion when he preached to the birds, which, as he spoke "began to stretch their necks, to spread their wings, to open their beaks, and to look intently on him."[5]

For Francis, everyone and everything is intimately related in Christ as brothers and sisters. This is memorably summarized in his "Canticle of the Sun," which he wrote a year before his death while staying with Clare and her nuns. In this short, sacred poem or hymn he praises God for all his works, listing various aspects of the natural world—"In beautiful things he saw Beauty itself," as Bonaventure wrote.[6] The hymn shows that Francis did not so much lose himself in creation as strike up a personal intimacy with its various elements, treating them as family members. There is Brother Sun, who fills the world with light, and Sister Moon and the stars, Brother Wind, Sister Water, and Sister Earth, "who produces varied fruits with coloured flowers and herbs." Francis even includes Sister Death, from whom no mortal can escape. The canticle ends with a verse that sums up the simplicity of Francis's spirituality: "Praise and bless my Lord and give Him thanks and serve Him with great humility."[7]

Bonaventure

The year that Francis died, Bonaventure, who was to become one of the great leaders and thinkers of the Franciscan order, was only five, and there is a story that Francis actually met the young boy and healed him of a life-threatening illness. Unlike the founder of the Friars Minor, Bonaventure was primarily a theological, philosophical, and mystical thinker who shaped and formalized the ideas and ideals of his Franciscan forebears. His writings, with their careful divisions, definitions, and erudition, show the influence of Scholasticism. But unlike many Scholastics, Bonaventure conveys great warmth in his works, and he declared that experiencing the "sweetness" of God was far better than intellectual research.[8]

Influenced by, among others, the Neoplatonists, Augustine, Dio-

nysius the Areopagite, and Hugh and Richard of Saint-Victor, Bonaventure is an important mystical writer for the manner in which he
brings order and system to the way of contemplation. Equally, he never
loses sight of the vital necessity of love and devotion to Jesus Christ in
the soul's progress to God. Despite his erudition, he stressed that a
simple, unlearned person could experience God as much as a theologian. Whether or not he personally enjoyed mystical experiences is
not entirely clear, although he does speak of once receiving a vision on
Mount La Verna. He was also admired for being pious, kindly, humble,
and without pretensions, qualities that earned him a place in Dante's
Paradiso (canto 12). It is said that when he was created a cardinal bishop later on in his life, the papal envoys bearing his cardinal's hat found
him busy washing up dishes and were told by him to hang the hat on
a nearby tree until he had finished his work.

Bonaventure, called the Seraphic Doctor, was born in about 1217
(he was baptized Giovanni di Fidanza) near the town of Viterbo in Tus-
cany. He joined the Friars Minor in either the late 1230s or the early
1240s and proceeded to study at the University of Paris. Bonaventure
went on to lecture at the university, continuing almost without inter-
ruption until 1257, when he was elected minister general of the Franciscan order. This appointment occurred at a time when there was a
serious conflict between the Spirituals and the Conventuals, and
Bonaventure played such a major role in resolving their differences that
he was hailed as the order's second founder. His tact, intelligence, and
leadership were qualities no pope could fail to wish to utilize, and in
1265 Clement IV asked him to become archbishop of York. Bonaventure modestly refused to accept what was a considerable honor, but he
failed to resist Gregory X eight years later, when that pope insisted on
creating him cardinal bishop of Albano. In the following year Bonaventure was a principal contributor to the Council of Lyons, at which the
pope hoped to bring about union with the Greek church, but he died
while the council was still in progress.

Bonaventure's mystical teachings are found in a number of works,
especially *The Journey of the Mind to God* (or *The Mind's Road to God*)
and *The Threefold Way*. In the prologue to *Journey*, Bonaventure says
that thirty-five years after Francis had received the stigmata on Mount
La Verna, he himself climbed the same mountain to experience peace

and meditate on the soul's ascent to God. He then witnessed the same vision that Francis had seen, namely the six-winged seraph with the figure of Christ's crucified body. The thought struck him—in a rather Scholastic way—that the number of the seraph's wings represented the six stages by which the soul passes into divine peace and wisdom, a journey achieved only through the "most ardent love of the crucified Christ."

So in *Journey*, the spiritual quest is a six-stage movement from the external and transient world to the interior realm of our souls and what is eternal and most spiritual. In the first two stages, we can discern God through and in his creation (Bonaventure's positive emphasis on creation echoes the joyful intimacy Francis had with it). From the world outside we pass into the interior of our souls, where, in the next two stages, we find that the soul's three powers of memory, intellect, and will are an image of the Triune God—the Father, Word, and Love. The soul, therefore, bearing the image of God, is close to him and can rise "as through a mirror" to contemplate the Trinity. Few of us, however, are able to see God within ourselves because of our fallen condition: suffering, distraction, and desires prevent any progress. Our only hope lies in Christ. No matter how intelligent or erudite we are, we must love and believe and hope in Christ to reach ultimate truth. And the divine image within our minds must be reformed or repaired through being purified, illuminated, and perfected.[9]

Bonaventure elaborates on these traditional divisions of purgation, illumination, and perfection, or union, in *The Threefold Way*. Purgation, or purification, includes facing up to past sins and present temptations; with illumination we grasp the reality of God's mercy, begin to contemplate, and recover our "spiritual senses," so that the soul can once again experience God's sweetness. After illumination comes union with God, when we are raised up "above all that is sensible, imaginable, and intelligible."[10]

In *Journey*, Bonaventure expresses the climax of the mystical ascent in slightly different terms. He says that the last two of the six stages involve the mind's contemplation of God through and in the divine light of eternal truth, since our minds are "immediately formed by truth itself" (as far as is possible in this life).[11] There is then a seventh stage, when the mind leaves itself and the world of senses behind and passes over, through Christ, into an ecstatic state of mystical union. To indicate how this can be attained, Bonaventure resorts to the suggestive, riddling language of Dionysius: we must find out from "grace, not instruction; desire, not intellect; the cry of prayer, not pursuit of study; the spouse, not the teacher; God, not man; darkness, not clarity; not light, but the wholly flaming fire which will bear you aloft to God with the fullest unction and burning affection."[12]

Angela of Foligno

If Bonaventure is a prime representative of the intellectual side of the Franciscan mystical tradition, the Blessed Angela of Foligno is, with her emphasis on poverty and humility, a more direct reminder of the fundamentals of Francis's teachings and the example of his life. Like the founder of the Friars Minor, Angela, too, came from a well-to-do family and enjoyed a pleasure-ridden, somewhat wayward lifestyle until her spiritual conversion. From then on, she, like Francis, pursued a life of holy poverty, outwardly and inwardly, in the service of God and her fellow human beings. She also received visions and divine consolations, and her writings, in contrast to Bonaventure's, abound with what it is like to experience ineffable mystical states—her descriptions of them, if ultimately inadequate to the task (as she points out), nevertheless give insights into the highest reaches of mysticism and its effects. Angela could be dramatic and intense in her spiritual ardor and her devotion to Christ as lover. On one occasion she felt compelled to disrobe in front of a cross and offer herself to Jesus. At other times she reached such a "blaze of love" that if she heard someone speaking of God, she screamed and could not have stopped even if "threatened with an axe."[13]

Angela was born in the Umbrian town of Foligno, which lies about ten miles south of Assisi, in 1248. Her early life appears to have been conventional enough for the times: she got married, had several children, and enjoyed worldly pleasures. But looking back at these years after her spiritual conversion, she regarded her former self as dissolute, self-centered, and sinful. Her moment of transformation came during a personal crisis in about 1285, when she was in her late thirties. She ended up praying to Francis for help and shortly afterward was able to confess her sins to a Franciscan friar named Brother Arnold, who seems to have been a relative of hers. About three years later her entire family died, possibly as a result of plague, and in the aftermath Angela sold her home and possessions and embraced a life of poverty.

In 1291, at the age of forty-three, she became a Franciscan tertiary, or a member of the Franciscan Third Order, founded for laypeople. In the same year she made a pilgrimage to the tomb of Francis at Assisi, where she experienced the presence of God so profoundly that when it left her she began to scream and shout, to the consternation of those around her. During the remaining eighteen years of her life, Angela gained a reputation for holiness, and in Foligno she attracted around her a number of Franciscan tertiaries, who together formed a community committed to spiritual living and charitable works. She eventually died in Foligno on January 4, 1309, and was laid to rest in the local Church of Saint Francis.

Angela recorded her mystical experiences for posterity by dictating them to a scribe, probably Brother Arnold, who wrote them down in Latin. The visions form the basis of what became known as the *Memorial*, which, with her writings on the spiritual life, known as the *Instructions*, comprise her surviving works. Angela emphasizes the importance of the traditional Christian, and especially Franciscan, values and practices of prayer, humility, poverty, and love in the spiritual quest. The soul cannot rely on its own labors to come to know God but must receive the gift of divine grace, which is brought about by ardent prayer. She stresses that prayer is not simply a matter of uttering words but a holistic act that engages the mind and heart, soul and body, accompanied by constant meditation on the life of Christ.[14]

Prayer, which is in effect a way of life, leads to the experience of God, from which is born true humility. The establishment of humility allows divine grace to increase in the soul, and this in turn deepens humility—grace and humility work positively and reciprocally on each other.[15] For Angela, humility is the source from which the other virtues spring, and through it the soul appreciates its own nothingness and sinfulness as well as the vastness of God's goodness. In the soul's increased state of self-knowledge and yearning for God, the other virtues flourish, the most important being the love of God and humanity. Realizing that it is nothing, the soul is consumed with an ardent love of God that transforms it into God, enabling it to love all God's creatures, since it sees God's presence in them.[16]

Prayer, humility, grace, and love are essential to the soul's ascent to God, and it is Angela's own direct experiences of God that give rise to her most compelling writing, for example in her description of the presence of God in the world: "The eyes of my soul were opened, and I beheld the plenitude of God, in which I did comprehend the whole world, both here and beyond the sea, and the abyss and ocean and all things. In all these things I beheld nothing except the divine power, in a totally indescribable way; so that through excess of marvelling the soul cried with a loud voice, saying 'This whole world is pregnant with God!'"[17] When Brother Arnold once asked her to describe her vision of God, she told him that what she saw was a "fullness, a brightness," that filled her so much that she was unable to describe or compare it to anything. She did not see a "bodily form," as such, but an ineffable beauty that seemed to her to be the ultimate beauty and total goodness.[18]

The highest mystical experience, union with God, is described by Angela in different ways. She speaks of her will becoming one with God's and realizing that her love originates not from her but from him.[19] She also speaks of having encountered the divine darkness— echoing Dionysius the Areopagite—in which she simultaneously saw nothing and everything, as well as seeing the face of the "God-man" (that is, Christ). It is the vision of God in darkness that is for Angela the ultimate mystical experience: It goes beyond all the other expressions of the divine presence because the good that she saw in it was "the All," whereas everything else was simply a part. "All the countless and unspeakable favors God has done to me," she says, "all the words He has said to me . . . are, I know, so far below the Good I see in that great darkness that I do not put in them my hope."[20] On her deathbed she was heard to cry out repeatedly, "O Unknown Nothingness! O Unknown Nothingness!"[21]

7

THE BEGUINES

She feels no joy, for she herself is joy, and swims
and floats in joy without feeling any joy, for
she inhabits joy and joy inhabits her.
　　　　　　　　　　—Marguerite Porete

T HE STATUS OF AND ATTITUDE TOWARD women in the Middle Ages was complex. In the songs of the Provençal troubadours and their German equivalents, the Minnesänger, the figure of the noble lady was central to the cult of courtly love, an idealized conception of love in which the woman was an object of unattainable desire and the cause of emotional pain to the frustrated suitor. In real life the honoring of women became part of the chivalric code of knights, and from the eleventh century this secular idealism was to some extent mirrored by the cult of the Virgin Mary. Indeed, the "Christianization" of courtly love can be seen in the writings of the Beguines, a religious movement for women, for whom the suitor represented the soul seeking the love of God.

There was also, however, an underlying misogynistic tradition in the church, going back to early times, which regarded women as daughters of Eve, the prime agent in the fall of man, and as sirens, ready to lure religiously inclined males onto the rocks of lust. The mastery of appetites and the prestige of sexual continence had become important in the church from the second century onward; celibacy and virginity were associated with spiritual potency, and for Christian men, "prolonged or lifelong abstinence . . . made women seem strange, lurid, dangerous."[1] This male wariness toward women continued down the centuries; to Bernard of Clairvaux, for example, "every woman was a threat to his chastity,"[2] an attitude that we can readily imagine was not uncommon in monasteries across Europe.

Although in medieval times there were convents that gave women a chance to escape the world and serve God, their numbers were relatively small, despite the monastic reforms of the eleventh and twelfth centuries. Cistercian convents did spring up, but these were barely recognized by the all-male General Chapter. The Franciscan Poor Clares also provided an outlet, but the nuns remained strictly cloistered, unlike their spiritual brothers. For women who wished to devote their lives to God but who found the strictures of the enclosed life too limiting, there were few, and sometimes not very orthodox, alternatives. The Beguines were one; and there were other groups, such as the Waldenses, who were judged by the church to be tainted by heresy.

The demarcation between orthodoxy and heresy was not always clear cut. The Waldenses, for example, had similarities with the Franciscans (some of whom, the Spirituals, also came to be branded as heretics)—both movements grew out of the idea of imitating the apostolic life of the first Christians. The Waldenses were named for Peter Valdes, a prosperous French merchant of Lyons who in the mid-1170s gave up his possessions and became an itinerant preacher wedded to poverty. In 1179 Pope Alexander III approved Valdes and his followers but forbade them to preach without the permission of local bishops. But the Waldenses would not bite their tongues, and in 1184 Pope Lucius III declared them heretics. Despite this pronouncement, however, they continued to spread into various parts of Europe, drawing most of their followers from the rural lower classes.

Other heretical groups did not fare as well as the Waldenses. Also condemned with them in 1184 were the Albigenses, a branch of the Cathars, a group that originated in Bulgaria. The Cathars were dualists, believing that were two eternal principles: good and evil. They rejected the flesh and material things as being evil, and they thought that Christ did not become a flesh-and-blood man but remained an insubstantial phantom. Therefore he did not suffer and die on the cross, nor was he raised from the dead. The Albigenses (their name comes from the town of Albi in Languedoc, southern France) could not be persuaded by orthodox preachers to see the error of their ways, so in 1208 Pope Innocent III launched a crusade against them. The crusaders came from the north of France and were motivated as much by winning land from the southerners as by extirpating heresy. A fierce, protracted war carried on until an uneasy peace was reached in 1229.

Another religious movement that was eventually viewed with suspicion and hostility was the Beguines (the name may derive from Albigenses, with whom their enemies associated them), who, by the end of the twelfth and beginning of the thirteenth century, had taken root in the Low Countries. The Beguines were women who expressed their spirituality by living alone or together with other women in small convents or larger communities, dedicating their lives to God in prayer, worship, and good deeds. What was remarkable about them was that they fell between the categories of lay and religious. Unlike the religious orders, they did not have a formal structure, common rule, or supreme central authority. Also, they were free to leave their way of life and return to the everyday world (or join an order). They committed themselves to chastity, but only so long as they remained Beguines. They were allowed to hold property and support themselves by, say, weaving, embroidering vestments, and teaching—indeed, this economic self-sufficiency was much praised by contemporaries. Also, they were unusual in being "basically a women's movement, not simply a feminine appendix to a movement that owed its impetus, direction, and main support to men."[3]

The attraction of the Beguines, who were also referred to as *mulieres sanctae* (holy women), was that they answered the need of women who wanted to lead mutually supportive spiritual lives but did not want to join an order. At the time, western Europe had a surplus of unmarried women, owing in large measure to the Crusades and other wars, which had decimated the numbers of potential husbands. Some women became nuns, but not all wished to live in an enclosed order. Whereas men were able to choose different ways of expressing their spirituality—for example, the vigorous asceticism of the Cistercians or the evangelical poverty of the Franciscan and Dominican friars— women had to choose between the home and the cloister. So the Beguine way of life, more spiritual than family life, less constricting than convent life, was a tempting alternative.

Although the first communities arose in the Low Countries, in places such as Liège and Nivelles in what is now Belgium, the movement spread to Germany, France, and other parts of Europe. In 1216 Pope Honorius III gave a qualified endorsement to the movement, which also attracted powerful benefactors, such as Louis IX of France, who established a Beguine presence in Paris in 1264. In time small discrete Beguine communities were often superseded by larger complexes, or beguinages, which could comprise a number of convents, a church, hospital, cemetery, and other amenities (the beguinage of Ghent, for example, had its own brewery).[4] Beguines could form a significant percentage of a city's or town's population. Writing in 1243, the English chronicler Matthew Paris reported that in Cologne and neighboring towns there were two thousand Beguines and Beghards (their male equivalents, who were less numerous and noteworthy).[5]

The church, however, was never entirely sanguine about the Beguines, with their halfway-house status and their sometimes untempered criticism of the clergy. With its ever-vigilant eyes watching for the slightest trace of heresy, the church from time to time focused its suspicions on the Beguines, particularly their alleged association with the heresy of the Free Spirit, a group said to believe in the irrelevance of morality and the holy sacraments once a state of spiritual perfection had been reached. In 1299 the Synod of Béziers decreed that the Beguines had "no approbation." Then in 1312 the Council of Vienne officially condemned them. Although ten years later Pope John XXII softened the decision, the movement lost momentum and continued in decline until the Reformation, when many of their convents were suppressed. Those in Belgium fared better than most, even growing in number during the seventeenth century and surviving the religious turmoil of the French Revolution.

Hadewijch of Brabant

In their spirituality the Beguines tended to emphasize the humanity and suffering of Jesus Christ and the central place of the Eucharist, and the spiritual marriage between the soul and God. Ascetic practices were common, as was the occurrence of supernatural phenomena, such as visions, ecstasies, and prophecies. The movement produced some outstanding mystics and teachers, especially Hadewijch of Brabant, in Belgium, Mechthild of Magdeburg, and Marguerite Porete, who was burned at the stake in Paris in 1310 for alleged heresy.

The Flemish Beguine Hadewijch is noted for her mysticism of love, which she expressed not only in letters and visions but also in poetry. Although she acknowledges the importance of the intellect, ultimately it is love alone that can reach God, abandoning itself to him, "plunging into the abyss . . . where fruition is reached."[6] Not much is known about Hadewijch's life apart from what can be inferred from her writings. She lived sometime during the first half of the 1200s, and allusions in her works to chivalric life may indicate that she came from a well-to-do family, possibly in or near Antwerp or Brussels. Judging from the fact that she knew Latin and French—although she wrote in medieval Dutch—and was knowledgeable about the scriptures, patristic writings, astronomy, music theory, and the art of writing poetry, she must have received a good education. It is likely that she was the head of a Beguine convent, and it seems that for reasons unknown she was compelled to leave it against her will, although she kept in contact with some of her former associates, writing letters of advice and encouragement to them.

Hadewijch's existing works are thought to have been written during a twenty-year period after 1221. They consist of fourteen visions, thirty-one letters, and about sixty poems, some written in stanza form, others in couplets. During the late Middle Ages her writings disappeared from the record and were only rediscovered in the early nineteenth century. Hadewijch did not systematically set out her spiritual teachings, which have to be patched together from what she wrote.

With regard to her own mystical experiences, she records in one of her visions that she encountered the living Christ in the Eucharist and felt that he was actually present in her body and that she was united with him.[7] In Letter 9 she again writes of mystical union, this time in reference to the spiritual lover and beloved: it is a state in which neither party can distinguish one from the other, with their mouths, hearts, bodies, and souls merged but with respective identities preserved: "sometimes one sweet divine nature transfuses them both, and they are one, each wholly in the other, and yet each one remains and will always remain himself."[8]

Central to Hadewijch's spirituality is love. It is clear that she had absorbed the prevalent ethos of courtly love; and she used the literary conventions of the genre in her own spiritual works. So, the devoted lover becomes the ardent soul, and the beloved, the Lady, is now the divine love of God. Hadewijch is keen to stress that love involves suffering. She points out that whereas everyone desires to live with God and partake of his glory, few are prepared to live after the model of his humanity and share his Passion. Suffering is not something to be avoided; rather, it is the means through which we reach the highest love, and it is this love that we must focus on single-mindedly, totally committed and trusting, before we can experience it. We must also practice virtuous works and be totally obedient to Lady Love if she is to penetrate us and take us out of ourselves into union with her.[9]

Obstacles to union, as Hadewijch explains in a letter, come from the fact that we are too self-centered and self-willed and too concerned with our rest and peace of mind, as well as being vulnerable to depression and dejection and attacks on our faith and honor. We care too much about gossip, socializing, nice clothes and food, beautiful objects, and entertainment, with which we try to escape from God (at the end of the letter she anticipates her reader's response to her strictures with the empathetic exclamation: "O Lord, how difficult it is!").[10] Hadewijch had no illusions about the travails of life, which she views in terms of being in exile from God. But we must desire to do what love asks us to do, no matter what the outcome may be.[11] We must also be aware that although love may bring us a "delightful sweetness," we should not measure it by this: the real fruits of love are found not in what we feel but what virtue it brings. Love can sustain qualities and virtues such as charity, mercy, humility, and reason—but they cannot sustain her: only her wholeness can do this.[12]

For Hadewijch, love is, ultimately, beguiling and mysterious. It is "beyond matter, immeasurable in God's great freedom, giving always from its superabundance."[13] In one poem, she describes love's paradoxical nature: to be imprisoned by her is to be free, her sweetest song is silence, her departing is her drawing near.[14] In another poem she beautifully evokes the mature effects of love on her: "But then she made me like hazel trees, / Which blossom early in the season of darkness, / And bear fruit slowly."[15]

Mechthild of Magdeburg

As is the case with Hadewijch, nothing much is known about the life of Mechthild of Magdeburg apart from what can be gleaned from her writings. Her great work, *The Flowing Light of the Godhead,* is a masterpiece of visions, prayers, allegories, reflective pieces, and aphorisms, written in prose and verse. It established her as one of the greats of German mysticism as well as a lyric poet of the highest order. For Mechthild, again like Hadewijch, the central realities of the spiritual life were the experience of divine love and the celebration of the Eucharist. Allied to these was the practice of prayer, which, she says, enables God to reside in the heart and also propels the soul to God: it is, in short, the means of union between God and the soul, who together "converse long of love" in bliss.[16]

Born in Saxony in about 1210, probably of a noble family, Mechthild received her first visionary experiences at the age of twelve. As a young woman she felt the call to lead a more intense religious life, and in her early twenties, she left home to join the Beguines at Magdeburg on the river Elbe. Here, for the next forty years or so, she lived an ascetic life devoted to prayer and continued to receive visions, which she began to write down. She eventually showed them to her friend the Dominican friar Henry of Halle, who collected them. Her psychic life did not, however, engross her to the extent that she was blind to the outside world: she was outspoken about the failings of the church and the local clergy.

Mechthild's time at Magdeburg came to an end in about 1270,

when she was in her late fifties. For reasons that are unknown, she left the Beguines and moved to the Cistercian convent at Helfta near the town of Eisleben. There she spent the last years of her life, dying sometime in the early 1280s. Earlier in her life she had confessed to God her fear about death and the passing of her soul from her body, and God had told her that when the time came he would draw his breath, and her soul would come to him "as a needle to a magnet."[17]

The visions Mechthild received were often powerful and sometimes cosmic. She describes how, when she was in rapture, her soul left her body and was elevated to a realm between earth and heaven where, in a state of bliss, she was able to see the shining figure of Jesus Christ and also the Holy Trinity.[18] In another vision she sees the world to come as a three-tiered realm consisting of hell, purgatory, and heaven, which also have subdivisions (some believe she may have influenced Dante in the writing of his *Divine Comedy*). She describes in some detail the horrors of hell, a structure that has three layers, with condemned Christians at the bottom, Jews in the middle, and pagans at the top. Lucifer himself lies chained in the deepest abyss, spewing pestilence, sin, and suffering from his mouth. The fate of those tormented in hell and purgatory exercised Mechthild, and she says that on one particular occasion she prayed for souls in purgatory and managed to free thousands of them from their bondage.[19]

Mechthild's major work, *The Flowing Light of the Godhead*, consists of seven books, six of them completed at Magdeburg between about 1250 and 1264, the last at Helfta. Mechthild wrote in a Low German dialect, but the two versions of her book that have survived are later translations into Middle High German and Latin. The book, which intersperses sections of prose with delicate verse, is full of imaginative and visionary power and exudes a sense of warmth and immediacy with its emphasis on love, frequently explored—as was the case with Hadewijch—through the literary conventions of courtly love. She often refers to the soul as the lover and Christ as the beloved in the sensual terms of the Song of Songs: "Many days have I wooed her / But never heard her voice. Now I am moved / I must go to meet her."[20] She also refers to love as "Lady love," who can bring "true safety" only through destroying a life attached to the world,[21] and to love "penetrating" the senses and capturing the soul, in which it grows with great desire for God until it expands and melts into the bodily senses, which then, like the soul, conform to love.[22] Elsewhere she compares the soul's drawing the senses along the path to God to a sighted person leading the blind,[23] and she says that the prolonged action of God's love on the soul has the effect of rendering it more pure, beautiful, and holy.[24] In a short, exquisite lyric she compares God's descending gently on the soul to dew falling on a flower.[25]

As well as focusing on the reality of divine love and its effects, Mechthild also emphasized the experience and necessity of suffering, which is bound up with identifying ourselves with the Passion of Christ. People experience the joy of God when they conform their will to his—so we must accept suffering with joy and consolations with fear; we must be one with him and rejoice in his will.[26] She also stressed the reality of sin. She was all too aware of how deleterious our desires are, along with self-willed obstinacy, hatred, anger, false piety, which, if we fail to deal with them, will deprive us of paradise.[27] Conversely, there is no substitute for practicing the virtues, especially humility, which is displayed in four ways: in our clothes and where we live, in our behavior toward others and the degree of loving-kindness we show to them, in our senses and how we "use and love all things rightly," and in the soul itself and the selflessness that raises us to heaven.[28]

Through the practice of virtue, through rigorous detachment from the world, and by inviting suffering we can reach the "true wilderness," a spiritual state of being emptied of false things and centered on love.[29] Virtues are essential to the harmonious spiritual life, a point Mechthild makes plain in an allegory that depicts a happily run convent staffed by various figures such as Charity, the abbess; Peace, the prioress; Meekness, the chaplain; and so on. In accordance with contemporary practice, all are subject to the male priest, Obedience. The virtues are not only good in themselves but are also, of course, the means of preparing the soul for the journey that ends in union with God. Mechthild describes the flight of the soul toward God in another allegorical illustration. She says that if a bird remains on the ground for too long, its wings grow feeble and feathers heavy. But the longer it flies, "the more blissfully it soars, . . . hardly alighting on the earth to rest. So it is with the soul: the wings of love have taken from it the desire for earthly things."[30]

Marguerite Porete

For several hundred years from the end of the thirteenth century, an anonymous mystical text entitled *Mirror of Simple Souls* circulated around Europe, describing the various stages of the soul's journey to God. In 1946 it was finally established that the book's author was Marguerite Porete, who in 1310 had been burned to death in Paris as a heretic. Despite the actions of the inquisitors, however, the book lived on in various translations down the centuries, spreading far and wide her spiritual thought.

The only substantial biographical details that exist about Marguerite concern her trial and execution. It is thought she may have originated in Hainaut in Belgium; by the end of her life she seems to have become a wandering preacher, and this irregular lifestyle, along with biting criticism of the church and some dubiously orthodox statements in the *Mirror*, combined to antagonize the church authorities, who branded her as a Beguine at a time when the name had become a term of abuse. Although Marguerite had secured the endorsement of three theologians for the *Mirror*, such support did not deter the bishop of Cambrai from warning her not to teach from or distribute her book, which he burned in public.

Heedless of his threats, and sublimely confident of her divinely revealed wisdom over theologians' book learning, Marguerite carried on her work as before and was duly arrested in 1308 and sent to jail in Paris. There she defied the Inquisition, refusing to disown her beliefs and teachings. Parts of her work, taken out of context, were then scrutinized by a team of theologians from the University of Paris, who found a number of alleged heretical statements. Still refusing to cooperate with the Inquisition, Marguerite was eventually condemned as a relapsed heretic and sentenced to be burned at the stake. She died, with dignity, on June 1, 1310.

Marguerite was unfortunate to have lived in an age when it was widely held by the church and other authorities that women should either be properly engaged in the religious life, that is, enclosed in a regular order, or committed to lay life as wives and mothers. There were other factors too. She made no friends, at least in clerical circles, by being an outspoken critic of the church, which she called, pejoratively, Holy Church the Less—as opposed to the ideal community of "free" or "simple" souls of Holy Church the Greater. She also emphasized the superiority of love over—and the "annihilated" soul's disregard for—the sacraments, the virtues, and reason, the latter being the mainstay of Scholasticism. There might also have been a political dimension to her death. The French king Philip IV had recently been engaged in suppressing the Knights Templar, who had had the backing of the pope. The king, it is suggested, might have been attempting to improve his standing with the pope by demonstrating his commitment to orthodoxy and the eradication of heresy in his kingdom.

Written in Old French, Marguerite's *Mirror of Simple Souls* is based around dialogues involving the figures of Love, Soul, Reason, and others, but it also includes poems and extended prose sections. A principal theme is the seven-stage journey of the soul that leads it to the point when it loses its will and reaches union with the Trinity. Marguerite summarizes these seven steps as follows: (1) The soul, touched by grace, resolves to keep God's commandments "to love him with all her heart, and her neighbor also as herself." (2) She, the soul, reaches a state where she scorns wealth, pleasure, and honors and does not fear material losses. (3) She renounces good works and abandons her will to that of her Lover. (4) She is exalted by Love through contemplation. (5) By an influx of divine light, she sees that she must abandon her will to the will of God, which, when it occurs, changes her into "Love's nature." Through divine knowledge she recognizes her nothingness, and yet she is everything and is drawn deep down into the abyss of her own evil, where she loses her pride. In the depths of herself, she can see divine goodness, which makes her reexamine herself: she becomes "wholly at rest." (6) She does not see herself or God, but God sees himself in her, for there is nothing but him. So the soul is illumined, but not glorified. (7) This last step is the state of glorification, about which we remain ignorant until death.[31]

Throughout her book, Marguerite is emphatic about how the human will is an obstacle to union. We lose our freedom when we will something—because the will strengthens the sense of "I." If we will nothing, then the soul can say: "I am alone in him, without myself, and wholly set free."[32] For those who no longer have any will, prosperity and adversity are of equal account: honor and shame, poverty and wealth, hell and paradise, are all esteemed at the same level.[33] She also describes those who operate by their own will as living by straw, stalks, and "coarse fodder," whereas those whose will has been replaced by God's live "by fine grain."[34]

The liberated soul is "completely dissolved, melted, drawn and joined and united in the exalted Trinity; and she can wish for nothing except the divine will through the divine operation of the whole Trinity. And a rapturous brilliance and light join her from ever closer at hand."[35] The soul has reached a level of spiritual transcendence at which it no longer seeks God through the sacraments, penitence, and thoughts, words, and deeds; nor does it seek or reject poverty and suffering, the Eucharist or sermons, fasting and praying. Also, without a will, it is prevented from sinning, since "without a will no one can sin."[36]

It is not surprising that the church authorities took exception to the idea of the soul jettisoning conventional religious observance and being incapable of sin. Similarly provocative is the moment when the liberated soul declares: "Virtues, I take my leave of you for evermore. . . . There was a time I was your serf but now I break away."[37] Nor would Marguerite have helped herself by her negative theology of the Dionysian tradition, which could easily be misinterpreted. Yet Marguerite did not confine her poetic imagination to negative statements, and she is at her most attractive when evoking states of union and transcendence, as when she says that the liberated soul "swims in the sea of joy—that is, in the sea of delights flowing and streaming down from the godhead. She feels no joy, for she herself is joy, and swims and floats in joy without feeling any joy, for she inhabits joy and joy inhabits her."[38]

8

THE RHINELAND MYSTICS

The eye with which I see God is exactly the
same as the eye with which God sees me.
—Meister Eckhart

THE SO-CALLED RHINELAND MYSTICS were a group of fourteenth-century German and Flemish mystics who were among the most influential spiritual thinkers of the medieval period. Three of them, Meister Eckhart, Johannes Tauler, and Henry Suso, belonged to the Dominican order, while Jan van Ruysbroeck founded a small community of Augustinian canons. It is perhaps not surprising that such able mystical thinkers were nearly all Dominicans, because the Blackfriars (as they were called because of their black mantles) placed great emphasis on study and scholarship. Their founder, the Spaniard Dominic de Guzman (ca. 1170–1221), realized the importance of education and the ability to preach effectively when he was trying to convert the heretic Cathars of Languedoc during the Albigensian Crusade. He also wished to see a clergy that could outshine the most pious and worthy of the heretics through personal morality and poverty. The Dominican Order of Preachers that he founded adopted the rule of the Augustinian canons and followed the Franciscans in insisting on mendicancy (begging) and corporate poverty. But more than the Franciscans, the Dominicans stressed the role of preaching and study, and they soon established friaries in university towns such as Paris, Bologna, and Oxford. Although never as numerous as the Franciscans, the order quickly spread; about a century after their foundation, there were approximately six hundred houses established throughout Europe.

The strong Dominican intellectual tradition peaked with the great Schoolmen Albertus Magnus and his hugely influential pupil Thomas Aquinas, in whose vast, encyclopedic *Summa Theologiae* medieval Scholasticism reached its peak. Born near Aquino in Italy in about 1225, Aquinas carried on the work of his master of trying to reconcile the thought of Aristotle with the Christian faith and the Augustinian intellectual tradition that had hitherto underpinned it. The works of Aristotle had been known since early medieval times only in fragmentary form. But in the twelfth and thirteenth centuries, through increasing contact with Muslim scholars—who had accessed and absorbed more of Aristotle's works than their Christian counterparts—in Moorish Spain and Sicily, and as a result of the Crusades (especially the capture of Constantinople in 1204), Aristotelian texts began to flow into Europe.

In essence, Aquinas made an important distinction between the realms of faith and reason, which he saw as complementary, not mutually exclusive. On the one hand he used logic to substantiate Christian doctrine, but he recognized that there were spiritual mysteries, such as the resurrection of the body, that lay beyond reason. He did stress, however, that matters of divine revelation should at least not be *contrary* to reason. But although Aquinas's teachings came to hold a central place in Catholic theology after the Reformation, they did not command universal assent among his contemporaries, and in the fourteenth century they were challenged by the Franciscans Duns Scotus and William of Ockham. William, with his emphasis on the gulf between faith and reason and the importance of empirical knowledge, marked the beginning of the end of the Scholastic era.

The 1300s also saw the start of a turbulent period for the papacy and an increasing assertiveness of nation states such as England and France, as well as the continuing growth and influence of towns. Early in the century, the French king Philip IV clashed with Pope Boniface VIII on an issue involving the authority of the papacy, and the quarrel eventually ended with the pope's having to be rescued from the clutches of the king's soldiers, but only after his dignity and health, and the status of the papacy, had been badly mauled. Then in 1305 a Frenchman was elected pope as Clement V and was pressured by Philip into moving the papal residency from Rome to Avignon in the south of France. For nearly seventy years successive French popes remained in what was ironically called the Babylonian Exile, a time when they were widely perceived to be susceptible to the bidding of the French monarchy.

The fourteenth century was also a time when the church sharpened its focus on irregular religious movements and individual heretics. At the Council of Vienne (1311–1312) Clement finally suppressed the Knights Templar, after Philip, desirous of their wealth, had conducted his own violent assault against them. In 1318 Pope John XXII had four Spiritual Franciscans burned as heretics and five years later officially pronounced their doctrine of poverty heretical. In 1327 John excommunicated Marsilius of Padua for his work *Defensor Pacis*, which asserted that the church should be subordinate to the state. And in the same year the German Dominican monk Meister Eckhart was summoned to Avignon to answer for alleged heretical statements in his works.

Meister Eckhart

Known as the father of German mysticism, Meister Eckhart was a profound mystical thinker, a charismatic and controversial figure whose influence on mystics, theologians, and ordinary believers, as well as poets and artists, continues to this day. His thoughts on the nature of God, the soul, and mystical consciousness are not methodically set out but scattered like sparks among the glowing prose of his sermons, treatises, and other writings, written in both German and Latin. Paradoxical, teasing, and provocative—a number of his statements were officially condemned by the church as heretical after his death—his sayings frequently challenge the mind to make leaps of imagination to grasp the truth behind them. "The eye with which I see God is exactly the same as the eye with which God sees me"[1] is the sort of statement that pressures our logical thinking in the way that the riddling Zen koans do ("What is the sound of one hand clapping?" "What did your face look like before you were born?"). Indeed, the great modern Zen master D. T. Suzuki believed Eckhart to be the profoundest of Western thinkers.

Eckhart was born in about 1260 in the small village of Hochheim near the town of Gotha in the province of Thuringia in central Germany. Not much is known of his early years. His family seems to have been reasonably well off, and at the age of about sixteen he entered the Dominican order at Erfurt (the capital of modern Thuringia). There he underwent the usual scholastic training, learning grammar, rhetoric, mathematics, and other subjects, before embarking on a three-year course in theology. After that he was ordained a priest and began a distinguished career in the service of the Blackfriars. That he was valued for his leadership and administrative acumen is shown by a number of senior appointments in the years to come: by his midthirties he was prior of Erfurt and vicar of Thuringia; in the early 1300s, at about the same time that he had completed his studies at Paris and become a Master of Theology (whence the "Meister"), he was elected head of the new Dominican province of Saxony; and in 1307 he was made vicar of Bohemia.

Later, after spells of teaching and administering in Paris and Strasbourg, he ended up in Cologne in the early 1320s. There he fell foul of the local archbishop, Henry of Virneburg, who accused him of heretical teachings. Eckhart believed there was a personal animus behind Henry's attack and decided to appeal directly to Pope John XXII. So in 1327, having publicly declared that he would gladly retract any statements found to be truly heretical, he made his way to the papal court at Avignon. But as the judicial proceedings rumbled on month after month, Eckhart suddenly died, possibly in early 1328. He therefore escaped the pope's declaration in the following year that seventeen of his statements were heretical. To take one example: Eckhart preached that it is wrong to talk of God's being "good." To anyone accustomed to the idea that God is the essence of goodness, the statement would seem perverse. But Eckhart's intention was to stress that nothing whatsoever can be predicated of God: he is beyond being and so far from our understanding that it is meaningless to attribute to him any qualities, even positive ones.

The judgment against Eckhart came too late to damage him while alive, although the process may have hastened him to his grave. But it did immediately cast a shadow over his reputation, and it was left to his loyal, mainly Dominican, followers to keep his inspiration alive, with Johannes Tauler and Henry Suso especially preserving the spirit of his teachings.

Although Eckhart exerted enormous influence on the Christian mystical tradition, there is little in his writings to indicate unambiguously that he himself enjoyed direct experience of the divine. Yet the confident authority of his works on mystical theology suggests that he probably did. His teachings were influenced by the Neoplatonists and the negative theology of Dionysius the Areopagite and include a number of important mystical themes, including the birth of God in the soul, the existence of a divine "spark" in the soul, and the necessity of detachment. He emphasizes that there is a distinction to be made between God and the Godhead (which he also sometimes, rather confusingly, refers to as God). The Godhead, like the Absolute of Plotinus, is the ultimate undifferentiated unity. Nothing can be predicated of it. It is beyond comprehension, beyond description, although Eckhart does refer to it as being "barren" and as a "desert," that is, a place where there are no forms or activity. So what is the relationship between the Godhead and God? According to Eckhart, the Godhead "reveals" or "manifests" itself as the Triune God—the Father, Son, and Holy Spirit.[2] So when he says rather startlingly, "Therefore let us pray to God that we may be free of God," he means that we need to get beyond the image or idea of God in his persons and back to the undifferentiated Godhead.

Eckhart also talks about the Father "ceaselessly generating the Son in eternity," while the Holy Spirit is the love that the Son reflects back to the Father. He goes on to say that not only does the Father beget the Son but he begets "me as his Son," that is, he transforms the individual into a being partaking of his divine nature. The birth of God in the soul, one of the Dominican's favorite images, comes about when the soul lays aside all its selfishness. Indeed, Eckhart says that the whole point of praying, fasting, performing devotions and good works, baptism, and the Incarnation is so that "God may be born in the soul and the soul born in God."[3] Elsewhere Eckhart talks about the birth in terms of God's pouring himself into the soul as light, which spills over into the body, making it radiant. Sinners, however, are deprived of this light because their sins block the channels of infusion. Eckhart therefore urges us to find the light by observing within ourselves the birth of God, which is something that God must do at all times, because it is part of his nature. We are blessed in the way we can passively receive God, and "the infinity of the soul's receiving matches the infinity of God's giving."[4]

Eckhart also stresses the importance of the divine image within the individual, which he calls variously the "spark," "crown," "light," and "ground of the soul." This image, which he equates with the intellect, lies beyond time and space and, like God, is one and simple. In fact it is God's presence in the depth of the soul through which the latter can unite with God. By turning away from the created world, we can become "unified and sanctified in the soul's spark," which desires only God—not the Triune God but God beyond God, the "still desert" of the Godhead, where no distinction of person exists. "There, in that most inward place, where everyone is a stranger, the light is satisfied and there it is more inward than it is in itself, for this ground is a simple stillness which is immovable in itself."[5]

For Eckhart the way of the mystic is founded on the individual's detachment from the world. This includes freedom not just from possessions but also from the images of objects that impede the mind. We need to strip away all images and to love God nonmentally in simplicity, without holding on to any idea of God as "spirit" or "person": we must love him as he is, "One, pure, simple, and transparent."[6] In order to enable God to make his home in the soul, the will's attraction toward finite earthly things and the pleasures they hold must be overcome. We must embrace true poverty by renouncing the will totally—even the will to do God's will: "I tell you by the eternal truth that as long as you have the will to perform God's will, and a desire for eternity and for God, you are not yet poor. They alone are poor who will nothing and desire nothing."[7]

Eckhart believed the mystic's path and the goal of uniting the soul with God was not reserved for the elite. What is important is the transformation of the inner person, and for this to happen it is not necessary to seek solitude, to escape the world, or to practice special religious rituals. For "whoever truly possesses God in the right way, possesses him in all places, in any company, as well as in a church or a remote place or in their cell."[8]

Johannes Tauler

Eckhart's most significant followers were Johannes Tauler and Henry Suso, the first of them renowned for his eloquent preaching and emphasis on practical spirituality, the second for the depth of his feeling about God. Tauler's sermons were hugely influential in Germany, being particularly dear to Martin Luther, who said that he had found "more true theology" in Tauler "than all the doctors of all the universities." Tauler was born in about 1300 in Strasbourg, the city with which he was associated for most of his life. He was educated at the local Dominican convent and subsequently spent most of the rest of his life in the city, preaching and acting as a spiritual director to Dominican nuns. His reputation as a good and holy man was enhanced during the Black Death in 1348, when Tauler administered to the sick and dying. He eventually died in Strasbourg in 1361.

Tauler's teachings are known primarily from his preaching, for which he became renowned (a contemporary said that he "set the world ablaze with his fiery tongue"). Some eighty sermons have survived, and although they do not have Eckhart's originality and verve, they compensate with their vigor, lucidity, and warmth. Like the Meister, Tauler talks about the birth of God in the soul, and he, too, uses the image of the desert or wilderness to refer to where the ineffable God exists beyond all categories—a place of "unfathomable darkness" and yet, paradoxically, of "essential light." Here the soul may find the simple unity of God, where distinctions and multiplicity are absent.[9] In Dionysian mode, he speaks of love that is stripped of self, characterized by "non-Knowledge," dead to sensible images, and that constitutes a state in which "we are reformed in the form of God, clothed with his divinity."[10]

Tauler does not refer to Eckhart's "spark" of the soul, but he does speak of "the ground of the soul" and of God's image lying in the hidden depths of the spirit. He also outlines the mystic's ascent to God, which begins with self-control and discipline, spurred on by a fear of damnation. We then progress to contemplation of Christ and the letting go of "forms and images," which allows God to enter us: the irruption of the divine may be sudden and dramatic or happen gradually and quietly.[11] Tauler describes union with God in different ways: for example, the individual, after the powers of his senses and reason have been unified, throws himself into the divine abyss, where the Godhead, descending into the soul, draws it up into union with its uncreated essence.[12] In Sermon 19, he talks about the blissful rapture when the soul is set on fire with love and the Holy Spirit floods the soul with radiant light.

Whether Tauler himself experienced the mystical states he refers to is a moot point, but he did state that it was easier to experience the divine than describe it, which he often attempts to do in terms of light. He says that "God illumines his true Friends, and shines within them with power, purity, and truth";[13] and he talks about the inner spirit of man being able to return to its divine origins, where it becomes the "light of lights," and when this shines into the soul, it is so dazzling that it appears as a darkness, in the same way, he says—in an echo of Plato— that the eyes see darkness when they "gaze at the disk of the sun."[14]

Tauler did not set the contemplative life against the active one, preferring to see them as complementary partners. People honor God in their various ways; it is not necessary to become a monk or a priest: "One man can spin, another can make shoes, and all these are the gifts of the Holy Ghost. I tell you, if I were not a priest, I should esteem it a great gift that I was able to make shoes, and I would try to make them so well as to be a pattern of all."[15]

Henry Suso

Of the three great German Dominican mystics, Henry Suso has the reputation of being the most passionate, colorful, and lyrical in his evocations of the mystical life. Subject for much of his life to ecstasies and visions, including one when the deceased Eckhart appeared to him, Suso was for a period one of the most ascetic of mystics, for many years following a regime of austerities that makes the eyes water (for example, he wore a tailor-made nightshirt fitted with specially sharpened nails).

The gory penances continued until one day he received an angelic message telling him that God did not require them of him anymore. From then on he realized that he should concentrate on detachment and abandonment of the self, and he advised others against severe penances.

Of aristocratic stock, Suso was born in about 1295 in or near Constance, where he joined the Dominican order at the age of thirteen. In the 1320s he went on to study in Cologne under the supervision of Eckhart, whose reputation he would later try to defend. For the rest of his life he wrote, preached, and gave spiritual guidance—especially to Dominican nuns—in Constance and various parts of Germany, Switzerland, and the Netherlands. The last years of his life were spent in the city of Ulm on the Danube in southwestern Germany, where he died in 1366. Centuries later, in 1831, he was beatified by Pope Gregory XVI.

Suso is interesting for his personal insights into mystical experiences. For example, just after his inward conversion to the mystical life at the age of eighteen, he describes an ecstatic vision he had on the feast of Saint Agnes. He was sitting by himself in the choir of a convent church, burdened with angst, when suddenly his soul left his body and he saw a "shining brightness" and became oblivious of the constraints of time—the sense of peacefulness and silence was such that he felt he was encountering the "sweetness of Eternal Life"; the ecstasy lasted for up to an hour, until he collapsed and came to. Afterward it seemed to him that he was "walking on air" or that he was like a vessel from which some perfumed ointment had been taken but which had left behind its scent.[16] On another occasion an angel directed him to look at his body, and he saw that the part over his heart was "as clear as crystal," enabling him to see his own soul embraced by the form of eternal Wisdom.[17]

Despite his own mystical experiences, Suso believed that the aim of contemplation is not to receive visions and raptures for their own sake but to go beyond the realm of images, which are based on ideas of the created world. The ideal for the mystic is the imageless vision and the experience of God in his pure simplicity: "Say farewell to the creature and in future let your questions be. Simply hearken to what God says in you!"[18] Like Eckhart, Suso conceived of the ultimate divine reality in apophatic, or negative, terms. The Godhead is a "dark stillness and a restful calm that no one can understand," a place that is a "nameless existing nothingness," where "the spirit encounters the nothing of unity."[19]

Yet Suso's apophaticism is more than matched by his enthusiasm and gift for lyric expression. His works were collected into a four-part volume called *The Exemplar*, which includes *The Little Book of Truth* and *The Little Book of Eternal Wisdom*, a devotional work on meditation that became a late medieval classic. He writes in a vivid, sometimes florid, style, using anecdotes, poetic turns of phrase, and images to make his point. For example, he celebrates the wonder of creation and its creatures, which reflect the divine light of God. The myriad stars, the planets, the fruitfulness of the earth, with its grass, flowers, and woods and fields echoing with the songs of nightingales and other birds, the animals who rejoice in spring after a harsh winter, and even the four elements of fire, earth, water and air—all of these praise and honor God.

In *The Little Book of Truth* Suso is eloquent in his description of the individual's union with God as a result of the abandonment of the self. Using traditional imagery, he compares the person who has entered the joy of God to a drunkard who has lost his sense of self and to a drop of water added to an abundance of wine. "For, as this is lost to itself, and draws to itself and into itself the taste and color of the wine, similarly it happens to those who are in the full possession of blessedness." Yet Suso refrains from saying the union involves complete loss of identity: the individual's "being remains, though in a different form, in a different glory, and in a different power."[20]

Jan van Ruysbroeck

Associated with Eckhart, Tauler, and Suso as one of the Rhineland mystics, Jan van Ruysbroeck is generally acknowledged to be the greatest Flemish contemplative. His books include *The Adornment of the Spiritual Marriage* (or *The Spiritual Espousals*), *The Sparkling Stone*, and *The Book of Supreme Truth*, which he wrote in the same Middle Dutch tongue as Hadewijch of Brabant. In them he describes and classifies the various stages of the contemplative life, using familiar Rhineland themes and motifs such as the divine darkness, the birth of

God in the soul, and the soul's spark, but also emphasizing the place of Christ, the Trinity, and the sacraments. He stresses the importance of both the contemplative and active lives, and he visualizes a spiritual rhythm whereby "the spirit of God blows us outside so that we may practice love and virtuous deeds"; then the spirit "draws us into itself as well so that we may give ourselves over to rest and enjoyment."[21] Ruysbroeck also had a reputation for being a humble, good-humored spiritual director, as well as an unflagging opponent of heresy. His saintliness is reflected in a pious tradition that later in his life he was once discovered sitting beneath a tree in a wood, where he used to write under the inspiration of the Holy Spirit, caught up in an ecstatic rapture and surrounded by a fiery glow of celestial light.

Ruysbroeck was born in 1293 in the small village near Brussels for which he was named. While still a child, he went to live with his uncle, Jan Hinckaert, who was a canon of the Collegial Church of Saint Gudule in Brussels. Hinckaert and a priest friend named Francis van Coudenberg brought up and educated Ruysbroeck, who, in 1317, entered the priesthood, becoming a prebend at the cathedral. He remained there for the next twenty-six years, living a simple, austere, pious life and, among other concerns, combating those believed to belong to the heretical Brethren of the Free Spirit, who were active in the area at this time.

In 1343 Ruysbroeck's life took a different turn. Now fifty years of age, he, along with his uncle and van Coudenberg, decided to leave Brussels to pursue a more contemplative life in a country retreat. The spot they chose was a hermitage called Groenendaal (Green Valley) in the forest of Soignes near Brussels. There the three men, living their quiet, holy lives, soon attracted disciples, and within a few years they decided to formalize the arrangement by creating a community of Augustinian canons, with Coudenberg the provost and Ruysbroeck the prior. For the rest of his long life—he died in 1381 at the age of eighty-eight—Ruysbroeck, wrapped in the silence of the woods, continued to write his mystical works and counsel the many visitors who came to the hermitage, drawn by its growing reputation as a spiritual center.

Ruysbroeck's best-known work is *The Adornment of the Spiritual Marriage*, which is divided into three parts. The first sets out the basis for the spiritual life. It deals with the "active life" and the need to develop virtues such as patience, gentleness, kindliness, compassion, generosity, temperance, and purity, as well as the importance of directing the will toward God in order to progress further on the con-templative path. When the moral foundations have been laid, a person may then feel "an unmeasured impulse" to see Christ himself, not just through his works on earth. Ruysbroeck compares this desire to the action of the tax collector Zacchaeus in Luke 19:1–10, who climbed a tree in order to see Jesus above the crowds in Jericho: the person who wishes to encounter Christ directly "must climb up into the tree of faith, which grows from above downwards, for its roots are in the Godhead."[22]

The second part concerns the interior life and how a person is transformed when divine grace, imagined as an inner living fountain, pours into the "higher powers" of the soul, that is, the memory, under-standing, and will. He or she is then filled with love and compassion toward God and humanity. Later on Ruysbroeck says that the contem-plative who has come this far can, through simple introspection, meet God without any intermediary. From the encounter with the divine unity, a spiritual light will shine into him and show him "darkness" (a state beyond intellectual comprehension), "nakedness" (losing the power of ordinary perception but being illuminated by a "simple light"), and "nothingness" (complete loss of activity), through which he becomes "one spirit" with God. Now he feels a profound spiritual contentment flowing into his heart, and "in the deeps of his ground he knows and feels nothing, in soul or in body, but a singular radiance."[23]

Yet there is still a higher spiritual stage, which is described in the third part of *Spiritual Marriage*. It is what Ruysbroeck calls the "superessential" or "God-seeing" life, that is, the contemplative's union with God, or the Godhead, the undifferentiated unity about which nothing can rightfully be said. To achieve this a person must fulfill three conditions. First, his virtues must be "perfectly ordered" and he must be completely "empty" within, untroubled by any "images." Second, he must, through his love and intention, adhere inwardly to God. Third, he must lose himself in the "divine darkness," where there is a brightness so powerful that the contemplative "sees and feels nothing but an incomprehensible Light; and through that Simple Nudity which enfolds all things, he finds himself, and feels himself, to be that same Light by which he sees, and nothing else."[24] He also refers to this ultimate goal of contemplation as "wayless" and "abysmal" and, in brilliant poetic phrases, "the dark silence in which all lovers lose themselves" and "the wild Sea, whence no created thing can draw us back again."[25]

9

ORTHODOX MYSTICISM
AND HESYCHASM

*God is Light, and those whom He makes worthy to
see Him, see Him as Light.*
—Symeon the New Theologian

THE WESTERN (Catholic) and Eastern (Orthodox) churches had been drifting apart on a sea of theological and cultural differences for several centuries before matters came to a head—more symbolic than substantial—in 1054, when the pope's representative Cardinal Humbert dramatically excommunicated the patriarch of Constantinople in the city's great church Hagia Sophia, only to receive an anathema in return. Relations between the Latin and Greek churches had been complicated ever since the West had succumbed to the barbarian incursions in the fifth century. At this stage Rome and Constantinople were only two among the five ancient patriarchal churches of Christendom, the others being Alexandria, Antioch, and Jerusalem. Rome, with its traditional, albeit diminished, imperial status and as the burial place of the two foremost apostles, Peter and Paul, was accorded the senior position. But in the seventh century the conquests of Islam changed the balance of power and influence. As Muslim armies swept east and west from Arabia, they quickly took Alexandria, Antioch, and Jerusalem, all of which henceforth ceased to play significant roles in the church.

The Muslim conquests left Rome and Constantinople—the latter having less spiritual prestige than the former but greater political status—as the two great remaining ecclesiastical centers. At first, from about the middle of the seventh to the middle of the eighth century, Greek influence at Rome was strong. Large areas of Italy were under Byzantine control, and many popes were of Greek stock. Eventually, however, the papacy realized that its political security was better placed in a power that was closer to hand and more dependable than the Byzantines. So it was that in the mid-eighth century, under threat from the Lombards, Pope Stephen II turned to the West and formed a political alliance with the Frankish king Pépin. This distancing between the papacy and the Byzantine Empire was given further dramatic expression in 800, when Pope Leo III crowned Pépin's son, Charlemagne, Holy Roman Emperor, forging an alliance between the papacy and Western emperors that would last for centuries, although in time the relationship would prove difficult for both sides.

In addition to the political realignment between the East and the West, there were also differences between the churches over doctrine and customs. Some of them seemed relatively slight: the Latins used unleavened bread during the Eucharist, whereas the Greeks used leavened; the Greeks fasted on Saturdays, the Latins did not. The most important issue concerned the creed and what was known as the "procession of the Holy Spirit." In accordance with the ancient councils, the Greeks held that the Spirit "proceeded" only from the Father. The Latins, however, had gradually accepted the formula, possibly originating in Spain in the 600s, that the Spirit proceeded from both the Father and the Son (*Filioque*), which for the Greeks seemed to compromise the position of the Father as the only source of being. In any case, the discord between the two churches came to a head in 1054 during a meeting in Constantinople to discuss plans to counteract the threat of the Normans in southern Italy. The subsequent acts of mutual excommunication were formally revoked only in 1965.

More important, however, in the worsening relationship between the Latin and Greek churches was the shocking sack of Constantinople in 1204 by a mainly Frankish and Venetian host during the Fourth Crusade. The crusade had originally been planned as an invasion of Egypt, seen as the weak spot in the Muslim Middle East. But, exploiting political divisions within the Byzantine government, Venice, the main backer of the crusade (and, significantly, the Byzantines' great trading rival), redirected the Latin army to Constantinople. There, in April 1204, the crusaders killed, maimed, robbed, and raped their fellow Christians before installing Baldwin of Flanders to be the new Latin ruler of the Byzantine Empire, which they now divided between the Venetians and the crusaders. For nearly sixty years the imperial throne was held by Latin Christians, until the Byzantine Michael Palaeologus regained it in 1261. But the memory of the crusaders' perfidy and sacrilege was perpetuated in Greek folklore. Even in 2001, Pope John Paul II, on a fleeting visit to Athens, was reminded of the behavior of his Catholic ancestors by leaders of the Orthodox Church.

In later times, as the threat from the Ottoman Turks increased, the Byzantines were forced to seek help from the West. But the price, it was made clear, was the Orthodox Church's submission to Rome. In 1439 the desperate Greek delegates at the Council of Florence finally agreed to Rome's demands, but the Greeks' humiliating acceptance was rejected by their people back home. Constantinople was duly left to its fate, and in 1453 the city fell to the Muslims.

The tradition of Orthodox mysticism goes back at least to the time of the Cappadocian Fathers and includes such notable spiritual figures as Dionysius the Areopagite and Maximus the Confessor (ca. 580–662). One important thread in the tradition is its mysticism of divine light, through which people can become deified or divinized. This idea of a divine, transforming light is rooted in the New Testament. Chapter 5 of Ephesians, for example, talks of true Christians being "light in the Lord" and "children of light." The Gospel of John describes Christ as "the true light that gives light to every man" (1:9), and the account of

Christ's transfiguration on Mount Tabor before Peter, James, and John—"His face shone like the sun, and his clothes became as white as the light" (Matt. 17:2)—was a particularly significant text in Orthodox spirituality. As the modern Orthodox scholar Vladimir Lossky has noted, "In the mystical theology of the Eastern Church, these expressions [of light] are not used as metaphors or as figures of speech, but as expressions for a real aspect of the Godhead."[1] Indeed, Lossky compared Western and Eastern approaches to spirituality to, respectively, the "solitude and abandonment of the night of Gethsemane" and "the light of the Transfiguration."[2]

Another distinctive feature of Orthodox spirituality was, and is, the practice of the mystical prayer known as "hesychasm," a word derived from the Greek *hesychia*, meaning "silence," "stillness," or "quietness." Beginning, it is thought, in about the fourth century, hesychastic prayer developed through figures such as Gregory of Nyssa, Evagrius Ponticus, John Climacus, and Maximus the Confessor, and it especially thrived in monastic communities. Hesychasts attempted to rise to a level of prayer that went beyond sensuous imagery and the workings of the rational mind and resulted in a profound sense of inner peace. This, however, was not the ultimate aim, which was the reception of divine grace and deification. The form of prayer that became most favored in hesychast practice was known as the Jesus prayer, a constant repetition of a simple imprecation: "Jesus Christ, Son of God, have mercy on me" (sometimes "a sinner" was added at the end).

It was in the thirteenth and fourteenth centuries that hesychasm and the Jesus prayer became most influential, especially within the monastic community of Mount Athos in northern Greece, when it became part of a spiritual revival that penetrated other Orthodox countries such as Russia and Bulgaria. By this time the Jesus prayer was practiced in conjunction with a set of particular body postures and breathing techniques. There are some similarities with yoga, but it must be stressed that the prayer's physical aspects were not obligatory. Typically, hesychasts would bow their heads, with their chins on their chests, and focus their eyes on the place of the heart. They would then synchronize the words of the Jesus prayer with their breathing while attempting to sink the mind or intellect into the heart, which was seen as the integrating center of the total person and the "dwelling-place of God."³ The emphasis on the "heart" was significant because it indicated that the prayer was not merely an intellectual activity but one that involved the spiritual, mental, emotional, and physical aspects of the individual. The merging of the intellect with the heart (which is why the prayer was also known as the prayer of the heart) might eventually lead, God willing, to the vision of the divine uncreated light.

Symeon the New Theologian

Hesychasm became particularly significant—and eventually controversial—in Orthodox spirituality in medieval times through Symeon the New Theologian (949–1022) and Gregory Palamas (1296–1359). It is also in the writings of Symeon, "the greatest of the Byzantine mystics,"⁴ that light mysticism is most persuasively expressed. He revels in describing the divine light, evoking it variously in terms of fire, the sun, the moon, or a shining pearl that grows in the heart.⁵ He also makes it clear that the divine light is synonymous with God: "God is Light, and those whom He makes worthy to see Him, see Him as Light. For the Light of His glory goes before His face, and it is impossible that He should appear otherwise than as light. Those who have not received this light, have not seen God: for God is Light."⁶ Symeon says that the divine light would often come to him, and that he would be desolate after its departure. When again he managed to achieve a state of complete humility, the light would return like the sun appearing dimly through a mist, growing brighter as a radiant orb, removing the inner darkness, insensitivity, passions, and sensuality.⁷ Elsewhere he describes the light as a sort of "luminous water" washing him.

Symeon placed great emphasis on experiencing the divine, which he felt all Christians had the potential to do, not just the select few. Although he created as many enemies as he did admirers within the Orthodox Church by his outspoken criticism of moral laxity and by placing greater value on encountering God than on doctrine, he was careful to back up his teachings with scriptural authority. Also, he was solidly orthodox in placing Christ at the center of his spirituality and stressing the importance of the Eucharist. In one of his hymns he praises the union with Christ brought about by the Eucharist, which he depicts in terms of a divine fire: "I, who am but straw, receive the Fire, and—unheard of wonder!—am inflamed without being consumed, as of old the burning bush of Moses."⁸ That Symeon was accorded the title "New Theologian" was a considerable honor, since it grouped him with only two other previous figures given the same appellation by the Orthodox Church, namely John the Evangelist and Gregory of Nazianzus.

The son of a minor Byzantine noble, Symeon was born in 949 in Paphlagonia in Asia Minor (modern Turkey). He studied locally until the age of eleven, when an uncle took him to Constantinople and the imperial court. There Symeon continued his studies and learned the niceties of the ways and protocol of the court. In 963 his life changed when he met a deeply spiritual monk named Symeon the Studite, so called because he belonged to the famous Studion Monastery near the Golden Horn in the west of the city. Inspired by the monk's aura of sanctity, Symeon yearned to join the Studion straightway; but the elder Symeon dissuaded him from doing so, feeling that his protégé needed to develop and test his spirituality further before contemplating such a move.

So in the following years Symeon spent his days in the service of the imperial court but devoted his nights to study and prayer. His spiritual commitment and awareness deepened over time, and when he was twenty he received a powerful mystical experience in which he saw or felt a divine light that was so pervasive it seemed to him as if he had turned into light. Seven years later, Symeon finally entered the Studion with the blessing of his mentor. But his launch into this new monastic world soon hit some unexpected rocks. Symeon's devout and uncompromising spirituality incurred the hostility of some of the Studion monks, and after a few months he left the community. He moved to the nearby monastery of Saint Mamas, where, within a few years, he was ordained a priest, then elected abbot. For more than twenty years Symeon devoted himself to transforming Saint Mamas into a model Christian community, but eventually his rigor and relentless emphasis on inner spiritual experience again aroused opposition from his fellow monks. In the end, in 1009, he was compelled by the church authorities to accept exile in a small village just across the Bosporus, where he founded a small monastery. Although the sentence of exile was soon quashed, Symeon decided to remain in his low-key locale, pursuing his spiritual path there until his death in 1022.

Symeon's sermons, hymns, and other works celebrate the glorious splendor of the divine light that can be experienced by all Christians, although he makes it clear that such an experience comes only when the right spiritual preparations have been made. He also says that raptures and ecstasies are really only experienced by beginners on the mystical path. He compares ecstasy to the experience of a man in prison who suddenly sees a vista of sunlit countryside through a crack in the prison wall. At first he is "ecstatic" because of his vision, but then his senses grow used to it. So, too, the soul that becomes accustomed to the spiritual life no longer holds ecstasies to be extraordinary.[9]

For Symeon, humility is one of the foundation stones of the contemplative life. We must be humble in heart and mind, taking care to carry out the precepts of the scriptures, ready to bear the trials and tribulations that may befall us.[10] Our model is Christ, who became incarnate and so swapped the glory of heaven for life on earth.[11] Through following the teachings of Jesus Christ, we will gradually become less subject to our passions and our hearts will soften and embrace humility, which is deepened by tribulations and affliction, and our souls will eventually be cleansed.[12] Symeon insists that humility cannot simply be manufactured. Ascetic practices, such as fasting, sleeping on the ground, and wearing hair shirts, cannot replace a humble spirit and contrite heart, through which alone God can dwell in us.[13]

Although our efforts to practice virtues such as abstinence and controlling anger can take us only so far, God will grant us spiritual gifts to perfect our labors, so that by his grace our hearts will be in easeful conformity with our acts: the effort to tame anger will be rewarded with not just the desired control but a sense of inner peacefulness.[14] Along with humility, repentance is another foundation stone, "the gate which leads from the realm of darkness into that of light."[15] The key to receiving the light is not to seek it directly but rather to repent and be humble, to follow God's commandment. By doing this we open a part of us that allows the light to enter: "The life of grace is an increasing progress in knowledge, a growing experience of the divine light."[16]

So when we are spiritually prepared we are rewarded with the experience of the divine light. Symeon attempts to describe the indescribable. He says God comes in a "definite form" but not with a particular appearance: simplicity is the keynote, along with a sense of "formless light." Symeon is acutely conscious of the paradox that God is invisible but in a sense can be seen, and that he speaks to those "whom by grace He has begotten as gods."[17] Symeon also says that the divine light brings great joy and peace, and that the light is a glimpse of the eternal light, a reflection of the light of "everlasting blessedness." The soul, as if looking in a mirror, sees its tiniest flaws and is drawn into the depths of humility, and it is then awestruck by the divine glory and filled with ecstatic joy. In this way a person is transformed—knowing God and being known by him. [18]

Gregory Palamas

If the divine light is crucial to the mysticism of Symeon, it also has a central place in the teachings of Gregory Palamas, one of the towering figures of Orthodox spirituality, who championed hesychasm and the distinction between God's essence and his energies, which, as we shall see, became an issue of great controversy in the Orthodox Church. For Gregory, too, God is light and is experienced in increasing intensity according to the spiritual worthiness of the individual. However, Gregory was clear that we cannot experience God directly in his essence, only in his energies. Those who participate in the divine energies become united to them and transcend both sensual and intellectual knowledge, and God, as light, dwells in those who love him.

Gregory was born in 1296, probably in Constantinople, to a noble family. He was drawn to the idea of becoming a monk from an early age and later managed to persuade his siblings, widowed mother, and various family servants to embrace the monastic life. He himself, in his early twenties, traveled to Mount Athos, where he was introduced to the practice of hesychasm and the Jesus prayer. After his ordination as a priest in 1326, he lived as a hermit in Beroea in Greece for several years before returning to the monks of Athos in 1331. Eight years later he became embroiled in a dispute over hesychasm with an Orthodox monk named Barlaam from Calabria in southwestern Italy. The controversy lasted more than ten years and drew in the highest echelons of church and government. In the end, Gregory was vindicated by an Orthodox Church council in 1351 and was able to enjoy the fruits of this success for another eight years before he died in Thessalonica in 1359. Nine years later he was canonized and became an Orthodox saint.

Barlaam, Gregory's principal theological opponent, was an exceptionally learned man who had been invited to teach in the university at Constantinople. Although he was at first critical of Latin Christianity, he was sympathetic toward the humanistic outlook of the nascent Italian Renaissance. He laid great stress on the apophatic tradition, reaching back to Dionysius the Areopagite, that God was totally transcendent and therefore unknowable: he could only be experienced indirectly. Therefore those who claimed to see the uncreated light of God through hesychastic practices were deluding themselves, for it was possible to see God only in the life to come. What they actually saw was a light that was natural and created.

Gregory rose to Barlaam's challenge, writing in defense of the hesychasts his important three-part *Triads*, a work enthusiastically supported by the Athonite monks. Gregory agreed with Barlaam about God's transcendence. In his essence, God is totally unknowable: "No single thing of all that is created has or ever will have even the slightest communion with the supreme nature, or nearness to it."[19] But Gregory emphasized an important distinction (found in the early church fathers) between God's essence and God's energies. God, in his essence, may be unknowable; but his uncreated energies, in which he is wholly present, can be known by divine grace. As Basil the Great said: "It is by His energies that we say we know our God; we do not assert that we can come near to the essence itself, for His energies descend to us, but His essence remains unapproachable."[20] It is as if God in his essence were the sun, which cannot be looked at directly, and his energies the visible rays streaming out. According to Gregory it was precisely God's energies that the three disciples saw as a dazzling radiance during the Transfiguration, when Jesus was transformed into glorious light on Mount Tabor. And it was this same light that it was possible for hesychasts to see through prayer. Gregory described it as "that Light which is the Glory of God, without end, and the splendor of Divinity, divine and eternal, uncreated, being itself the Majesty of God."[21]

The Transfiguration was a key event for Gregory, for whom it displayed the effect of divine grace and its transformatory power on human beings. As Christ appeared to Peter, James, and John, so does he continue to manifest himself to true Christians: "He is not experienced in his essence, . . . but in a most mysterious manner, he shines upon them the radiance of his proper nature and grants them to participate in it."[22]

Barlaam, in common with other antihesychasts (many of them in sympathy with the ideas of the Scholastic thinkers of the West), asserted that God was a simple unity and could not be divided into essence and energies, which smacked of ditheism, the doctrine that there are two Gods. He also made fun of the idea that hesychasts prayed while directing their eyes to their own bodies, referring to them as "omphalopsyches" (that is, those with souls in their navels).

While not viewing the physical practices of hesychasm as indispensable, Gregory defended them by affirming that a human being was a unified combination of body and soul. He stressed the importance given to the physical body in the Bible, especially with the Incarnation. When the Bible states that people were made in God's image, this refers to the entire psychosomatic entity. And by assuming human form, Christ made the body "an inexhaustible source of sanctification."[23] So the hesychasts were not guilty of materialism, as their opponents claimed, but were staying true to the biblical tradition that gave due honor to the flesh. The body had its part to play in hesychasm and receiving divine illumination, and those praying could meet God halfway in an ecstasy of union: "Our mind, then, comes out of itself and becomes united with God after it has transcended itself. God also comes out of himself and becomes united with our mind by condescension."[24]

The hesychast controversy came to a head in 1341 at the first of a series of councils held to settle it. Convened in the church Hagia Sophia in Constantinople on June 10, the council was a resounding success for the hesychasts, who trounced Barlaam and his supporters. Barlaam himself was compelled to retract his accusations and soon departed for Calabria, where he became a Roman Catholic. But the disagreement rumbled on. Barlaam's place was taken by other able opponents, and the matter was complicated by the fact that it took on a political dimension, with leading members of the Byzantine government and the church split between the two sides. Gregory himself suffered a downturn in his fortunes when he was arrested in 1343 and imprisoned for four years—the virtue from this necessity was that he was able to continue writing. Matters improved for him in 1347 when the prohesychast John Cantacuzenus came to power and Gregory was consecrated archbishop of Thessalonica. Then in 1351 the sixth the last of the councils held to debate the hesychast issue took place, and the Palamite side won a decisive and enduring victory, with hesychasm declared the official teaching of the Orthodox Church.

As a short postscript to the hesychasm affair, it should be noted that after the fall of Constantinople to the Ottoman Turks in 1453, hesychastic practice continued to hold an important place in the Orthodox tradition. In the late eighteenth century it was brought to much greater public notice after the appearance of a work named the *Philokalia*, published in 1782. Edited by Macarius of Corinth and an Athonite monk named Nicodemus, the *Philokalia* is a collection of writings by the great Eastern Christian teachers of the past, focusing on hesychasm, the Jesus prayer, and other aspects of mysticism. Soon after its publication, it was translated into Slavonic, and in the nineteenth century it came to make a great impact on the spirituality of Russia. Here the Jesus prayer became popular through teachers such as Seraphim of Sarov (1759–1833), and especially after the publication in the middle of the century of a short spiritual work called *The Way of a Pilgrim*, which emphasizes the supreme value of the prayer.

The anonymous author of the *Way*, which became a classic, is a thirty-three-year-old widower who travels around the wilds of Russia and Siberia in search of someone who will enlighten him over the meaning of Paul's words "Pray without ceasing." At first his inquiries prove fruitless, but eventually he comes across a monk who teaches him the words of the Jesus prayer and encourages him to read the *Philokalia*; the pilgrim later obtains a copy of the book and becomes its ardent advocate.

The monk instructs his protégé to repeat the prayer first three thousand, then six thousand, and finally twelve thousand times a day, which he finds induces a state of profound contentment. The pilgrim then continues his journey, living on water, bread, and salt, sleeping rough, taking on odd jobs, having memorable encounters with peasants, criminals, monks, and priests, and receiving in dreams spiritual guidance from his now-deceased mentor. He learns how to coordinate speaking the prayer with concentration on his heart, which brings about euphoric spiritual states: "My heart would feel as though it were bubbling with joy, such lightness, freedom, and consolation were in it." He also experiences a "burning love for Jesus Christ and for all God's creatures" as well as a profound spiritual understanding.[25]

10

The English Flowering

*Would you learn your Lord's meaning in this
thing? Learn it well; love was his meaning. Who
showed it to you? Love. What did he show you?
Love. Why did he show it? For love.*

—Julian of Norwich

THE ENGLISH MYSTICS of the fourteenth century—Richard
Rolle, the anonymous author of the *Cloud of Unknowing,* Walter
Hilton, and Julian of Norwich—stand out in an age that saw a
burgeoning of spiritual writings, including translations of the Bible
into English, sermons, practical manuals for priests, and poetry (for
example, William Langland's epic religious poem *Piers Plowman*).[1]
Although the individual mystics differ from each other in approach
and temperament, they did share traits that were typical of English
spirituality of the time, for example, a preference for the pragmatic
over the speculative, a humane asceticism, and fidelity to church
teachings. They also expressed their wisdom and serenity against the

background of arguably the most turbulent century of the Middle Ages, with its catalog of plague, war (particularly the Hundred Years' War between England and France), and widespread social unrest. From about 1347 to 1351 Europe suffered the horrors of the Black Death, a plague that wiped out some twenty million people, about one-third of Europe's population.

The devastation wrought by the plague had further social consequences. Depopulation suddenly gave an economic advantage to the peasants and laborers who had survived it and an impetus for better pay and working conditions. When governments tried to impose a freeze on wages and preserve the status quo, tensions rose and precipitated violent responses. In 1358 the so-called Jacquérie revolt in France, prompted by the aftermath of the plague and the disastrous effects of the Hundred Years' War, was savagely put down. In 1381 in England Wat Tyler and his peasant army tried to enforce radical reforms and were crushed.

The church, meanwhile, was continuing to lose its prestige and authority. At the start of the century the papacy had moved to Avignon, where it was widely believed to be under the sway of the French king. Toward the end of the century it returned to Rome, but there soon followed another calamity: the Great Schism, with two rival popes struggling unedifyingly for the papal throne. Apart from difficulties at its head, the church was widely perceived as being too worldly and corrupt, as the satirical eyes of the English poets Geoffrey Chaucer and Langland make clear. Although at the grassroots level parish priests were often hardworking, pious souls, bishops and abbots and others high up in the hierarchy were frequently indistinguishable from any other large landowners.

In England dissent toward the church emerged not only through writers such as Chaucer and Langland: another, more-radical voice was that of John Wycliffe, a theologian who became increasingly critical of church doctrine and practices. Wycliffe opposed the hierarchical structure of the church, emphasized the central place of the Bible, and attacked the use of the Eucharist. Condemned by the pope, he continued to write his anticlerical treatises in retirement, and after his death in 1384, his ideas were perpetuated by his supporters, known as the Lollards. With their own well-trained preachers, the Lollards were effective enough to provoke suppressive measures by the English government—the first Lollard was burned in 1401. But after a failed Lollard rebellion against King Henry V in 1414, the movement went underground, although the Lollards' influence continued until the Reformation.

Richard Rolle

The first of the great English mystics during these troubled times was Richard Rolle. Hermit, spiritual counselor, poet, and mystic, Rolle is important not so much for his mystical theology as for his witness to how it *feels* to experience the heights of mystical consciousness. In his best-known work, *The Fire of Love*, Rolle writes with the enthusiasm of someone who is trying to convey what it is like to be filled with the deep, penetrating heat and "sweetness" that comes from the mystic's ardent love of God. For Rolle the mystical path was not confined to monks, priests, and other clerics but was open to anyone who would shun the vanities of the world and set his heart on loving God.

Rolle was born in Thornton in Yorkshire, probably in about 1300. He studied at Oxford for a short while before leaving to pursue the life of a solitary dedicated to God. He returned north to Yorkshire but soon left his home and family for good, dressed in his idea of an authentic hermit's robe—a patchwork of two of his sister's tunics and his father's rain hood. Then with the help of the local squire, who provided him with clothes, food, and shelter, Rolle began his life as a solitary, living in places remote from towns and villages, writing his mystical works in both English and Latin, and providing spiritual counsel to anyone who sought him out.

Whether acting within the authority of the church or as "freelancers," hermits were a feature of medieval life. They were sought out for their counsel and wisdom, especially by those who cared little for the local priest. Certainly Rolle was as enthusiastic about the eremitical life as he was scathing about the representatives of the church. He chastises theologians for their bookishness and arguments—all for the purpose of getting good reputations and jobs—instead of concentrating on the love of Christ, the "sweetness" of which is dispersed by useless debates and "unbridled curiosity": an old woman, he avows, can know more about love than an erudite theologian.[2] Hermits, on the other hand, base their lives around loving God and their fellow human beings: they scorn the good approval of men, they shun laziness, they resist sensual pleasures, they yearn for spiritual things, they believe everyone to be more worthy than themselves, they take delight in prayer.

Apart from the clergy, another object of his criticism was women. Perhaps fearing that his hermit's resolve might be fatally tested by the opposite sex, Rolle strongly warns against the company of women, who have the power to befuddle man's reason and distance his affections from God.[3] Elsewhere he complains of the latest fourteenth-century women's fashions—braided hair, makeup, and "wide-spreading horns on their heads, extremely horrible, made up of hair not their own."[4] Yet whether he was a misogynist or simply conforming to the ascetic's dread of sensuality remains open to doubt. What is clear is that there were some women whom he met and admired, including a local anchoress named Margaret Kirkby. Also, toward the end of his life (he died in 1349, presumed to have been a victim of the Black Death), he moved to Hampole, near the town of Doncaster, where he gave spiritual direction to the nuns of the Cistercian convent there.

The turning point in Rolle's interior life occurred a couple of years after his commitment to the eremitical way. He was, it seems, praying in a certain chapel when he felt a strange but "sweet" heat welling up from within his body. Then, still in the same chapel, he heard while he was reciting some psalms the sound of singing above his head—his desire for heaven conveyed by his prayers was met by what he describes as a "symphony of song" corresponding to a harmony in his mind. This spiritual music turned his thoughts and prayers into tuneful songs, accompanied by an "inner sweetness," which caused him to sing, but only inwardly, for God. After this initial awakening, there passed four more years before he was able to reach the "heights of loving Christ," and consolidate his spirituality.[5]

Heat (*calor*), song (*canor*), and sweetness (*dulcor*) play a significant part in Rolle's mysticism. To love Christ truly involves these three experiences, which in turn need profound quietness (Rolle found that only by sitting still, as opposed to walking around or lying on the ground, could he maintain the requisite tranquillity). More specifically,

Rolle describes heat or fervor as a state of being when both mind and heart are ablaze—not metaphorically but as a physical sensation—with the fire of divine love. Song refers to the condition of the soul when it is brimming over with praise of God and thoughts have been transmuted into songs. From these two experiences, which are maintained only by committed devotion, comes a third one, ineffable sweetness.

Rolle also distinguishes between two types of rapture. With the first, a person suddenly loses all bodily feeling (he cites the example of Paul being raised to the "third heaven" in 2 Corinthians 12:2–4) and may appear to others to be stricken. This type of rapture can even be experienced by sinners, who may see visions of the blessed and the damned. The second type, and for Rolle the more desirable one, comes when true lovers of God lift their minds up to him in the act of contemplation, when they are rapt by love, experiencing a seizure—but unlike in the first type of rapture, bodily feeling is never lost.

Most important to Rolle, however, is the mystic's ardent love for God. Throughout *The Fire of Love* Rolle cannot emphasize enough the need for love, as well as its effects. To reach the point of burning love of Christ requires commitment and discipline, the rejection of the world and all its empty values. Then the ingress of the "sweetness of eternal love" will destroy lustful and other impure thoughts and compel complete attention to Christ; and those who attain this love will then turn away from human consolation "as if it were smoke hurting his eyes" and be utterly transformed. Just as "the air is stricken by the sunbeam, and by the shining of its light is altogether shining, so a devout mind, enflamed with the fire of Christ's love and fulfilled with desire for the joys of heaven, seems all love, because it is altogether turned into another likeness."[6]

The Cloud of Unknowing

After the warm, positive, spiritual exuberance of Richard Rolle, the anonymous author of *The Cloud of Unknowing*, which was written in the second half of the fourteenth century and is one of the great mystical treatises of medieval England, seems much more sober and measured in its apophatic approach. Yet *Cloud of Unknowing* is equally rewarding, with its acute psychological insights and its insistence on the importance for the contemplative of "a naked intent directed unto God."[7]

Just who the *Cloud*'s author was remains a mystery. Those who have debated the issue believe he was a priest or a monk, possibly of the Carthusian order. Whoever it was wrote in the same East Midlands dialect of English used by Chaucer and wrote a number of other works, including a translation of the *Mystical Theology* of Dionysius the Areopagite, whose negative theology is much in evidence in the *Cloud*. From his various writings, it can be inferred that the author was an experienced contemplative as well as a confident and original thinker who possessed a keen satirical wit. In chapter 53 of the *Cloud*, for instance, he wryly exposes false contemplatives and their affectations: "Some set their eyes in their heads as they were sturdy sheep beaten in the head, and as they should die anon. Some hang their heads on one side as if a worm were in their ears. Some pipe when they should speak, as if there were no spirit in their bodies."[8]

The book's central theme is the practice and rewards of contemplative prayer and the idea of the "cloud of unknowing." The would-be contemplative must try to forget the things of the sensual world and develop a longing for God.[9] But having embarked upon the spiritual quest, he will soon encounter a sort of "darkness," which the author terms a "cloud of unknowing" (that is, a lack of knowledge). This cloud blocks the way to God. It prevents an understanding of him and the experience of the "sweetness" of his love. The contemplative's task is not to give up but to maintain desire for God. For the cloud is a fact of spiritual experience, and God can be felt, or seen, only in it.

To progress as far as the cloud of unknowing, which is, paradoxically, both a barrier and the means of access to God, it is first necessary to reject the world and the thoughts and memories it produces. This is done by putting what the author calls a "cloud of forgetting" between yourself and the things of the world.[10] For the very process of thinking about something causes the soul to focus on it—just as someone about to shoot stares at the intended target. So unless you forget the world and direct your thoughts solely at God, a barrier is created, preventing any sort of contact with him. Similarly, it is necessary to suppress the "sharp stirring" of your "understanding," or imagination, which presses upon you during contemplation: failure to suppress it means it will suppress you.[11] What is crucial is that you maintain "a blind stirring of love unto God for Himself," and keep secretly pressing on the cloud of unknowing: this is what is healthy for the soul, not pleasant visions of heaven with its angels, saints, and celestial music. You must direct your love to the cloud of unknowing or, rather, let it be drawn up by God.

There are other matters the apprentice contemplative must attend to in order to progress to the cloud and God, including reading, thinking, and praying. To read God's word (or hear it in a sermon) is like looking in a mirror. As a mirror reveals a speck of dirt on your face, so God's word enables the soul, otherwise blinded by sin, to see the dirt within its conscience. Prayer, for those who are some way along the contemplative path, consists of unpremeditated thoughts or words directed toward God. If words are used, then the fewer there are of them the better. In fact a word of one syllable is best. For just as a man or woman frightened by a fire will simply yell out "Fire!" to attract attention directly and quickly, so a one-syllable word deeply felt "pierceth the ears of Almighty God" more effectively than "any long psalter unmindfully mumbled in the teeth."[12]

The mystic's path involves discipline, persistence, and hard work, as the author freely admits. Contemplatives must "beat upon" the cloud, toiling to eradicate memories of the sensual world, and subject themselves to the cloud of forgetting. But help may come in the form of divine grace. Operating within the soul, the action of grace can happen out of the blue, shooting out to God like a spark from a fire, causing the soul to forget in a flash the things of the world (although it can quickly backslide).[13] If the contemplative perseveres, God may sometimes reward him or her by sending out a beam of spiritual light that will pierce the cloud of unknowing that separates them. If this happens, the recipient will feel inflamed with the fire of God's love to an indescribable extent—the author says he would not dare to attempt to speak about it with his "blabbering fleshly tongue."[14]

In chapter 71 the author distinguishes between those who receive the grace of contemplation as an ecstasy only once in a while and those who are so spiritually attuned to God that they can experience his grace whenever they like (and in this state they are still able to participate fully in everyday life). Indeed, the author says that the practice of contemplation results in a number of benefits that enrich life in the world. Even plain-looking contemplatives will look attractive and be happy and cheerful company. They will feel comfortable with everyone they meet, whether they are sinners or not, and they will be able to discern people's personalities and needs and inspire others through their graceful nature to pursue the contemplative way. A self-portrait, perhaps, of the anonymous author?

Walter Hilton

The third peak of the mystical mountain range that rose in England in the fourteenth century was Walter Hilton, a man of great spiritual insight and practical wisdom. His greatest work was *The Ladder* (or *Scale*) *of Perfection*, which enjoyed great popularity up to the Reformation and was described as being "more precious than gold" in its first printed edition in 1494. Divided into two books, the first addressed specifically to an anchoress, the *Ladder*, with its implication of a progressive upward journey and its echo of Jacob's ladder connecting earth to heaven, describes various aspects of the spiritual life and the stages to be followed in order to reach contemplation of God, a journey that is centered on Christ (Hilton emphasizes the central role of Christ in the spiritual journey more than Rolle and the *Cloud* author do).

Not much is known about Hilton. It is thought he may have studied at Cambridge and that he may have been a hermit for a while. More certain is that he became an Augustinian canon at Thurgarton in Nottinghamshire. His date of birth is unknown, but he is said to have died on March 24, 1396. What can be inferred about him is that he was a sensible, conscientious, humble, and devout soul who was extremely learned—his works indicate that he had studied Augustine and Bernard, among others. His temperament was such that he avoided the more speculative theology of the *Cloud* author and was wary of the highly experiential mysticism of Rolle. Yet, although he claims not to have had profound mystical experiences himself, his sensitivity toward and quiet enthusiasm for the contemplative life indicate that he was able, at the very least, to empathize strongly with such experiences.

The first of the *Ladder*'s two books gives sound guidance on how to develop the spiritual life. It talks of the merits of the active and contemplative lives, the former based around religious externals and good deeds, the latter concerned with the inner journey to God. The contemplative life has different stages. The first consists in getting to know God, through reason, teachings, and the scriptures, which, however, do not bring any direct "inward savour of God."[15] The second stage—more suited, he says, to uneducated, less sophisticated people—is simply loving God without the need for intellectual understanding. If blessed with divine grace, a person meditating on God may feel great love or a sense of trust or awe, and even an outpouring of emotion that can cleanse the heart of its sin.[16] The third and highest stage of contemplation involves both knowing and loving God, which happens when the soul, through perfecting the virtues, is "reformed" or restored to the "image of Jesus." This may result in the soul's being rapt and having such a perfect vision of ultimate truth— accompanied by a "soft, sweet, burning love"—that for a time it becomes one with God and bears the likeness of the Trinity.[17] Although the beginnings of this third stage can be experienced in this life, its fulfillment occurs only in heaven.

The second book of the *Ladder* begins by saying that the soul is the image of God, filled with love and light, and that it was corrupted by the sin of Adam, before God ensured the possibility of its being reformed by the atonement of Christ. The process of reforming can happen in two ways: by faith, through the sacraments of baptism and penance, which is enough for salvation, and, second, by faith and by feeling, which is rewarded by the bliss of heaven.[18] Suitable for contemplatives, this second way takes a long time and needs great effort, but it results in the destruction in the soul of sensuality and worldly desires and paves the way for the ingress of grace. The soul and its faculties are made new, and the reformed soul comes, bit by bit, to know and see God.[19]

In an extended passage, Hilton compares the reform of feeling in the soul to a pilgrimage to Jerusalem. In the same way that a pilgrim leaves behind his home and family, the spiritual pilgrim must leave behind his good and bad deeds and embrace poverty, setting his heart on the spiritual Jerusalem, which represents "contemplation in perfect love of God."[20] He also talks about the "night" that the pilgrim must travel through. The transition from the light of this world (that is, crea- turely love of it) to the light of heaven, or love of God, does not happen suddenly—the night intervenes. Less daunting than John of the Cross's "dark night," Hilton's night represents the withdrawal of thoughts and affections from the world in order to focus on Jesus: it is a "good, glow- ing darkness" that excludes false, worldly love and leads to the light of truth. The night may be a painful experience, but if pilgrims can get used to it, they will experience peace, gradual spiritual enlightenment, and the destruction of impure thoughts and desires. When this takes place, the goal is near at hand and they will glimpse Jerusalem far off "because of the twinkling rays of light shining from it."[21]

Julian of Norwich

The last, and perhaps the greatest, of the medieval English mystics was a woman known as Mother Julian of Norwich, who lived as an anchoress dedicated to a life of solitude and prayer in a cell attached to the city's Church of Saint Julian (from which she took her name). Her *Revelations of Divine Love*, which exists in shorter and longer ver- sions, is a classic of the contemplative life. It continues to fascinate modern believers, many of them drawn by Julian's emphasis on humil- ity, her view of God as being "homely and courteous," her devotion to the suffering Christ, and her espousal of the idea, articulated before by Anselm and others, of the motherhood of God—a view that stresses the tenderness and procreative power of the deity. Julian is also attrac- tive for her optimism in the saving power of God, encapsulated by her oft-quoted words "And all shall be well and shall be well, and all man- ner of things shall be well" (lines made famous by T. S. Eliot in his poem "Little Gidding").[22]

Julian's life is mostly shrouded in mystery. She is thought to have been born in about 1342 and to have died in about 1420. The turning point in her life came in May 1373, when, at the age of thirty during a life-threatening illness, she experienced a series of sixteen "shewings" or revelations in the form of visions and spiritual truths and insights. In the first shewing she saw an image of Jesus during the Passion with blood trickling down from the crown of thorns. Over the course of one day, she experienced another fourteen visions, mostly of the Passion.

Then, in the following night, she received the sixteenth and last one, when God reassured her that all the shewings she had received had come from him and were not hallucinations.

At some point after the revelations, Julian became an anchoress and wrote down the essential substance of her mystical experience. But she continued to ponder them over a period of twenty years and ended up writing a longer, more substantial account that includes her reflections on their meaning. She describes herself as being a "simple, unlettered creature"—she may in fact have dictated her thoughts to a secretary—but it is clear that she was well versed in the Bible and the thought of Paul and John. She could also write vividly. With an artist's eye she describes the moment during her first revelation when she watched blood falling like "pellets" in such number that it was like water dripping from "eaves after a great shower of rain" and that the drops of blood on Jesus's forehead were round "like scales from a herring."[23]

In her book, Julian is concerned with important theological issues such as the efficacy of prayer and the primacy of divine love. She is also preoccupied by the problem of sin. In a vision, Julian sees that God is present in everything, and she is certain that he can do no sin, which leads her to believe that sin has no substance: it is an absence of good, nothing. But in an age when sin and suffering abounded (indeed, many believed that the plague and other disasters were directly attributable to sin), Julian was not entirely happy about this concept of sin. She puzzles about it throughout the book, looking at it from different angles. She recognizes that sin is "behovable"—a necessary part of life—and asserts that people have a "beastly will" that chooses what is bad but also a "godly will" that can never assent to sin.[24] And God reassures her that because the Fall—the worst event ever to have happened to mankind—had been more than counteracted by Christ's atonement, any lesser sins could also be put right by him.[25] She comes to the conclusion that what people see as sin God sees from a different, eternal perspective, and that through the atonement of Christ, "whenever God looks at any of us, even in our sin, God sees Christ."[26]

Julian is also instructive about prayer. In the fourteenth shewing, in response to her admission that she sometimes feels as dry and barren after prayer as before it, God tells her that he is the "ground of her beseeching"—the foundation of her prayer; it is his will that she should pray, and it is he who makes her will it and speak it. Prayer, she then goes on to say, is a "true, gracious, lasting will of the soul, united and fastened into the will of our Lord by the sweet inward work of the Holy Ghost." She also paints the attractive image of God taking prayer and sending it up above and placing it in the heavenly treasure, "where it shall never perish." So, despite any feelings of dryness, we must continue with our prayers—God will receive them with delight: our mood is irrelevant to their effectiveness since God accepts good intentions and work "howsoever we feel."[27]

Throughout her book Julian emphasizes the central place of the love of God for his creation—his "homely loving," as she calls it. She is granted a visual embodiment of this when God shows her in the palm of her hand a small object, as round as a ball and the "size of a hazel nut." She looks at it with "the eye of understanding" and wonders what it is. She receives the divine intuition that the object is "all that is made." It seems so small and fragile, however, that she wonders how it might last, but then receives the assurance that it will last and "last forever because God loves it." This little object teaches her three things—applicable to all creation and revealing the Triune God—namely that "God made it, God loves it, and God keeps it."[28]

The supremacy of God's love is reaffirmed at the end of the book. In response to Julian's long search for the meaning of her visions, God reveals the answer in unambiguous and memorable terms: "Would you learn your Lord's meaning in this thing? Learn it well; love was his meaning. Who showed it to you? Love. What did he show you? Love. Why did he show it? For love."[29]

11

THE LATE MIDDLE AGES

In this world, the rays of God's love,
unbeknownst to man, encircle man all about,
hungrily seeking to penetrate him.
                                    —Catherine of Genoa

THE DOMINANT CONCERNS OF THE CHURCH in the late fourteenth century revolved around the return of the papacy to Rome from its exile in Avignon, which eventually occurred in 1377, and immediately following this homecoming, the Great Schism, when two popes, each with his own set of cardinals and bureaucratic machinery, claimed to be the rightful head of the church. The crisis gave momentum to what is called the conciliar movement, which asserted that the supreme authority of the church should reside not in the papacy but in a general council that had the power to depose popes if necessary.

Although the Avignon popes were able to count a number of positives during their seventy years of office, such as the expansion and efficient running of the papal bureaucracy, and although faults such as nepotism could be found before and after their time, the papacy's very presence in the south of France and the vast preponderance of French cardinals led many in Europe to believe that its universalist aspirations were irretrievably compromised. Eventually, Pope Gregory XI, realizing acutely the need to return the papacy to the church's ancient spiritual center, and under pressure from influential individuals such as Catherine of Siena, made the momentous journey back to Rome in January 1377. However, his death in the following year created a worse crisis than the popes' exile. The newly elected Italian pope, Urban VI, formerly the archbishop of Bari, soon showed a despotic temperament, and the French cardinals, who made up the majority of the Sacred College and felt they had been pressured by the Roman mob to choose Urban, decided to elect another man, Robert of Geneva, as the antipope Clement VII, who duly returned to Avignon. So now there were two popes, with Europe split over its support for them: France, Spain, and Scotland backed Clement, while Urban could count on England, Germany, and Hungary.

To the despair of churchmen and theologians throughout Europe, the Great Schism lasted beyond the death of the two popes. Successors were chosen to fill their shoes, perpetuating the division. For many, the only hope seemed to lie in a general council that could depose the two rivals and elect a new pope who could unify the Western church. This nearly happened at the Council of Pisa in 1409; the problem was that after the election of the new pope, Alexander V, the Avignon and Roman popes refused to step down, so the church now had three pontiffs!

The schism was finally resolved, however, at the Council of Constance in Germany (1414–1418), when all three popes were replaced by a new one, Martin V. The council was also notable for the execution of the Czech reformer Jan Hus, a priest and university lecturer in Prague in Bohemia (modern Czech Republic). Hus, who was much influenced by John Wycliffe, emphasized the centrality of the Bible and condemned the lax morality of the clergy and practices such as the sale of indulgences, certificates that were believed to bring about a reduction or complete remission of the deceased's time in purgatory. Hus was summoned to Constance to defend his beliefs, and despite promises of a safe conduct by Emperor Sigismund, the ruler of Germany, Bohemia, and Hungary, he was condemned as a heretic and burned to death in 1415.

Although Constance seemed to vindicate supporters of the conciliar movement, the aftermath proved to be a disappointment to them. The principle that general councils were superior to popes and that they should be held on a regular basis eventually foundered, despite the efforts of the Councils of Pavia (soon moved to Siena because of plague) in 1423 and Basel (1431–1449). By the time Pope Pius II (r. 1458–1464) described conciliarism as a "pestilent poison,"[1] the papacy had regained its preeminence, if not its prestige.

Constance may have healed the schism, yet it not only failed to establish the conciliar principle but was also unable to implement much-needed church reforms. Wycliffe and Hus had been two militant figures voicing their disenchantment with the church establishment. But there were other, more-mainstream voices at this time expressing their disquiet: the French churchman and theologian Jean de Gerson warned his sister not to expose herself to corruption by entering a convent, and the monk and scholar Ambrogio Traversari advised the Franciscan Bernardino of Siena not to compromise his evangelical spirit by becoming a bishop.[2]

Catherine of Siena

One of those who did the most to persuade Pope Gregory XI to move the papacy back to Rome was Catherine of Siena, who, like Teresa of Ávila—both women were honored by being declared doctors of the church in 1970—was one for whom the contemplative and active lives were mutually supportive. Joyful, determined, fearless, and charismatic, Catherine led a highly disciplined religious life, practicing austerities and enjoying profound visions and other religious experiences. Yet far from tempting her to remain in solitude, her inner spiritual world nourished her public mission to help the sick and poor, to heal the divisions of a fractured society, and to reform the church. It was as if she could not bear fragmentation at any level and that for her the ideal of the unity and wholeness of the church was like an outward reflection of the soul brought to perfection in union with God. Her spirituality was marked by her devotion to Christ, whom she described as a bridge between man and God, and to his Passion and all-encompassing love—she once said that "nails would not have held the God-man fast had not love held him there."[3] Her sympathetic understanding of Christ was dramatically expressed when, at the age of twenty-eight, she experienced the stigmata, the five wounds of Christ.

Catherine was born with her twin sister (who died shortly afterward) in Siena in 1347—her mother had already given birth to twenty-two children. Her father, Giacomo Benincasa, ran a cloth-dyeing business and seems to have been reasonably prosperous. From her early years Catherine showed signs of a religious temperament, and she received her first vision, of Jesus, at the age of six or seven, after which she took a vow of perpetual virginity. Her parents did not encourage her spiritual aspirations and wanted her to marry and live a conventional life. Catherine determined otherwise: at the age of sixteen she joined the Dominican order as a tertiary, or lay sister, adopting the habit and lifestyle of a nun but remaining in the world. In fact she lived at home: for three years she confined herself to her room, except for excursions to Mass, and spoke to no one except her confessor. During this time she fasted, slept little, and prayed and recited the divine office.

This period of her life ended in about 1366 or 1367 after she received a vision of her mystic marriage to Christ: she saw the Virgin Mary take her right hand and hold it out to Christ, who placed a ring on her finger. The vision was also a summons to take up the active life, inspired by Christ's love, and Catherine responded by breaking her self-imposed seclusion and performing charitable works for the poor, lepers, and sick of Siena, doing the rounds of prisons and hospitals. She also attracted a number of followers, men and women from all sections of society, who formed a loyal and devoted "family," much to the derision of other Sienese townsfolk.

In 1370 Catherine received another powerful mystical experience during which Christ exchanged her heart for his and she was bidden to engage more widely in the world. Although illiterate until very late in her life, Catherine began dictating and sending letters—382 of them have survived—to people from all walks of life, including popes, kings, queens, and princes. In 1375 her devotion to Christ was confirmed by her receiving the stigmata. During Communion in a church in Pisa, she saw rays of light from the wounds of Christ stream toward her and pierce her hands, feet, and side, but in accordance with her prayer, the marks remained invisible while she was alive.

A year later, in 1376, Catherine became personally embroiled in the armed struggle that had broken out between Florence and the papacy and had led to the revolt of most of the papal states (territories, mostly in Italy, under the sovereign authority of the popes). At the same time she also found herself playing a pivotal part in ending the Babylonian Captivity. This occurred when she traveled to the papal court to negotiate with Pope Gregory XI on behalf of the Florentines. Although her mission was unsuccessful, she made a great impression on the pope and helped to persuade him to return the papacy to Rome, despite formidable pressure against this move by the king of France and most of the cardinals of the Sacred College. She carried on her crusade for church unity during the Great Schism. Despite having reservations about Urban VI, who was widely regarded as mentally unstable, Catherine recognized the legitimacy of his election and was prepared to fight his cause. At his request, she took up residence in Rome and sent letters across western Europe to drum up support for him. She stayed in Rome for the rest of her life, succumbing to a stroke on April 29, 1380. She was canonized in 1461.

Catherine's teachings are found principally in her work *The Dialogue*, completed in Siena in 1378 before her departure to Rome, as well as in her letters. Much of her spiritual thought came from divine inspiration received during mystical experiences. It is said that her ecstatic states would last for hours, during which she was unconscious to the world—to the extent that she did not respond to being pricked with a needle.[4] In *The Dialogue*, which takes the form of exchanges between God and Catherine herself, representing the human soul, she gives an insight into the nature of ecstasy. God explains to her that the soul unites with him through love, at which point the body loses its powers: the memory is filled only with God, the intellect rises up and gazes on the object of divine truth, and the affection loves and unites with the same object of truth. Because these powers are immersed in God, the body loses its ability to see, hear, and speak (except for divine utterance), and its members cannot move.[5]

Catherine emphasized the importance of self-knowledge in the spiritual quest. In a letter to a friend, she advises her to create within herself a spiritual abode, a "cell of true self-knowledge" that she can carry with her at all times. Self-knowledge, which leads to knowledge of God, is founded on humility.[6] Associated with humility is the need to get rid of self-will, which traps us in selfishness and prevents us from realizing the love of God. When the soul feels this divine love within, it becomes emptied of ordinary desires and love, and it surrenders itself entirely to God. It becomes a vessel for God's goodness and extends the love received from God to all God's creatures.[7]

Anticipating "the dark night of the soul" of John of the Cross, Catherine says that on the road to union with God, the mystic must face the pain of God's withdrawing himself and the deprivation of his consolations. God does this to perfect the soul, to teach it humility and make it love him without any consciousness of self and attachment to sensuality. The soul, although acutely aware of God's withdrawal, must remain steadfast in its humble pursuit of self-knowledge, and it must wait in faith for the Holy Spirit to come to it.[8]

Humility, self-knowledge, faith, and perseverance lead to union with God, a state in which the soul no longer has its own will but is so ablaze with God that it is like a brand in a furnace that cannot be drawn out because it has turned into fire. Likewise, it is impossible to draw those united with God away from him—God tells Catherine in *The Dialogue* that he will stay in their souls both "by grace and feeling" so that whenever they want they can unite their spirits to him through love. Their union with God's love is so intimate that separation is impossible, and "every time and place for them is a time and place for prayer."[9]

Catherine of Genoa

Like her Sienese namesake, Catherine of Genoa combined a life of asceticism, prayer, and mystical states with action in the world—in her case laboring for many years in her local municipal hospital. For the first twenty-six years of her life, however, there was little to suggest that she would reach the spiritual heights that enabled her to serve her fellow citizens with such compassion and energy. Marriage at the age of sixteen to a husband who proved to be faithless and neglectful seemed to be the lifelong cross she would have to bear. The extraordinary transformation that turned the chaff of her wretchedness into the gold of divine peacefulness and a new sense of purpose in life occurred in the form of a mystical experience when she was at her lowest ebb. From then on she became, in the words of Evelyn Underhill, "in fruition and activity, in rest and in work, not only a great active and a great ecstatic, but one of the deepest gazers into the secrets of Eternal Love that the history of Christian mysticism contains."[10]

Catherine was born in the great Italian maritime city of Genoa in 1447. Her parents were prominent members of Genoese society: her father's family, the Fieschi, boasted two popes, Innocent IV and Adrian V, among their forebears, and he himself became the viceroy of Naples. Catherine developed a religious sensibility from an early age, and by the time she was thirteen she was eager to enter a convent; her request was turned down because of her youth. Three years later she was married off to a certain Giuliano Adorno, a young Genoese nobleman, who quickly showed himself to be a dissolute philanderer.

For the first five years of marriage Catherine bore her misery with passive resignation; for the next five years she tried to adopt a more extravert lifestyle, seeking consolation, or at least distraction, in society—in vain. Then in March 1473 her life changed permanently when she underwent a sudden spiritual conversion. Her sister, who was a nun in a local convent, encouraged Catherine to make her confession to the nuns' confessor. As Catherine knelt before him, she felt in her heart "the wound of unmeasured love of God" and saw her faults and unhappiness beside God's goodness so clearly that she nearly collapsed. Now filled with boundless, ardent love, she vowed inwardly to cease from worldly desires and a sinful life.[11]

This mystical experience was the spiritual foundation on which the rest of her life was built. That life was mainly devoted to sharing with the sick in the Pammatone, Genoa's hospital, the infinite divine love she had received. She was aided in her work, surprisingly, by none other than her husband, Giuliano, who had also felt the call of God and become a Franciscan tertiary. In 1479 the couple, who had agreed to live in continence, moved into the hospital to be nearer their charges. Catherine was eventually given a senior administrative position, and she continued to work tirelessly and selflessly, especially in 1493 when Genoa was ravaged by plague. She herself caught the disease but managed to survive, as did Giuliano (although he died four years later). All this time Catherine had led a rather idiosyncratic religious life. She regularly fasted for long periods and received Communion on a daily basis, at a time when it was rare for laypeople to do so, but she did not have a spiritual director and rarely went to confession. Then in 1499 she found a congenial confessor in a priest named Cattaneo Marabotto, who for the rest of her life gave her spiritual guidance and listened to her innermost thoughts and concerns. She finally died, after a painful illness, in 1510.

Catherine's life and teachings were recorded in an anonymous work called *Vita e Dottrina* (Life and Teaching), which was published about forty years after her death and includes material, mainly supplied, it seems, by Marabotto, on which her treatise on purgatory and her *Spiritual Dialogue* were based (in modern times Baron Friedrich von Hügel made a pioneering study of her in his *Mystical Element of Religion*, published in 1908). Scholars still debate the extent to which Catherine's works, which she did not write herself, record her actual thoughts, and the consensus seems to be that the important treatise on purgatory, at the very least, is an authentic reflection of her beliefs.

It is also clear that Catherine's postconversion life was underpinned by mystical experiences and an awareness of the divine presence. Her whole being appears to have been dominated by a sense of God, to the extent that nothing could distract her from him. Even when attending church she was oblivious to what was being spoken or done because she was absorbed in an inner divine light. Her attention to God would make it difficult for her to converse with anyone, and she would become so enrapt that she would go off and find a secluded place. Sometimes she was discovered lying on the ground, face in hands, evidently caught up in a transport of indescribable joy and could not be disturbed by being shouted at. Equally, she could lie as still as a corpse for hours on end but then when called would immediately get up and go about her duties.

For Catherine such mystical consciousness and bliss is the result of a process directed by God, who "revivifies the soul with a special grace of His. In no other way could the soul renounce its self-centredness."[12] God finds the soul he calls to him to be initially full of sin, which is "the object of God's hatred, for it prevents his love from transforming us."[13] And so he inspires the soul with a sense of virtue and encourages it to reach a state of perfection; then, through his grace, he leads it to self-annihilation and transformation. At this point the soul does nothing of itself—whether it is speaking, willing, or feeling—because it is God who guides it directly. The soul itself is now in a state of blissful serenity, as if "immersed in an ocean of utmost peace."[14]

Throughout her life Catherine was only too well aware of suffering, mental, emotional, and physical, both in her own life and in the lives of those she tended. For her, spiritual suffering from an acute sense of sinfulness was a necessary condition of the soul, which begins the process of purification here on earth and continues it after death in purgatory—as she herself put it, the soul's "ardor in transforming itself into God is its purgatory."[15] It is a process that eventually ends with the soul's reaching the joyful state of being in God's presence without the impediment of sin. She compares the soul in purgatory encrusted with sin to an everyday object that has been covered up and cannot reflect sunlight. In the same way that the object reflects the sun in proportion to how much it is uncovered, so the soul will mirror the light of the true sun, God's love, as its sinful excretions are burned away by the purgatorial fire, and the more it is exposed to divine love, "the more the soul responds to that love and its joy increases."[16]

During her life Catherine felt this love firsthand—"All that I have said is as nothing compared to what I feel within, the witnessed correspondence of love between God and the soul"[17]—and she was able to channel it into selfless actions. She was fully aware of the constant struggle between self-will and God's will, the false self and the true self, and the way in which the individual could triumph only through the grace of pure love. And she was confident that her own experience of divine love was potentially open to everyone: "In this world, the rays of God's love, unbeknownst to man, encircle man all about, hungrily seeking to penetrate him."[18]

12

PROTESTANT MYSTICISM

*I knew nothing but pureness, and innocency,
and righteousness; being renewed into the image
of God by Christ Jesus, to the state of Adam,
which he was in before he fell.*

—George Fox

SCHOLARS STILL DEBATE THE CAUSES of the Protestant Reformation in the sixteenth century, which should probably be seen not as a sudden eruption but as the culmination of a reform movement whose tremors can be traced back to the likes of Hus, Wycliffe, and others before them. But in the early 1500s the forces of reform surfaced with even greater vehemence and tenacity, most notably through the protest of the German monk Martin Luther—who in fact had not intended to break away from the church, only to correct its abuses—and then through Huldrych Zwingli and John Calvin. The Protestants' attack on, and eventual split from, the church ushered in a new chapter in its history. The effects were felt at all levels of the ecclesiastical structure. Reformers debated, challenged, and often modified or rejected church doctrine and practices, such as the theological basis of the Mass, and in the process they did much to undermine popular piety, including pilgrimages, the cult of holy relics, and recitation of prayers for the dead.

The Reformation affected the tradition of mysticism in various ways. For example, the reformers' bias against what they spurned as "superstitions" could easily extend to other nonrational aspects of religion, and such a climate was generally unconducive to those who claimed to hear divine voices or to see the face of Christ or to feel the presence of God. In a more practical way, the decline in Protestant lands of the religious orders and their monasteries—the great seedbeds of mysticism—destroyed or at least reduced some of the most favorable habitats for contemplatives. But despite the fact that the Protestant churches had removed themselves from the mainstream tradition of contemplative prayer, mystics still appeared in Protestant lands, but they were as likely to be shoemakers (for example, Jacob Boehme and George Fox, the subjects of this chapter) or poets as priests.

One of the main instigators of the Reformation, Martin Luther was born in Saxony in 1483 and became an Augustinian monk and, later, a professor at the University of Wittenberg. He was profoundly influenced by Paul's Letter to the Romans, which convinced him that people were justified by faith in God and not by good works (a tenet that implied that priests and the church were unnecessary as mediators between people and God). At the time this seemed, as the church historian Diarmaid MacCulloch has noted, "an exhilarating, liberating idea, because it ended the tyranny of religious observance and of external demands on the human soul."[1] Luther also became increasingly critical of clerical morality and practices, particularly the sale of indulgences and the implication that human effort could affect a soul's destiny in the afterlife. Eventually, in 1517, he was moved to nail to the door of Wittenberg's castle church his Ninety-five Theses, a document that excoriated the practice of indulgences and invited a debate about them.

The church was slow to react to this challenge to its authority, but finally, in 1521, the pope excommunicated Luther. With the help of the newly developed printing presses, however, the "new opinion" of Luther and his followers, with its emphasis on the central place of the Bible as against the traditional authority of the church and papacy, leaped across Europe, causing debate, division, and violence. Politics further complicated the religious turmoil, for example in Germany, where the local princes were often guided in their decisions whether or not to support Luther as much by a need to make prudent political alliances as from a concern for doctrine. The hostility between the Lutheran and Catholic sides was partially resolved by the Peace of Augsburg in 1555, when it was established that people should adopt their particular ruler's faith, whether it be Catholic or Lutheran.

Elsewhere in Europe, the momentum of reform was continued in Switzerland, by Huldrych Zwingli (1484–1531) in Zurich and, especially, John Calvin (1509–1564) in Geneva. Calvin, who more than Luther stressed the idea of absolute predestination (the belief that God, before creation, had predestined people to either salvation or damnation), established in Geneva a theocratic and puritanical regime that was fearless in using severe punishment to ensure "good moral behavior." Calvinism later spread to France, the Netherlands, England, and Scotland (under the charismatic leadership of John Knox), and parts of Germany, although it was excluded from the terms of the Peace of Augsburg.

Meanwhile, in England, Henry VIII, in conflict with Rome over his desired divorce from his childless wife, Catherine of Aragon, declared himself the head of the Church of England; in 1536 English monasteries began to be "dissolved," their pews torn out and roofs stripped of lead. In fact Henry, whose previous enthusiasm for the papacy had been rewarded by the title Defender of the Faith, was conservative in doctrinal matters. Reform ideas took root during the reigns of his successors Edward VI and, after the rule of the reactionary Catholic Mary (r. 1553–1558), Elizabeth I, when the Anglican Church stabilized on a compromise position between extreme Calvinism and Catholicism. In the following century the Calvinist party within the church did emerge victorious after the Parliamentarians under Oliver Cromwell defeated King Charles I and the Royalists during the English Civil War (1642–1649). But their victory was only temporary. When Charles II restored the monarchy in 1660, he reestablished Anglicanism.

The period during and after the war was something of a spiritual melting pot in England. There was a proliferation of religious and quasi-religious movements, although some of them wilted before too long. Apart from the bigger groups such as the Presbyterians, Independents, Baptists, and Unitarians, there were smaller, more-radical sects such as the Ranters, Diggers, and the exotically named Fifth Monarchy Men. There was also the Seekers, many of whom became absorbed into the Quaker movement, founded by the mystical visionary George Fox. The diarist Samuel Pepys gives an idea of how disturbing individual members of the sects could be: his diary entry for July 29, 1667, states that in a city hall in London "a Quaker, came naked through the Hall, only very civilly tied about the privities to avoid scandal, and with a chafing-dish of fire and brimstone upon his head, did pass through the Hall, crying 'Repent, repent!'"[2]

One of the principal characteristics of Protestant mysticism is its emphasis on the idea, found in medieval spirituality (especially in Rhineland mysticism), that the divine can only truly be found within: the kingdom of heaven—often described as the "inner light" or "true light" or the "spark"—lies within us, in the innermost part of the soul. This emphasis can be found in the thought of a number of Protestant mystics, for example, the sixteenth-century Catholic-priest-turned-Lutheran Sebastian Franck (1499–1542), who declared that "no man can see or know himself, unless he sees and knows, by the Light and Life that is in him, God, the eternally true Light and Life."[3] And for the Lutheran pastor Valentin Weigel (1533–1588), the "Spirit and Word of God are within us. God is Himself the eye and light in the soul, as well as the object which the eye sees by this light."[4] This stress on the divine within was also central to two of the greatest Protestant mystics, the German Jacob Boehme and the Englishman George Fox.

Jacob Boehme

Jacob Boehme lived at a time when the Lutheran Church was becoming doctrinaire and authoritarian, a tendency against which he revolted, conducting his life according to the divine illumination he claimed to receive. His inclination toward mysticism, however, did not make him withdraw from the world. On the contrary, in 1599, at the age of twenty-four, having completed his training as a shoemaker, he set up shop in his local town of Görlitz and married Katharina Kuntzschmann, the daughter of a local butcher, by whom he was to have four sons. Conversely, his conventional lifestyle did not seem to block his ability to receive mystical experiences, on which he drew for his teachings. Not that what he wrote was always pure inspiration: many of his concepts and terms were drawn from astrology, the Rhineland mystics, and the writings of alchemists, especially those of the Swiss physician Paracelsus (1493–1541), and they often make his books complex and obscure. The eighteenth-century English bishop William Warburton said they would "disgrace Bedlam at full moon."[5]

Yet Boehme's self-conviction and vivid, colorful, and authoritative style won him many contemporary admirers as well as influencing a number of later mystics and thinkers, including William Law, William Blake, and Hegel. One of his best-known concepts is the *Ungrund* (literally "unground"), which is sometimes translated as "abyss" and bears resemblance to Eckhart's unknowable "Godhead." The *Ungrund* refers to the primal, undifferentiated state, devoid of dualities such as good and evil, from which God is eternally becoming self-aware, manifesting himself in the light and wisdom of the Son.

The offspring of German peasants, Boehme was born in 1575 in the village of Alt Seidenberg near the town of Görlitz. He learned enough at school to be able to read and write well, but he never enjoyed a formal higher education, remaining an autodidact for the whole of his life. After school he became an apprentice shoemaker, learning his trade for three years. It was during this time that he had a striking encounter with a stranger who came to buy shoes at the shop where Boehme worked. Having bought his shoes, the man left the premises, then stopped and called Boehme outside. The apprentice did what he was told, and the man gripped his hand and told him he would astonish the world and should study the scriptures. For Boehme it was a fateful encounter, a call to the spiritual life. His vocation was later confirmed during his time as a journeyman cobbler (the grade up from apprentice), when, after a period of intense prayer, he received an infusion of divine light and joy, the effects of which lasted for seven days.[6]

In 1600, the year after his marriage, Boehme received his most profound illumination to date. It seems to have been triggered by reflected light. One day he was staring at a pewter bowl when the sunlight flashing off its surface induced in him an ecstatic state during which he formed the impression that he could see into the inner workings of nature, the fundamental principle of things. Thinking that it might only be his fancy, he went outside to snap out of his rapture. But as he stared at the town green, he found he was able to see into the essential nature of "grass and herbs." Many years later he recalled that this sensation was accompanied by a feeling of God's love and of being reborn.[7]

Over the next decade Boehme began to record his spiritual experiences, thoughts, and reflections, which coalesced into his first book, *Aurora*, completed in 1612 when he was thirty-seven. A dense, difficult work, *Aurora* explores fundamental spiritual themes such as the relationship between God and creation and the nature of good and evil. Unfortunately for Boehme, the local Lutheran pastor, Gregorius Richter, took violent exception to its content and pressured the town council to take action: Boehme only just avoided being banished from Görlitz, but he was ordered to cease writing. He obeyed this command for several years, but by 1618 he was writing a number of treatises (later collected and published in 1623 as *The Way to Christ*), and over the next few years these were followed by several other weighty works, including *The Signature of Things* and *Mysterium Magnum*.

In early 1624, however, his old foe Richter exploded when he read *The Way to Christ* and splenetically denounced Boehme from the pulpit and in a pamphlet. At the instigation of the town council, Boehme left Görlitz and took refuge in Dresden at the court of the elector prince of Saxony, where he was well received. By the time he returned to Görlitz a few months later, Richter had died. But Boehme enjoyed only a short triumph before he, too, passed away, in November 1624. His last words were reported to be "Now I am going into Paradise."[8]

Boehme's writings, as noted, can try the patience of even the most dedicated reader, especially when he is yoking alchemical and astrological lore to his spiritual teachings. But he can also be admirably clear, for example in the two dialogues that comprise his short work *Of the Supersensual Life*, in which a scholar questions his master as to how he may see and hear God.

During the course of the first dialogue in this work, Boehme emphasizes the need for stillness and complete surrender in order to experience the divine: when the intellect and will are quiet and the soul has risen above the sensual world, then the human spirit, being now the organ of God's spirit, will hear the divine voice. What prevents the encounter with God is self-will and a concern for the things of the world, which trap the soul in its self-created jail. The scholar asks how, since human nature leads to this self-imprisonment, it is possible to rise above nature without destroying it. The master replies that there are three things a person must do: resign the will to God, resist the dictates of the will, and bow the soul to the way of the cross in order to overcome the temptations of the flesh. This entails a rejection of the world and its values, a course the scholar despairs of achieving: success lies in surrendering constantly and totally to the mercy of God and to the sufferings of Christ and his intercessory power. Only then will the soul receive the strength to conquer death and be impervious to temptation. Belief in Christ and self-surrender bring their reward. If the will could "plunge itself into that where no creature is, or can be; presently it would be penetrated and clothed upon with the supreme splendor of the divine glory."[9]

As a soul receives the gifts of God, it finds paradoxically that it both loves and hates itself simultaneously. It loves the divine wisdom, goodness, and beauty that have become part of it but hates the self that is still wrapped up in the world and its snares. Love and hate, the master explains, are a necessary duality, since they define themselves through each other. The master then launches into a paean in praise of love, whose power "supports the heavens and upholds the earth." Love is higher than the highest, greater than the greatest, and whoever "finds it, finds nothing and all things"—"nothing" because love is so incomprehensible and so much deeper than everything that nothing can be compared to it: it is an ineffable mystery. Yet the discoverer of love also finds "all things" because love is the beginning and the end of everything—"all things" are "from it, and in it, and by it."[10]

In the second dialogue, the scholar complains that his ability to receive the divine light is blocked by an inner wall. The master replies that the wall is the "creaturely will," which can be broken only by the "grace of self-denial." This cannot happen through the soul's own effort—it must passively obey God's divine light, which penetrates the darkness of its "creaturely being." Boehme distinguishes between the superior light of God and the inferior light of nature or reason and insists that the first must inform the second to bring about true enlightenment and harmony in the soul. We must seek "the fountain of light," and wait in the "deep ground" of the soul for the "sun of righteousness" to rise, increasing the light of nature sevenfold, since it "shall receive the stamp, image, and impression of the supersensual and supernatural."[11]

Later on in the second dialogue, Boehme again emphasizes the role of the will in encountering God and his love. When the will desires something, it enters that object, which then takes it over and fills it with darkness. But if the will desires nothing, then it enters nothing, whereby it can receive God's will and reside in the light.[12]

The total surrender of the will means that the love of God becomes part of human nature. Giving up self-will is a sort of death—to the world—but in doing so people allow God to live within them. Few reach this state, because they seek love in *something*, an *object*, in which they find only that object. Finally, the soul arrives at that nothing "out of which all things may be made" and says to itself, "I have nothing . . . I can do nothing . . . I am nothing . . . and so sitting down in my nothingness, I give glory to the Eternal Being, and will nothing of myself, that so God may will all in me, being unto me my God and all things." By embracing nothing, the soul allows the entry of divine love, which needs a place that is still, before it can make its home there. When it does so, it rejoices with its "love-fire," which burns up the center of selfishness, the "I", and increases in heat until it has accomplished its task within the soul, which cannot bear to be separated from it.[13]

George Fox

The year that Jacob Boehme died, 1624, saw the birth of George Fox, the English visionary, mystic, and founder of the Quakers, or Society of Friends, who are still renowned for their tolerant spirit, pacifism, and acts of charity. There were parallels between the two men. Like Boehme, Fox received only a basic school education and was apprenticed to a shoemaker. Fox, too, experienced mystical visions of reality, including one in which, like Boehme, he was able to see into the heart of nature: "Now I was come up in spirit through the flaming sword, into the paradise of God. All things were new; and all the creation gave unto me another smell than before, beyond what words can utter. I knew nothing but pureness, and innocency, and righteousness; being renewed into the image of God by Christ Jesus, to the state of Adam, which he was in before he fell. The creation was opened to me; and it was showed me how all things had their names given them according to their nature and virtue."[14] Furthermore, Boehme's writings were beginning to circulate in England at about the period when Fox had started his itinerant spiritual mission, and it is said that the German's works were studied by Fox's followers.

Central to Fox's spiritual vision was the Bible, and in common with other fringe religious groups of the civil war period, he saw the world in dualistic terms, as a cosmic struggle between light and dark, love and death, God and Satan. Underpinning his spirituality, however, was "an earthy wisdom and salt entirely his own, and an insistence on the love and light of Christ which is centrally Christian."[15]

Fox was born in the village of Fenny Drayton in Leicestershire. His father, Christopher, was a weaver and a devout Christian (his neighbors called him "Righteous Christer"), while his mother could claim as an ancestor a Protestant martyr who had died during the reign of the Catholic queen Mary I (r. 1553–1558). George felt a strong religious instinct from childhood, and at one point his family considered making him train as a priest. Instead, he worked for a shoemaker and wool trader until, in 1643, at the age of nineteen, he experienced a direct call from God, who said to him: "Thou seest how young people go together into vanity, and old people into the earth; thou must forsake all, young and old, keep out of all, and be a stranger unto all."[16] Impelled to leave home, Fox felt the great weight of spiritual despair on his shoulders, and he set out to find an answer to it. For the next three years he wandered around the Midlands and the north of England, seeking out priests who he hoped might remedy his depression and sense of sin. None could offer him any comfort. One of them, Fox says, told him "to take tobacco and sing psalms"; another man seemed to him to be "like an empty, hollow cask"; another suggested Fox should undergo some blood-letting.[17]

During this time of seeking, however, Fox experienced what he called "openings" or revelations—divinely revealed knowledge of the truth of which he was inwardly certain. It was "opened" to him, for example, that all believers, whether Protestants or Catholics, were born of God; that attendance at the universities of Oxford and Cambridge was not a sufficient training for the priesthood; and that God did not dwell in man-made temples or churches. Meanwhile, Fox continued his travels, fasting, reading his Bible, and reflecting upon life in "hollow trees and lonesome places," or pitching up at some town, where he would take a room for a time. Having given up on the priests of the established Anglican Church, he sought out those of the dissenting faiths, such as the Baptists and Congregationalists. But even though he found some of them to be "tender" (one of his most positive adjectives), they could not help his wretched condition. This only strengthened his desire for God without the mediation of any person or book.

Then on one occasion, after a period of solitude, he received a mystical revelation accompanied by a profound experience of divine love. "One day, when I had been walking solitarily abroad, and was come home, I was taken up in the love of God, so that I could not but admire the greatness of His love; and while I was in that condition, it was opened unto me by the eternal light and power, and I therein clearly saw that all was done and to be done in and by Christ, and how He conquers and destroys this tempter the devil, and all his works, and is atop of him; and that all these troubles were good for me, and temptations for the trial of my faith, which Christ had given me."[18]

The experience gave him a solidity of faith, "as an anchor in the bottom of the sea," but the divine light also served to intensify his awareness of the darkness in his life, with all its trials and temptations. From then on, however, he began to draw large numbers of followers, especially among craftsmen and yeomen. His new recruits were borne along by their leader's glowing spirituality, self-conviction, keen sense of justice, charity, and bravery in the face of persecution. For Fox inevitably made enemies wherever he went. Apart from taking constant issue with priests, judges, schoolteachers, and other establishment figures, he refused to doff his hat to his social superiors, and he showed a puritanical streak in his attitude toward those activities which he considered made people "vain" and "loose," including "feasts, May-games, sports, plays, and shows." (In a similar vein he referred to the days of the week by numbers, not by their names, because the latter reflected the names of pagan gods.) He was rewarded for his advice and warnings to all and sundry with beatings, stonings, whippings, the stocks, and jail. But nothing could prevent him from his aim to declare "the Word of life and reconciliation freely, that all might come to Christ."[19]

In 1652 Fox's mission became firmly established after he took residence at Swarthmoor in northwest England. There he got to know the aristocratic judge Thomas Fell, who gave valuable support to the nascent movement. In the following years Fox began to give the Quakers organizational shape, instituting regular monthly, quarterly, and yearly meetings between members. Later, in 1669—the year he married Thomas Fell's widow—Fox took his message abroad to the people of Ireland, then to the West Indies and America in 1671–1672, and to the Netherlands in 1677 and again in 1684. For the rest of his life he continued preaching and overseeing the organization of the movement. He died on January 13, 1691, and his *Journal*, which became a spiritual classic, was published three years later.

For Fox the central spiritual reality of existence was the divine inner light, which is received directly from God and which transforms and guides a person through life. This meant that churches and priests were unnecessary and the scriptures secondary (for the light precedes the scriptures) to what was a God-given inner certainty. He sums up the essence of this teaching in his *Journal*: "Now the Lord God opened to me by His invisible power that every man was enlightened by the divine Light of Christ, and I saw it shine through all; and that they that believed in it came out of condemnation to the Light of life, and became the children of it; but they that hated it, and did not believe in it were condemned by it, though they made a profession of Christ."[20]

Fox echoes the sentiments of the first chapter of John's Gospel, but he stresses that his insights were revealed to him, not learned from holy writ. "For I saw, in that Light and Spirit which was before the Scriptures were given forth, and which led the holy men of God to give them forth, that all, if they would know God or Christ, or the Scriptures aright, must come to that Spirit by which they that gave them forth were led and taught."[21] There is, then, a divine principle that is found in every soul and manifested outwardly in righteous actions. It is our disobedience to the calling of this inner spirit of God that causes disharmony. But heeding it brings enlightened self-knowledge; for example, we see that by harming our neighbor we really are harming ourselves.

It was Fox's mission to restore people to their spiritual selves, which in turn would bring about true religious devotion, charity, and justice.

So, inspired by Fox's writings and example, the Quaker movement was founded on spiritual and radical egalitarian principles on the basis that the divine light and spirit reside with everyone, not just "qualified" priests. Quakers abandoned the rigid structures of the established churches, preferring to emphasize the need for each individual to acclimatize and tune in to his or her own inner, divine voice.

13

THE GOLDEN AGE OF SPAIN

*If a man wishes to be sure of the road he travels
on, he must close his eyes and walk in the dark.*
—John of the Cross

LTHOUGH THE PROTESTANT REFORMATION gave impetus to the Catholic Church to bring about internal change, currents of reform had been felt within the church before and during the ructions caused by Luther's protest. At the end of the fifteenth century, for example, the puritanical Dominican friar Savonarola in Florence denounced the corruption and laxity of the clergy and papacy with a careless fanaticism that brought him excommunication and later death at the stake. In Spain, Cardinal Ximénez de Cisneros (1436–1517), impressive in his personal asceticism and piety, presided over important reforms and patronized learning, founding the University of Alcalá. Yet it is clear that the revival of the church known as the Counter-Reformation, or Catholic Reformation, was made more urgent by the Protestant movements. One response to the latter was the formation of new religious orders, such as the Theatines, established in Rome in 1524, and the Capuchins, a branch of the Franciscans, in the late 1520s. In 1534 a former Spanish soldier named Ignatius Loyola founded the Society of Jesus, or Jesuits. Formally approved by Pope Paul III in 1540, the Jesuits became renowned for their superb organization and flair for teaching and missionary work, which they carried abroad to the New World and the Far East.

The principal doctrinal conduit for the renewal of the church was the Council of Trent (a city in northern Italy that was part of the Holy Roman Empire), at which, intermittently from 1545 to 1563, Catholic prelates and theologians attempted to define doctrine, correct abuses, and implement reforms. The council had far-reaching effects on the life of the church. Protestant teachings were repudiated and traditional doctrines, such as on the validity of the seven sacraments, relics, and purgatory, affirmed; the position of the pope as the supreme head of the church was confirmed; extra provision was made for the education of the clergy; and the Latin Vulgate Bible was endorsed as the authoritative text, with the church preserving the sole right to interpret it.

There were, however, less-attractive aspects of the Catholic reform movement. The Index of Prohibited Books, first issued in 1557 (and finally abolished in 1966), forbade the reading of certain books deemed inimical to the faith. More serious was the role of the Inquisition, which was first established in the 1200s and gained added notoriety during Renaissance times with the founding of the Spanish Inquisition at the end of the fifteenth century. Initially aimed at rooting out baptized Jews and Muslims who were believed to have reverted to their original faiths, the Spanish Inquisition later included Protestants in its web of violence. Then in 1542 Pope Paul III founded in Rome another version of the Inquisition, officially known as the Holy Office and mainly restricted to the confines of Italy.

The combination of discipline and reforms did much to bolster and revitalize the Catholic Church in the face of rival denominations. At a practical level, Catholicism was able to reclaim from the Protestants Poland, southern Germany, and other parts of Europe, as well as stake claims in North and South America. Yet the Counter-Reformation also had its interior spiritual side, notably in Spain, a country that had been recently unified by the marriage of Ferdinand of Aragon and Isabella of Castile and had become the dominant European power under Emperor Charles V (r. 1516–1556).

Confident and aggressive in its colonial adventures in the New World, Spain was a faithful supporter of the pope and wielded significant influence at the Council of Trent. Spanish spirituality bubbled up in the Alumbrado (Illuminated) movement—small informal groups of individuals whose devotion toward mystical prayer and emphasis on the interior, as opposed to the externals of piety, brought some of them into odium with the Inquisition. But the greatest flowering of Spanish spirituality was seen in the writings and lives of the Carmelite reformers Teresa of Ávila and John of the Cross, two of the church's greatest mystics.

Teresa of Ávila

Teresa of Ávila was remarkable for being able to combine practice of the most profound mystical prayer with a dynamic involvement in the world, seen particularly in her reform of her own Carmelite order and the foundation of seventeen new convents. Ebullient, courageous, patient, humble, and humorous, she gives an insider's guide to contemplation, which she saw as a journey of the soul from the outside world to its innermost depths and union with God. More a describer than an analyzer, unlike her more intellectual friend and fellow Carmelite John of the Cross, she was eloquent about the various supernatural concomitants of mysticism, such as ecstasies, visions, locutions, and raptures, which she described as a "powerful eagle rising and bearing you upon its wings."[1]

The daughter of a well-to-do merchant named Alonso de Cepeda, Teresa was born in 1515 in the town of Ávila in central Spain. She grew up to be a good-looking girl, sociable and confident, and with an adventurous, romantic streak—the story is told that at the age of seven she set out from home with an elder brother in order to seek martyrdom at the hands of the Moors (their efforts were thwarted at the city gates by an uncle).

Sometime after her mother died in 1529, Teresa was sent to be educated at an Augustinian convent in Ávila. The onset of poor health, however, forced her to return home after eighteen months. During her convalescence she read the letters of Jerome, which consolidated her desire to become a religious. But the opposition of her father prompted her to run away and join the Carmelite's Convent of the Incarnation in Ávila in November 1535. Faced with this fait accompli, Alonso relented and dropped his objections. A year later Teresa's convent life was disrupted by a serious illness that continued for years, despite the best efforts of doctors. In 1539 her health deteriorated and she fell into a coma for four days; when she regained consciousness, she found herself partially paralyzed, a condition she endured for the next three years, until finally her health improved through, she believed, the intercession of Saint Joseph.

During the following years, Teresa practiced mental prayer and occasionally enjoyed supernatural experiences, but this was generally an unexceptionable period of spirituality for her. In 1555 her contemplative life deepened after she experienced a "second conversion" while praying in her oratory before a small statue of Christ being scourged at the pillar. From this time the number of visions, locutions, and other divine favors she received increased—causing alarm to some of her confessors, who believed they were inspired by the devil. Any doubts Teresa may have had were dispelled by an inner consolation from God, culminating in 1559 with the dramatic experience of the "transverberation," when she felt an angel piercing her heart with a red-hot spear. She was also supported by a number of friends and close associates, especially Peter of Alcántara.

In the early 1560s Teresa turned her attention to reforming the Carmelite order. For some time she had been less than happy with the relatively relaxed lifestyle at the Convent of the Incarnation. Finally, on August 24, 1562, despite opposition from her own convent and the townspeople of Ávila, she founded a new house of Discalced (Shoeless, or Barefoot) Carmelites, dedicated to Joseph and obedient to a more strict, ascetic rule. Four years later the general of the Carmelite order visited the new convent and was so impressed by what he saw that he gave the go-ahead for the foundation of more Discalced houses for both nuns and friars, a process recounted in her *Book of Foundations*, written in the 1570s. During this time she also began to write her greatest work, *The Interior Castle*, an account of the different stages of mystical prayer. Opposition to the expansion of the Discalced Carmelites continued, however, until in 1580, with the backing of the Spanish king Philip II, they were finally granted the right to have a distinct province of their own. By this time Teresa was frail but still able to found houses at Palencia, Soria, and Burgos. She eventually died in Alba de Tormes in October 1582. She was beatified in 1614 and canonized eight years later.

Teresa's great contribution to mysticism is the intimacy, honesty, and vividness that she brings to her descriptions of the different stages of spiritual growth and contemplation, including the highest state, of "spiritual marriage." In her autobiographical *Life of the Mother Teresa of Jesus*, for example, she compares the four stages of mystical prayer to four ways in which a garden may be watered, an image used by Augustine and others. The four ways, which proceed with decreasing personal (and increasing divine) involvement, are: (1) by well water drawn by hand, (2) by well water drawn with the help of a waterwheel and a windlass, (3) by a stream or spring, and (4)—best of all—by heavy rain.

She then goes on to explain the simile. Irrigating the garden with water laboriously drawn from a well corresponds to beginners in prayer who strain to recollect their senses while trying not to succumb to distracting sights and sounds. There may come a period when they feel "dryness" and lose heart. But they must remember that their work is not for their own sake but for the Lord and that their labors will be rewarded.[2]

The second way (well water drawn with the help of a windlass) results in a greater abundance of water with less effort and is like the soul when it is more advanced in recollection and receives some mystical experiences. It still has to make some effort, but because it feels divine grace to a greater degree, the labor is less intense. Also, the soul loses its appetite for sensual and worldly things and enjoys a sense of peace and contentment.[3]

The third way (an irrigating stream or spring) involves much less labor than the first two methods, although a degree of effort is needed to channel the water to the right place. This represents the soul that has reached a point when, with its faculties dormant, it enjoys considerably more sweetness and delight than before. At this stage it is not only immersed in contemplation but can also participate in the active life, for example, doing charitable works.[4]

The fourth and final way, which involves downpours of heavy rain and therefore no human effort, corresponds to the soul that has progressed to a state in which it feels nothing but delight—a delight that has no object. This is the condition of divine union, which Teresa does not attempt to analyze, saying that she cannot differentiate between "mind," "soul," and "spirit" (although she does liken the soul to a flame that sometimes leaps out of a fire, the substance of which it shares). Yet although she does not analyze union, she does describe its effects, for example, the way the soul feels it is fainting with peacefulness and joy, its faculties being in suspension and the body almost catatonic. She also says that on one occasion, when experiencing this state, she was wondering what was happening to the soul when she heard God say to her that it "dissolves utterly, my daughter, to rest more and more in Me. It is no longer itself that lives; it is I." [5]

Teresa's most sustained work on contemplation is *The Interior Castle*, which she wrote at top speed in 1577 after she had received a vision. In the book she depicts the stages of the soul's inner spiritual quest for divine union in terms of a journey through seven sets of rooms, or "mansions," located within a castle made of crystal or diamond. The soul's destination is the innermost room, where it will find ultimate union with God.

From the castle's outer courtyard, the soul passes through the castle gate, representing prayer and meditation, to the first three sets of rooms, where it learns the importance of virtues such as humility, prayer, and perseverance. It then moves on to the fourth lot of rooms, where it begins to learn the prayer of recollection and of quiet. The fifth rooms concern the prayer of union and spiritual betrothal. At this point, Teresa introduces the memorable image of the soul as a silkworm that eats mulberry leaves until, when it is fully grown, it spins a silk cocoon from which it emerges as a white butterfly. Similarly, the soul feeds on outer nourishment provided by the church, such as sermons, confessions, and holy books, until it, too, becomes fully grown. It then begins to spin its cocoon—that is, Christ—in which it can hide itself. And just as the silkworm has to die to become a butterfly, so the soul must die to its attachment to the world and emerge transformed by its proximity to God.⁶

In the sixth set of rooms, the soul, seeking to progress from betrothal to marriage, has to undergo further physical and spiritual suffering. But when it finally arrives at the seventh rooms it experiences union with God and receives a wondrous vision of the Trinity. The very last room—the center of the soul itself—is the locus of the spiritual marriage between the soul and God. Teresa clearly distinguishes between permanent spiritual marriage and betrothal, in which separation may occur. She compares spiritual betrothal to two candles that have been joined together near the tops so that their wicks combine to give a single flame but that can be pulled apart into two separate objects. Conversely, spiritual marriage is like rain falling into a river, when the river's water is impossible to distinguish from the rain; or it is like a stream entering the sea or a room in which light pours in through two large windows—"it enters in different places but it all becomes one."⁷

John of the Cross

Teresa's cofounder of the Discalced Carmelites and one of the great analysts of contemplation, John of the Cross, once wrote that "if a man wishes to be sure of the road he travels on, he must close his eyes and walk in the dark."⁸ "Darkness" and "night" are words popularly associated with John, particularly through his famous description of the "dark night of the soul," during which the soul is gruelingly purged so that its will can be united with God's. For John, the soul's attachment to the world and to spiritual practices has to be completely broken— he compares the situation to a bird that cannot fly away to freedom until the cord that grounds it has been cut. To do this, we must always seek the road less easy: "In order to arrive at having pleasure in everything, / Desire to have pleasure in nothing."⁹

But although his teachings can seem daunting, John was no cheerless pessimist. A diminutive man, just over five feet tall, he was warm and saintly, and he himself emphasized that at the end of the night came the reward—the glorious light of God. In *The Living Flame of Love*, he describes how the soul, when it is on fire with love, feels as if an angel has struck it with a burning brand, and how at the moment of contact it suffers a wound that is "unimaginably delicious" and enjoys the sense of diffusion of heat through its "spiritual veins" until it feels like an "immense sea of fire."[10]

John was born in 1542 at Fontiveros near Ávila. The following year his father, a nobleman who had been disinherited by his family for marrying a poor weaver, died, leaving John and his two brothers to be brought up in poverty by their mother. At the age of seventeen he studied at a Jesuit college in Medina del Campo; then, convinced he had a religious vocation, he joined the Carmelite order, taking the habit in 1563. But he still continued with his education, embarking on a three-year course at the University of Salamanca, during which time he was reckoned sufficiently proficient to teach students himself. In 1567 he was ordained a priest, and in the same year, at Medina, he fatefully met Teresa, who persuaded him to help her reform the Carmelite order and set up a Discalced monastery. Next year John and two other Carmelite friars established such a house in Duruelo, the first of fifteen he was to found.

For the next four years John was involved in various administrative duties for the reform movement before becoming confessor to the nuns of Teresa's original Convent of the Incarnation in Ávila, staying there until 1577. In the same year he was imprisoned by the mainstream Carmelites, who were hostile to the radical reforms that he and Teresa had been implementing. Interrogated and flogged, John was kept prisoner in a tiny windowless cell in the Carmelite priory at Toledo. Thrown back on his spiritual resources and faith in God, he responded by writing some of his finest poetry, including part of the "Spiritual Canticle," which became the wellspring of his mystical treatises. After eight months' incarceration he managed to escape, taking with him his precious writings. From then on he continued to administer Discalced monasteries, act as a spiritual director, and write his mystical works. He died in 1591, and his last words were reputed to be "Tonight I shall sing matins in heaven." He was beatified in 1675, canonized in 1726, and declared a doctor of the church in 1926.

John plumbed great depths of mystical experience and wrote about them in a carefully considered, meticulous way. But he is also one of the greats of Spanish lyric poetry, and his mystical poems form the basis for longer prose commentaries. In the "Spiritual Canticle" he draws on the bridal mysticism of the Song of Songs, interpreting the love between man and God in terms of that between bride and bridegroom, with the stages of the relationship representing the stages of the mystical path. His lines are often simple in diction but haunting in resonance, both sensual and spiritual at the same time:

> *My loved one is the mountains*
> *The lonely wooded valleys*
> *The strange islands*
> *The rushing streams*
> *The hushing of the amorous winds.*[11]

John is best known, however, for his description of the soul's "dark night"—a painful but inevitable stage of its journey toward union with God—which he elaborates fully in *The Ascent of Mount Carmel* and *The Dark Night of the Soul*. These two unfinished treatises, based on two poems, really form one continuous work and were designed to be read by monks. John says that to reach union with God, the soul has to undergo purgation by passing through two states of darkness, or "nights"—John's terminology ultimately goes back to Dionysius the Areopagite, but he expands and enriches it. (It should be noted that John's "nights" are not necessarily sequential, since different aspects of the journey may be experienced at different times.)

In the night of the senses, the soul is purged of its desire for things of the world as well as emotional attachments. The second, more-painful state, the night of the spirit, relates to those who are further along the contemplative path and involves purgation of any residual spiritual consolations, whereby the soul feels itself agonizingly abandoned by God before its final union with him. (With regard to this union, John says that God is "substantially present" in every soul, whether that of a sinner or a saint. But John distinguishes between this divine presence, naturally occurring in every creature, and the union of the soul with God through love, when the soul's will and God's will are in perfect consonance.)

John also says that both nights have their active and passive phases. The active one involves the soul's making efforts to effect the necessary purgation. So, in the active night of the senses, the soul must try to imitate the life of Christ and reject anything that does not glorify

God. The emotions of joy, hope, fear, and grief must be mortified and the soul should try to pursue the most difficult, despised, and unpleasant things in life. The active night of the spirit concerns the higher part of the soul. The use of the imagination and meditation, for example, picturing Christ on the cross, must come to an end, since the soul must stay in darkness, emptied of sensual images. Also the memory must be stripped of its knowledge of sense objects, and the soul must not reflect upon supernatural experiences, such as visions and inner voices (of which John, unlike Teresa, was extremely wary). It must simply focus on God in loving affection.

The passive stages of the two nights require the soul to do nothing but allow God to work on it. John says that there are three indicators that the soul is going through the passive night of the senses: it derives no comfort in divine or created things, it feels "dryness" owing to God's transferring "to the spirit the good things and the strength of the senses,"[12] and it is unable to meditate or stimulate the imagination. It also feels forsaken by God and is tempted to revert to its old habit of meditation—which it may lapse into, unless guided by a spiritual director. The soul should remain quiet, letting its faculties remain inoperative, and so allow God to do his work in it, "for by not hindering the operation of infused contemplation, to which God is now admitting it, the soul is refreshed in peaceful abundance, and set on fire with the spirit of love."[13]

Finally, the more-demanding and painful passive night of the spirit, in which the soul keenly feels the lack of spiritual consolation, ultimately leads to loving union with God. This last phase of the dark night involves the soul's doing nothing except attending to God in love and allowing his light to enter it. The divine light is like a "ray of darkness" because it leaves the soul in a darkness that comes from nonunderstanding and a sense of its own impurity. This light overcomes the light of natural reason and is so radiant and pure that the soul it enters recognizes its wretched state and suffers greatly, thinking it has been removed from God's grace. But the darkness, which can last for years, is in fact purifying the soul "as fire consumes the rust and moldiness of metal,"[14] and the soul must allow itself to be refined so that it can become united with God in love. God, in short, makes "the soul die to all that is not God" so that being "denuded and stripped" it may become renewed. "This is nothing else," John says, "but the supernatural light giving light to the understanding, so that the human understanding becomes divine, made one with the divine."[15] In *The Living Flame of Love*, John states that the substance of the soul cannot be changed into the substance of God. Nevertheless, the soul can be "united in Him and absorbed in Him, and is thus God, which comes to pass in this perfect state of the spiritual life, although not so perfectly as in the next life."[16]

14

French Mystics and Quietism

Our only business is to love and
delight ourselves in God.
—Brother Lawrence

URING THE COURSE of the seventeenth century, France became the dominant European state. The country gained a reputation not only for the cultural brilliance of the court of its
"Sun King," Louis XIV, whose absolutist ambitions impacted all levels
of society, including the life of the church, but also for its influential
thinkers, churchmen, and mystics, including René Descartes, Blaise
Pascal, and Francis de Sales. Yet France's national confidence and preeminent status had come only after many years of civil war, known as
the Wars of Religion, in the second half of the sixteenth century, as well
as its involvement in the bitter conflict of the pan-European Thirty
Years' War in the early 1600s.

The tension that existed between Catholicism and the newly
formed Protestant churches had added a distinctly religious dynamic

to a number of conflicts in post-Reformation Europe—struggles that also involved territorial ambitions, political power broking, and dynastic disputes. This was certainly true of the Wars of Religion, fought intermittently from 1562 to 1598 between France's Catholic majority and its Protestant minority, who were Calvinists known as Huguenots. The war finally drew to a close only when the Huguenot Henry of Navarre, who had ascended the French throne as Henry IV in 1589, converted to Catholicism in 1593 and, five years later, proclaimed the Edict of Nantes. This granted the Huguenots civil rights and the freedom to worship in certain cities within the country. (Almost a century later, in 1685, Louis XIV revoked the edict, precipitating the migration of some three hundred thousand Huguenots to Prussia, Holland, England, and other parts of Europe, as well as to South Africa and America.)

At the start of the seventeenth century, France also became involved, along with most of the other European countries, in the immensely complex Thirty Years' War (1618–1648), in which politics and religious convictions again combined to produce widespread brutality, death, and destruction, particularly in Germany. Hostilities eventually came to an end with the Peace of Westphalia in 1648, which realigned territorial boundaries and reaffirmed the principle that a state's ruler should determine his people's faith. The war had other effects: Germany lay in ruins, exhausted by the effects of the fighting; the Holy Roman Empire was now virtually impotent; and France emerged as the most powerful European state.

French spirituality during the latter half of the seventeenth century was marked by Louis XIV's attempt to draw the French church away from the orbit of Rome and more into his own gravitational field. Also, his reign saw the rise of significant religious controversies, especially over Quietism and Jansenism, a spiritual doctrine named for Cornelius Jansen (1585–1638), a theology professor who became bishop of Ypres. Jansen and his followers were deeply influenced by Augustine and, like the Calvinists, emphasized predestination and the idea that only a small group of Christians—the "elect"—will be saved from damnation.

The Jansenists were pessimistic about the human condition and the all-too-numerous travails of life, and they advocated strict moral discipline and asceticism. They were also hostile to the Jesuits, who were influential at court and therefore dangerous enemies. One of the notable champions of the Jansenist cause was the brilliant French thinker Blaise Pascal (1623–1662), whose sister attended the Jansenist-dominated convent at Port-Royal near Paris. In his *Provincial Letters,* which sold in their thousands, he attacked the Jesuits and what he saw as their worldliness and argued for a return to more austere forms of worship. The conflict between the Jansenists and the Jesuits—as well as the French king and the papacy—continued for the rest of the century. But in 1713 Jansenist teachings were condemned by a papal bull and the tide was turned decisively against them.

Francis de Sales

Francis de Sales, who grew up during the Wars of Religion and lived to see the start of the Thirty Years' War, once wrote that "it is an error—no, a heresy—to wish to banish the devout life from the army, from the workshop, from the courts of princes, from the households of the married folk."[1] An aristocrat by birth, a prominent churchman, and eventually a doctor of the church and the patron saint of writers, Francis was especially concerned to help ordinary people, not just the ecclesiastical professionals, to achieve a profound intimacy with God. His spiritual approach to the divine may lack the intensity and soul-searching of other mystics, but in his writings, especially his classic *Introduction to the Devout Life,* he unfolds a sane, achievable, and attractive way by which the soul may be led into the fulfillment of the spiritual life.

The eldest of six boys, Francis was born in 1567 in the small duchy of Savoy, which lay between France and Italy. He was educated by the Jesuits at Clermont College in Paris, where he experienced an inner conversion. For some time he had been filled with despondency about the church's debate on predestination and the likelihood that he would fail to be one of the elect saved from damnation. One day, exhausted with anguish, he prayed on his knees before the statue of the Virgin Mary in a local church and afterward felt a profound sense of liberation and healing. He subsequently vowed himself to chastity and to the service of the Virgin. It remained his deep conviction that everyone had the ability to receive God's abundant grace and be saved, and this became the basis of his spirituality.[2]

After Clermont, Francis went to Padua to study law, completing his studies there in 1592. In the following year, against the wishes of his father—at least initially—he entered the church and embarked on a mission to convert the region of Chablais, on the southern side of Lake Geneva, which had become a Calvinist stronghold after the Reformation. Despite the danger to his life, he traveled throughout the area, preaching, teaching, and above all impressing people with his personal sanctity, eventually leading many back to the Catholic fold. Over the following years he gained a reputation for his diligence and spirituality, and in 1602 he was appointed bishop of Geneva, administering his diocese from Annecy in Savoy, since Geneva itself was still solidly Calvinist. Two years later, while he was in Dijon, he had a momentous meeting with a woman named Jeanne de Chantal: he became her spiritual director, and, bound by a deep friendship and love of God, they together founded in 1610 the new contemplative Visitation order, intended for women who were unable to bear the asceticism of the traditional orders. For the remaining twelve years of his life, Francis continued his preaching, spiritual direction, pastoral care, and writing. He eventually died in 1622, at the age of fifty-six, while visiting Lyons.

Francis's teachings are found in a number of works, including his letters and sermons and in particular his two spiritual classics, *Introduction to the Devout Life* and *Treatise on the Love of God*, which were published in 1609 and 1616 respectively. He developed his *Devout Life* from a spiritual manual intended originally for the private use of a relative. Its commonsense practicality, full of encouragement to reflect fruitfully on life and to practice meditational exercises, shines through as it attempts to show how religious devotion is possible amid the everyday concerns of the world.

Devout Life is addressed to "Philothea" (that is, the "God-loving" soul) and consists of five parts, which deal with (1) purging the self, (2) the importance of the sacraments and prayer, (3) practicing the virtues, (4) remedies against temptations, and (5) exercises for the soul's spiritual renewal. Francis emphasizes throughout the importance of being aware of the ubiquitous presence of God and the need to develop devotion, which bursts forth from charity as flame from a fire.[3]

Francis's style and approach can be gleaned from his method of meditation in the second part of the book. The meditation is divided into four parts. The first begins with the soul's preparation, which entails being aware of the presence of God and asking him for help. To become truly conscious of God, it is important to realize that "just as wherever birds fly they always encounter the air, so also wherever we go or wherever we are, we find God present."[4] We should also try to imagine Christ literally standing by our side, like a friend. Then, having become aware of God and of our own unworthiness, we must ask him for grace to serve and worship him. We should also conjure up in our minds a particular Gospel scene or spiritual truth to meditate upon; for example, we might picture Christ on the cross and try to sense the actual sights and sounds of Golgotha, or meditate, perhaps, on death or hell. Beginners should stick with subjects that can be pictured in some way, rather than abstractions, which are more suitable for those further along the contemplative path.

The second step is to reflect upon meditations such as the Crucifixion in order to understand them better. Francis makes the point that meditation differs from reading a book or from ordinary thinking in that it entails spiritual growth and an increasing love of God. So we should not only picture something but also consider its deeper import: "Imitate the bees, who do not leave a flower as long as they can extract any honey out of it."[5]

The third part concerns exercising our affections and resolutions. Meditation rouses our emotions: through it we feel love of God and of our neighbors or a general sense of compassion or shame for our past sinful life—and we should allow ourselves to feel these positive feelings as much as possible. Yet it is not enough just to be aware of them. We must use them to achieve practical ends, to correct some personal failing, such as getting annoyed by "the disagreeable words" uttered by "some man or woman who is my neighbor, a manservant, or maid."[6]

The meditation concludes with the fourth and last part. We should thank God for his help in the meditation process, offer him our affections and resolutions, and ask him for his blessing, so that our meditation will bear fruit. Francis ends by suggesting that we should gather "a little devotional bouquet," that is, pick out a couple of points from the meditation and savor them, just as a person can enjoy throughout the day a handful of flowers plucked from a beautiful garden.[7]

Further along the spiritual path is contemplation, which Francis considers in his *Treatise on the Love of God*. Contemplation, Francis says, is born from the marriage of meditation with love. Love rises from meditation and enables us to contemplate, and this in turn inspires us with a more ardent love.[8] He also describes contemplation as "simply the mind's loving, unmixed, permanent attention to the things of God." Through contemplation, the soul enters a grace-given state of tranquillity in which it and its faculties are in abeyance—memory and imagination are not needed, and only the will "drawing gently at the breast" imbibes the milk of divine providence.[9]

Brother Lawrence

One of those who fought in the Thirty Years' War was a certain Nicholas Herman, a young Frenchman who would later metamorphose as Brother Lawrence of the Resurrection, a lay brother and mystic of the Carmelite order. Working in a monastic kitchen for some thirty years, he was able to practice being in the presence of God to such an extent that his inner peacefulness and radiance gained him a reputation for holiness that spread way beyond the confines of the monastery. He spoke of his ability to remain constantly aware of the divine presence in terms of "an habitual, silent, and secret conversation of the soul with God, which often causes in me joys and raptures inwardly, and sometimes also outwardly, so great that I am forced to use means to moderate them, and prevent their appearance to others."[10]

Herman was born in about 1605, in Lorraine, in eastern France. His career in the army was cut short by a leg wound, and then for a short time he became a footman to the treasurer of the king of France, a post he remembered primarily for his clumsiness and propensity to break things. He then decided to commit his life to God, having already had in his late teens a profound conversion experience: one day in winter while he was reflecting upon a stripped tree and realizing that soon in the coming spring its leaves, blossoms, and fruits would appear again, he "received a high view of the providence and power of God, which has never since been effaced from his soul."[11]

After this experience he first became a hermit, then in 1649 he joined the Carmelite monastery in Paris. Now adopting the name Brother Lawrence, he worked in the kitchen for most of the rest of his life, developing over time the saintly demeanor and cheerfulness for which he became famous. Among those who met him was a priest named Joseph de Beaufort, who recorded four conversations with Lawrence, later publishing them along with some of the latter's sayings and letters shortly after his death in 1691. Although Lawrence's posthumous reputation in France suffered from his being quoted by François Fénelon, bishop of Cambrai, who was condemned for his association with the Quietist movement, his writings were influential elsewhere, particularly in England, where de Beaufort's book was translated in the early eighteenth century as *The Practice of the Presence of God*.

One of the most significant points of Lawrence's teaching is that there is for those who practice God's presence no separation between the different activities of life. It is not a case of doing mundane tasks without the awareness of God, then going off to chapel to reconnect with him. Life, when lived in true faith and commitment to God, is not compartmentalized: a person's relationship with the divine continues uninterrupted whether he or she is peeling potatoes, gardening, or kneeling down and praying. There are parallels with Zen Buddhism, in which the sacred is not so much searched for beyond the self as realized in the total awareness of the present moment.

The divine peacefulness that Lawrence found by not looking or thinking beyond anything that was not God allowed him to retain his composure and inner joy, day in, day out. All tasks, great and small, he said, must be dedicated to God and done out of love for him. In fact, he claimed that he felt closer to God when occupied with his daily duties than when he withdrew to pray. Even when the kitchen was at its most hectic, he is said to have kept calm, with his focus on heaven. He neither dallied nor rushed around but did the right jobs at the right time, professing that "in the noise and clutter of my kitchen, while several persons are at the same time calling for different things, I possess God in as great tranquillity as if I were upon my knees at the Blessed Sacrament."[12]

Brother Lawrence also emphasized that he did not arrive at his awareness of God through books but through simple faith and love. Love is the key and the bedrock of all activities: acts of penance and mortification and other exercises that are performed without love are of no use. His philosophy can be summed up by his words, "Our only business is to love and delight ourselves in God."

Miguel de Molinos

After Louis XIV's government clamped down on the convent at Port-Royal for its support of Jansenism in the 1660s, it "signalled the anti-mysticism which characterized the latter part of the seventeenth century," and from then on there was a "subtle restraint on open discussion of the interior life, an attitude which endured [in France] until well into the twentieth century."[13] It was, therefore, an unpropitious time for the appearance of the Quietists, who believed that people should abandon themselves totally to God through complete self-abnegation, passivity, and annihilation of the will. Quietists thought that any mental or emotional activity that involved self-awareness, including meditation and petitionary prayer, was counterproductive to attaining the desired state of perfection: the aim was simply to surrender oneself into God's hands in an act of pure, careless faith.

The best-known proponent of Quietism at this time was a Spanish priest named Miguel de Molinos, who was eventually found guilty of error and spent his last years in jail. However, the Quietist tradition was continued in France in a moderated form by Madame Guyon and François Fénelon. All the aforementioned were involved in bitter disputes with the church authorities, who objected to the way Quietists seemed to elevate themselves above ecclesiastical authority and the norms of external worship. They also feared that Quietist teachings could lead people to believe that having reached enlightenment through passivity, they were incapable of committing further sins and were therefore free to lead immoral lives.

Miguel de Molinos was born in about 1628 near the university town of Saragossa in northeastern Spain. He studied at Valencia, where he was also ordained a priest, and then in 1663, at the age of twenty-five, he moved to Rome, where he soon gained a reputation as an extremely able spiritual director. Twelve years later, in 1675, he attracted great attention, not to say notoriety, through the publication of his *Spiritual Guide*, a work that was translated throughout Europe.

In it he advocated meditation, contemplative prayer, and the value of silence, and he emphasized the need for the complete resignation of the self to God's will and the avoidance of harsh asceticism. The Jesuits and Dominicans, however, accused him of doctrinal error. At first Molinos was defended by Pope Innocent XI himself. But in 1685 the church authorities ordered his arrest and imprisonment; two years later he was condemned by a papal bull, which specified sixty-eight propositions in his book as being heretical or offensive. His recantation failed to gain him release, and he languished in prison until his death in 1696.

Molinos taught that people must practice total self-abandonment and that they should desire and do absolutely nothing: only in this state of passivity can God dwell in the soul. We should not concern ourselves about our lives nor worry about our fate in the afterlife but simply let God's will guide us in all things, neither petitioning him for anything nor giving him thanks for any boon. Prayer should be conducted without mental concentration on images or thoughts but as a quiet, loving commitment to God's presence. Thoughts that bubble up in prayer, even if impure or evil, should be ignored rather than resisted, since a conscious struggle against them only serves to acknowledge and therefore strengthen them. The soul eventually reaches a point when it is devoid of passion and exists in a state of undisturbable serenity. Only in this way will we "sink and lose ourselves in the immeasurable sea of God's infinite goodness, and rest there steadfast and immoveable."[14] With regard to the liturgy, although Molinos was in favor of taking Holy Communion, he did not believe any preparation was required for it except for the soul's state of passivity. He also thought that confessions and acts of penance were unnecessary, except for beginners.

Clearly, Molinos's views challenged the structure, traditions, and authority of the church, and it is easy to imagine how the alarm bells must have rung when some nuns under Molinos's direction abandoned their rosaries, stopped going to confession, and flouted the rules of their convents. It is also easy to see how a doctrine that advised that evil be ignored, not actively resisted, could easily be distorted by minds less subtle than Molinos's. Yet it should be said that Molinos practiced the sort of self-abandonment that he preached, bearing his captivity with the serenity he advocated in his book.

Madame Guyon

One of those influenced by Molinos—as well as by Francis de Sales—was a Frenchwoman named Madame Guyon. She, too, taught that people should renounce their self-centered lives and abandon themselves totally to the will of God. By doing this they will enter a state of complete passivity and be indifferent about what the future might hold. Like Molinos, she suffered for her views, being imprisoned for several years in the Bastille in Paris. Yet despite the hostility she encountered, she remained, in her own eyes, a devout Catholic until her dying days. After her death her ideas, although largely neglected at home, were taken up by Protestants in England, Germany, Switzerland, and elsewhere.

Madame Guyon was born Jeanne-Marie Bouvier de la Motte in 1648 in the town of Montargis about fifty miles south of Paris. She was a delicate, religiously inclined child whose education was interrupted by her parents' constantly moving (nine times in ten years). In 1664, at the age of sixteen, she married a thirty-eight-year-old invalid named Jacques Guyon. The union, which lasted twelve years, was a miserable experience for Jeanne, who produced five children, two of whom died. But thrown back on her own inner resources, she did find time to explore and deepen her mystical bent through books and the spiritual direction of a priest named François Lacombe.

After her husband passed away in 1676, Madame Guyon was able to devote herself fully to her religious life, feeling called to make public the fruits of her spiritual experiences. In 1685 she published her influential *Short and Easy Method of Prayer*, and in the following year, accompanied by Père Lacombe, she moved to Paris. But her attempts to promulgate her ideas were ill timed. It was only a year since Molinos had been imprisoned for his Quietism, and in Paris Louis XIV was eager to clamp down on those who held similar views. Lacombe and Madame Guyon were duly sent to jail, in 1687 and 1688, respectively: Lacombe remained incarcerated for the next twelve years, while Madame Guyon was released several months later through the influence of the king's second wife, Madame de Maintenon.

On her release, Madame Guyon managed to establish herself in the royal circle and through it came into contact with François Fénelon, who was to become her most illustrious supporter. Yet the opposition to her teachings did not diminish, and in an effort to clear her name she asked for her writings to be examined by an ecclesiastical commission. Her request was granted, but at the Conference of Issy in 1695 she was condemned and again imprisoned, despite a signed retraction. She was released in 1703 and allowed to live with her son in Blois, where, until her death in 1717, she spent the time in seclusion, receiving occasional visits from those interested in her ideas and devoting herself to writing religious verse and letters to her friends.

Madame Guyon's teachings spring from personal experience, the most significant moment of which was her spiritual conversion when she was nineteen years of age. Throughout the first years of her unhappy marriage, she had tried to find solace in God, but in vain. The turning point came when she went to see a visiting Franciscan friar, who told her that she was "seeking without that which you hold within" and that she would find God in her heart. His words had an almost instant effect: "They were to me like the stroke of a dart, which penetrated through my heart. I felt a very deep wound, a wound so delightful that I desired not to be cured."[15]

From this time on her practice of contemplation was devoid of sensual imagery—indeed, she taught that prayer should be one of simple abstraction, empty of visual meditation, even on God's attributes and the person of Christ. The soul, she believed, passes through three stages on the journey toward union with God: first there is the withdrawal of the senses and the will from the external world and an apprehension of the divine presence. The soul then realizes that its pleasure in the divine is in danger of becoming a substitute for God himself. This results in a stage of spiritual desolation in which the loss of God's favors is felt, like John of the Cross's "dark night." The last stage is an "apostolic state" in which the emptied soul is possessed by God, its will replaced by his. The soul now feels joy and a "holy indifference," a complete detachment from what might befall it, including even the prospect of being saved from damnation.[16]

François Fénelon

François Fénelon, who was appointed archbishop of Cambrai in 1695, was a great admirer of Madame Guyon's personal spirituality and the ideas set out in her works (but not always of the way she expressed them), and he defended her in writing. In doing so he incurred the wrath of his former friend, the formidable Jacques-Bénigne Bossuet, bishop of Meaux, which led to a protracted and bitter controversy about Quietism. Eventually, although Fénelon escaped imprisonment, he was sentenced by Louis XIV to stay in his diocese of Cambrai indefinitely.

Fénelon's mysticism, like that of Francis de Sales, was eminently temperate. It was not a matter of having supernatural experiences. He did not deny that saints in the past had had these experiences, but they did not by themselves constitute holiness. For him "faith working by love" was the guiding principle, which led the soul to a profound sense of inner peace: "It would be a mistake to suppose, that the highest state of inward experience is characterized by great excitements, by raptures and ecstasies. . . . One of the remarkable results in a soul of which faith is the sole governing principle, is, that it is entirely peaceful. Nothing disturbs it. And being thus peaceful, it reflects distinctly and clearly the image of Christ; like the placid lake, which shows, in its own clear and beautiful bosom, the exact forms of the objects around and above it."[17]

Fénelon was born in 1651 in Périgord in the Dordogne into an old aristocratic family that had fallen on hard times. In about 1672 he entered the celebrated seminary of Saint-Sulpice in Paris, and after his three-year course, he was ordained. Then in 1678 he was appointed head of the "New Catholics," a community designed to educate recent Protestant women converts. Fénelon soon became renowned as a spiritual director, educator, and preacher, and in 1681 his reputation led to his being appointed tutor to the young Duke of Burgundy, grandson of Louis XIV. Of much greater significance to him was his meeting Madame Guyon in 1688, for his personal admiration of her and his warm espousal of her teachings would now shape the course of his life. In 1697 he published a defense of her position in his *Explanation of the Maxims of the Saints*, in which he attempted to show that her ideas were part of the Catholic mainstream mystical tradition. Immediately attacked by Bossuet, the book was finally condemned by Rome two years later. Fénelon, who accepted the judgment, was ordered to remain in his diocese of Cambrai for the rest of his life.

After his death in 1715, his reputation, damaged at home, blossomed abroad, especially in Britain, where the Anglican writer Alexander Knox (1757–1831) proclaimed that "no Catholic was more popular in Protestant countries than Fénelon."[18]

Fénelon taught that it was possible to experience a love of God that was completely pure, untainted by any desire for future bliss or dread of damnation: God should be loved simply for himself, without any other motive. Having reached this unitive state, the soul practices "holy indifference" and insofar as it allows God's grace to work within it, it desires only what he desires for it. Fénelon stresses that holy indifference is not the same as inactivity: it means indifference to anything not encompassed by God's will, and the highest activity when enjoined by that will.[19]

The trials and temptations encountered in life are the way in which our love of God is purified; it is the means by which we lose our selfish desires. Love is sought not for any personal happiness but because God desires it of us; sins are confessed not for personal salvation but because it is something God wants us to do for his sake. With regard to worship, Fénelon believed that souls that had progressed far along the way toward disinterested love do not have the same need for organized church services as others, since their love is strong enough for them to be united with God inwardly at any time and in any place. This, however, does not mean that they should disregard outward observances, if only because it would set a bad example to beginners.[20]

As our love becomes purified of self-interest, so the soul is led through states of detachment and self-abnegation. It eventually reaches a state of passivity in which its will is replaced by God's: there is no further motive for actions beyond what God desires. Fénelon likens the transformed soul to a ball on a flat surface, which can be moved in any direction with the same facility: its sole motivating power comes from God.[21]

15

THE AGE OF THE ENLIGHTENMENT

*The divine will is a deep abyss of which the
present moment is the entrance.*
—Jean-Pierre de Caussade

HE PERIOD KNOWN AS THE ENLIGHTENMENT, or the Age
of Reason, lasting approximately from the late seventeenth century to the end of the eighteenth, embraced a wide variety of
attitudes and interests that generally emphasized the central place of
reason and empiricism as well as a commitment to greater tolerance
and justice. The foundations for the Enlightenment had been laid by the
scientific and philosophical revolution begun by the likes of Galileo,
Descartes, and Newton, and it was carried forward particularly in
France, at this time the most sophisticated state in Europe, by thinkers
known as the *philosophes*, men such as the writer and satirist Voltaire
and the encyclopedist Denis Diderot, who explored a variety of intellectual pursuits, spurred on, at least initially, by their optimism and
faith in the idea of progress through rationalism.

The Catholic and Protestant churches, some of them bound closely to their national, often absolutist, governments, differed from place to place in their response to the new rationalist zeitgeist, which found much greater acceptance in the salons and coffeehouses of the intelligentsia than with the masses, for whom the nonrational mysteries of traditional religion still remained strong. Those who subscribed to the latest philosophical thinking but did not want to jettison God completely could turn to Deism; others who were less sanguine about Enlightenment ideals and found mainstream religion too tepid took refuge in revivalist movements such as Pietism and Methodism, which should, as the historian Jane Shaw has noted, be put into a "pan-European and transatlantic context of religious revivals which stressed a 'religion of the heart' or affective piety."[1]

The Deists advocated "natural religion," that is, they believed that knowledge about God was discoverable by human reason without the need for divine revelation. For Deists, God was like a divine inventor who had fashioned the universe like a machine, then left it to carry on without his intervention. They challenged the nonrational aspects of Christianity, such as mystical experiences, prayer, and miracles, which seemed to contradict the idea of a noninterventionist god, and although their religion seemed to many to be devoid of warmth and intimacy, it did have the positive effect of promoting tolerance (for example, its antisupernatural bias helped to end the persecution of witches). Deism was relatively small in England, where it was made known by writers such as John Toland, author of the influential *Christianity Not Mysterious* (1696). But the movement proved to be more popular in France, where it was championed by Voltaire, and also in Prussia during the reign of Frederick the Great (1740–1786).

If Deism appealed to the rationalist instincts of believers, Pietism, founded by the Lutheran minister Philipp Jakob Spener (1635–1705), aimed at their hearts. At a time when the Lutheran Church had become dry and rigid in its dogmatic teachings, Spener attempted to introduce more warmth and life into religion through an emphasis on personal conversion as well as by prayer meetings and Bible groups, and he also sought to get more laypeople involved in the church. Spener's revivalist movement quickly spread throughout Germany—although it varied from place to place—especially through

Spener's follower August Francke, whose Pietist ideals translated into the founding of an orphanage and a home for vagrants in Halle in northeastern Germany, and through his godson, Count von Zinzendorf, who gave spiritual care and leadership to a group of Protestants known as the Bohemian, or Moravian, brethren, whom he had allowed to take refuge on his estate of Herrnhut in Saxony in 1722 (John Wesley was to visit them in 1738).

The Enlightenment affected the tradition of mysticism by asserting values that were inimical to the nonrational, suprasensual basis on which it was founded. The idea of "enthusiasm," defined by Dr. Samuel Johnson as "a vain confidence of Divine favour or communication," was repellent to many orthodox churchmen, as in the case of the Anglican bishop Joseph Butler, who told John Wesley, the founder of Methodism, that "pretending to extraordinary revelations and gifts of the Holy Spirit is a horrid thing; a very horrid thing!"[2] In fact Wesley himself was wary of supernatural visions and voices, and it would be interesting to know what Butler would have made of a Hildegard or Teresa. Visions and voices are not of course synonymous with the direct apprehension of the presence of God, but it is easy to believe that even profound mystical experiences without the visionary pyrotechnics would have elicited considerable skepticism at this time. In truth, the eighteenth, like the seventeenth, century was not a fruitful period for mysticism, especially in its more dramatic manifestations: the mystical outlooks of the French Jesuit Jean-Pierre de Caussade and the English writer William Law were serious but understated, unlikely to outrage any rationalist.

Jean-Pierre de Caussade

Jean-Pierre de Caussade was much influenced by his fellow countryman Francis de Sales, and his own teachings can be seen as a sort of epilogue to the controversy over Quietism, of which he was critical. De Caussade was little concerned with the more extreme approaches to contemplative prayer, and although he refers in a letter to the experience in prayer of "sweet tranquillity" and an "intense sweetness" that has "a charm that draws almost all the soul's attention to the heart,"[3] the focus of his mysticism was on the idea that divine grace was freely available to all Christians who surrendered or abandoned themselves to God's will. Like Brother Lawrence, he tried to convey the importance of living in the present, and he coined the memorable phrase "the sacrament of the present moment" to suggest the religious import of concentrating exclusively on the here and now, a practice that leads to a radical spiritual liberation: "It is necessary to be disengaged from all we feel and do in order to walk with God in the duty of the present moment. All other avenues are closed. We must confine ourselves to the present moment without taking thought for the one before or the one to come."[4]

Not much is known about the details of de Caussades's life. He was born in France in 1675 and at the age of eighteen joined the Jesuit order in Toulouse as a novice. In 1705 he was ordained a priest, and three years later he took his final Jesuit vows. Over the following years he excelled as a teacher, confessor, and preacher in Toulouse and elsewhere; then in 1729, at the age of fifty-four, he moved to Lorraine in eastern France, where, in Nancy, he became spiritual director to some of the nuns of the Visitation (the order founded by Francis de Sales and Jeanne de Chantal). His conversations with the sisters were sometimes noted down, and these, along with letters to nuns imparting spiritual advice, were later published, in 1860, by a priest named Henri Ramière as *Abandonment to Divine Providence.* The book established de Caussade's reputation as a deeply perceptive spiritual writer with marked mystical leanings.

De Caussade himself published just one book during his lifetime, *Spiritual Instructions,* in 1741. This work took the form of a series of imaginary dialogues with Jacques-Bénigne Bossuet, the formidable bishop of Meaux, who had died in 1704 but who still remained an influential spiritual figure in France. De Caussade tried to show that true contemplative prayer, the reputation of which had suffered in France during the Quietist saga, was actually supported by the traditional teaching of the church, and he quoted from Bossuet to substantiate his point. For the last decade of his life he resided at Perpignan, Albi, and Toulouse, where he died in 1751.

The keystone of de Caussade's mysticism, as suggested by the title of his posthumous book, is the idea of abandoning the self to divine providence. We must surrender ourselves totally and unconditionally to God and accept as the right thing any situation we are in at any moment, even if it is fraught with hardship or danger. He urges that we give up the pleasures of our senses and withdraw from a self-oriented outlook on life, with its illusions, pretenses, and vanity, and commit ourselves to God's will. This commitment is not to be a long-thought-out act of determination but a spontaneous and instant commitment to the present moment, to the flotsam and jetsam of life's everyday dealings, big and small, that come our way. For it is not our external circumstances that affect our relationship with God but the way in which we accept them: "The divine will is a deep abyss of which the present moment is the entrance. If you plunge into the abyss you will find it infinitely more vast than your desires."[5]

God uses the events and people we encounter every day to draw us closer to him. The challenge is for us not to filter out those things that we do not enjoy or think will not help us to grow spiritually: we must accept whatever comes our way in the knowledge that it has a divine provenance and is moving us toward union with God. "Every moment of our lives may be a kind of communion with the divine love,"[6] and may be, he says, as spiritually efficacious as receiving the Eucharist—de Caussade does not seek to denigrate the latter and lower the spiritual to the realm of the mundane but, rather, to raise the mundane, the quotidian, to the sphere of the spiritual.

Underlying our abandonment to the will of God is faith. Lacking faith "we wander like madmen in a labyrinth of darkness and illusion."[7] But with faith we can see that what is created is ultimately hollow: the veil of illusion is ripped away and eternal truth is revealed. The key to faith and abandonment does not lie in books, history, or the saintly exemplars of the past. De Caussade emphasizes that it is a pointless exercise harking back to the age of the saints for inspiration. Instead, "we must listen to God from moment to moment" and reach out to discover "the fountain of living waters" that flows at hand. The divine commandments are declared by the present moment, which is the "ambassador of God." With total attentiveness to the divinity of the now, there is no need to choose or distinguish between alternative states of being. Categories such as health and sickness, solitude and society, verbal prayer and silence, become irrelevant.[8] Whatever is encountered comes from God and must be surrendered to. "Thus, the present moment is like a desert in which simple souls see and rejoice only in God, being solely concerned to do what he asks of them. All the rest is left behind, forgotten and surrendered to him."[9]

De Caussade's mysticism is simple in outline but difficult in practice. Abandonment to the present requires a mind that is empty of the past and the future—a mind that can ignore the events leading up to the present and can resist speculating about the future. Filled with the inspiration of grace, we must obey the impulse that comes to us at any given moment—whether it is to read a book, for example, or speak or listen to someone—without chewing it over or making an effort or steeling ourselves if something unpleasant is involved: "Give yourself up to these things for as long as God wishes without doing so through any self-will." For those who can surrender, the soul is "as light as a feather, liquid as water, simple as a child" in the way it receives and follows the dictates of grace. It is like molten metal, which can be shaped by different molds, or a blank canvas on which God can create beautiful patterns, or a stone being sculpted into a statue. As work proceeds, the soul can only feel the blows of the chisel and, blind to what it is to become, can only trust its master, the sculptor, enduring the work with resignation. We must cooperate "with all these divine operations by a constant submission, a forgetfulness of self, and an assiduous application to duty."[10]

Constant submission is not easy, especially during times of physical and spiritual trial. The soul's journey is compared to that of a traveler who, passing through trackless fields at night in a foreign country, has to rely totally on his guide. Yet given this trust, the soul, liberated from expectations built up from study and secondhand experience, can experience the renewing vitality of the unknown, because the "divine action is ever fresh, it never retraces steps, but always marks out new ways. . . . It acted in one way yesterday, today it acts differently."[11]

William Law

In "an age of religion without mystery, of a theoretical God and a mechanical universe, of Christianity, not as something to be lived, but as something to be proved,"[12] William Law and his younger contemporary John Wesley attempted, each in his own way, to bring new meaning,

depth, and fervor to the Anglican faith. Opposed to the cold imperson-
ality of Deism, William Law was at pains to emphasize that the riches
of the spiritual life could only be found within. Christ, the eternal Word
of God, lies hidden in the soul "as a spark of the divine nature," able to
conquer sin and regenerate the "life of heaven." Against those who were
content to find God in books, debates, and church structures, Law proclaimed: "Seek for Him in thy heart, and thou wilt never seek in vain,
for there He dwells, there is the seat of His Light and Holy Spirit."[13] Law
did not deny the value of the scriptures, but he saw them primarily as a
signpost to the divinity within. The word was overshadowed by the
Word, "the light, life, and salvation of fallen man," and the Bible was an
"outward, verbal direction" pointing toward him.[14]

Law received his mystical understanding from the writings of,
among others, Dionysius the Areopagite, Ruysbroeck, Tauler, Fénelon,
and when he was in his forties, Jacob Boehme. His best-known work,
A Serious Call to a Devout and Holy Life, attempts to stir people to
commit themselves to the Christian way *wholeheartedly*, and to cultivate ascetic living, meditation, and virtues such as humility and temperance, dedicating all their activities to the glory of God. The book's
directness, spiritual warmth, and clear, elegant style all contributed to
its success. John Wesley praised its "beauty of expression" and "depth
of thought." Even the pragmatic Dr. Samuel Johnson recalled that the
first time he thought in earnest about religion was after reading Law's
book as an undergraduate at Oxford.

The son of a tradesman, William Law was born in 1686 in King's
Cliffe, near Stamford in Northamptonshire. In 1705 he went up to
study at Emmanuel College, Cambridge, becoming a fellow of the college in 1711, the same year that he was ordained a deacon. In 1714,
however, he refused to swear the oath of allegiance to the new Hanover-
ian king of England, George I, and so became a Nonjuror, one who
pledged loyalty to the Stuart dynasty, whose last representative, James
II, had been deposed in 1688. Because of his stance, Law was deprived
of his fellowship and had to earn his living by other means. One way was
by teaching, and in 1727 he became tutor to the father of the great historian Edward Gibbon, living in the family home in Putney in London.
His post lasted for ten years and allowed him time to publish, in 1728,
A Serious Call, which soon became a spiritual classic.

In 1740 Law's life took a radical change of direction: along with two middle-aged women, an affluent widow named Mrs. Hutcheson and Hester Gibbon, sister of his former pupil, he retired to King's Cliffe, where they established a small religious community devoted to pious living and good works. They founded schools and almshouses and gave out clothes, food, and money to the poor to such an extent that vagrants from all around were beating a path to their door, much to the dismay of the local inhabitants and the parish priest. For more than twenty years Law remained in his home village, studying, writing, and performing good works. He died in 1761.

Law's mysticism is most apparent in his later Boehme-influenced treatises, *The Spirit of Prayer* (1749) and *The Spirit of Love* (1752). In *The Spirit of Prayer* he taught that the only way of discovering God is by reverting to the divine light he believed everyone possessed; for although God is omnipresent, he is only present to the individual in the depths of the soul. The bodily senses are helpless in trying to effect union with God, as are the faculties of understanding, will, and memory: these can grasp at God but cannot provide a dwelling place for him.

There is, however, a place at the "bottom of the soul" from which the mental faculties spring ("as lines from a centre or as branches from the body of a tree") which is the "unity, the eternity," and this cannot be satisfied except by the "infinity of God." The treasure of this inner sanctum should be the object of our desire, to be won at any price: "Begin to search and dig in thine own field for this pearl of eternity that lies hidden in it; it cannot cost thee too much, nor canst thou buy it too dear, for it is all; and when thou hast found it thou wilt know that all which thou hast sold or given away for it is as mere a nothing as a bubble upon the water."[15]

Like other Protestant mystics, Law suggests that everyone has a spark of divine light and spirit, given to the soul by God so that it can regenerate the paradisiacal life that was lost with the fall of man. This inner spark has an innate and almost infinite disposal to seek and return to God's eternal light and spirit, from where it originally came and in whose divine nature it partakes. Our inner light and spirit, therefore, are always tending toward God, who has the endless and immutable desire to fill our soul with his riches, "just as the spirit of air without man unites and communicates its riches and virtues to the spirit of the air that is within man."[16] God's love toward the soul was such that he gave his son to conquer the soul's enemies and enable us to be reborn according to the divine image in which we were originally created.

Law also refers to the inner treasure of the soul as a "seed of divine life" and as a "seed that has all the riches of eternity in it." In the same way that the sun nourishes natural seeds in the earth, so Jesus Christ, the sun of righteousness, is always shining on the soul's seed to "kindle and call it forth to the birth."[17]

In an echo of Eckhart, Law expressed his emphasis on the divine aspect of humanity in the idea of the birth of Christ within the soul. Christ, as the Word, existed from the beginning and lives inside us, wanting only our faith and good will in order to have in us "as real a birth and form as He had in the Virgin Mary." We must give ourselves over totally to nurturing the innate desire we have of God: then we will be led to the birth of Jesus "not in a stable at Bethlehem in Judea, but . . . in the dark center of thy fallen soul."[18]

In *The Spirit of Love*, Law again contrasts the limited value of "outward, verbal instruction" with the true efficacy of an "inward birth of divine light, goodness, and virtue in our own renewed spirit."[19] The "spirit of love" itself cannot simply be embraced easily and casually: we must deny our creaturely nature absolutely to bring forth its birth within, dying to our selves through patience, humility, and resignation to the divine will.[20] For Law, the spirit of love is not just the means to personal happiness but a cosmic force, identical with God, bringing peace and harmony wherever it is allowed to blossom. With its birth, "every hunger is satisfied, and all complaining, murmuring, accusing, resenting, revenging, and striving are as totally suppressed and overcome as the coldness, thickness, and horror of darkness are suppressed and overcome by the breaking forth of the light."[21]

John Wesley

One of those deeply influenced by William Law was John Wesley, one of the principal founders of Methodism—a movement within the Church of England, from which it eventually separated—and one of the great spiritual figures of the modern era. His status as a mystic is a matter of debate. Although he is usually included in surveys of mysticism, he was not a contemplative and is even recorded to have said "the same poison of Mysticism . . . has extinguished the last spark of life," a remark that seems to have referred to the unwelcome state of passivity to which some mystical teachings could lead. He was also wary of visions, voices, and revelations—manifestations of the "enthusiasm" that was much despised at the time. On the other hand, as one modern commentator has noted, "At least on a broad definition of mysticism, as communion or union with God, Wesley always showed himself mystical."[22] He was greatly inspired by the simple, otherworldly piety of the Moravians; and he himself enjoyed a profound conversion experience that altered his personal spirituality and paved the way for his immense evangelical activities. He was also an avid reader of mystics, and between 1749 and 1755 he published extracts from his favorite Christian writers that he published in his fifty-volume *Christian Library*, which included the likes of Miguel de Molinos and François Fénelon.

John Wesley was born in 1703 in Epworth in Lincolnshire, the fifteenth child of Samuel and Susannah Wesley. His father was an Anglican clergyman, and the seeds of John's piety were nurtured in his early years by the Bible and the Book of Common Prayer. At Oxford University he and his younger brother Charles formed a religious group of Christians who met to read the Bible and pray together. Others scoffed at the earnestness and methodical worship of these sincere, studious individuals and labeled them Bible Moths, the Holy Club, and—the name they adopted for themselves—Methodists.

In 1735 John and his brother left Oxford to go abroad to America to preach the word of God in Georgia, both to the colonists and to the Native Americans. The trip was largely a failure: John fell out with the colonists, whose morality he criticized, and an unhappy love affair did not improve his state of mind. One positive outcome was his encounter with Moravian missionaries both in America and on the voyage home, when during a violent storm he was impressed by the way they calmly sang hymns. Back home Wesley's spiritual life changed for good after a conversion experience on the evening of May 24, 1738, which he recorded in his journal. It occurred while he was attending a small religious gathering in London. He was listening to a reading of Martin Luther's preface to Paul's Letter to the Romans, when: "I felt my heart strangely warmed. I felt I did trust in Christ, Christ alone for salvation, and an assurance was given me that he had taken away my sins, even mine, and saved me from the law of sin and death."[23]

From then on, Wesley devoted his life to promoting what he called "vital practical religion," and to this end he rode around Britain and Ireland preaching, especially to the rural and urban poor, often in the open fields, where thousands gathered to hear his message. By the time of his death in 1791, there were more than seventy thousand Methodists in Britain and forty-three thousand in America, where Methodism had developed during the 1760s.

The immediate source of Wesley's spiritual vitality was his inner conversion, after which his life became truly Christ centered. As he says in his journal entry for May 25, 1738, the morning after the experience, he found as he woke up that "'Jesus, Master,' was in my heart and in my mouth" and that all his strength "lay in keeping my eye fixed upon Him and my soul waiting on Him continually." In the afternoon he went to a service at Saint Paul's Cathedral, and it was there that a moment of doubt crept in, when an inner voice asked why there was not more of a dramatic change in him: "I answered (yet not I), 'That I know not. But, this I know, I have now peace with God.' And I sin not today, and Jesus my Master has forbidden me to take thought for the morrow."[24]

It was this inner experience of peace and profound sense of release from sin and the anxieties of the future that Wesley felt impelled to convey to his audiences, most of whom were starved for spiritual nourishment. Wesley spoke to them with the authority of one who had himself been reborn in Christ; he was able to impress not by declaiming cold doctrine and creeds but by describing what it was like from the inside to live a completely different life, guided by the spirit. In one of his sermons he conveys the excitement and immediacy of what happens to one who is reborn: "But the 'eyes of his understanding are opened.' . . . He feels 'the love of God shed abroad in his heart.' . . . And now he may be properly said to live. . . . From hence it manifestly appears, what is the nature of the new birth. It is a great change

. . . wrought in the whole soul by the almighty Spirit of God, when it is 'created new in Christ Jesus,' . . . when the love of the world is changed into the love of God; pride into humility; passion into meekness; hatred, envy, malice into a sincere, tender, disinterested love for all mankind."[25]

16

ROMANTICS AND NATURE MYSTICISM

If the doors of perception were cleansed
everything would appear to man as it is, infinite.
—William Blake

THE FRENCH REVOLUTION (1789–1799), which swept away France's old order and sent seismic tremors throughout Europe, marked a low point for French Catholicism. The revolutionary leaders reorganized the church, prohibited the taking of monastic vows, and sold off church lands. Central clerical appointments were replaced by local clerical elections, and the clergy were obliged to give their assent to the new constitution by oath: the vast majority of bishops refused, as did many local priests. But in 1792 these nonjurors, their loyalty to the new regime suspect, suffered repressive measures, with thousands being deported, executed, or lynched. Later the government tried to replace Catholicism with new, ephemeral cults dedicated to Reason and the Supreme Being. Matters changed, however, when Napoléon Bonaparte, backed by the army, took control of the government in 1799. A religious skeptic himself, Napoléon realized that religion could help to bolster patriotism and social stability, and in 1801 he agreed to a concordat with Pope Pius VII that formally restored Catholicism in the country.

The Revolution is often considered to be a watershed between the so-called Age of Enlightenment and that of Romanticism, which began toward the end of the eighteenth century and continued throughout the nineteenth. Romanticism was not so much a concerted movement as a distinctive attitude or intellectual cast of mind that informed many influential thinkers and artists of the time. In general, Romantics felt unsatisfied by the Enlightenment's rationalism and its predominant values of balance, harmony, urbanity, and politeness. Instead, they stressed the importance of the imagination, the individual, introspection, the emotions, and nature in its wild, unpredictable aspects.

Two early influential figures of Romantic philosophy—although they were sons of the Enlightenment—were the French author Jean-Jacques Rousseau (1712–1778) and the German philosopher Immanuel Kant (1724–1804). Rousseau was one of the first to voice the Romantics' suspicion of the artificiality of civilization by championing the "noble savage," the idea that human beings living in a primitive state according to their instincts attain a natural happiness that civilized society corrodes. Kant, meanwhile, had anticipated the Romantics' shift of emphasis from objective to subjective knowledge by his assertion that we cannot gain direct knowledge of the outside world—"things in themselves"—but only of our own perceptions, which we order by imposing on them innate mental structures, such as notions of time and space.

Later, Kant's fellow countryman Friedrich Schleiermacher (1768–1834), a theologian who had been raised by parents who had become Herrnhuter brethren, echoed the Romantic approach to spirituality by emphasizing the place of feeling and intuition as a basis for religion. "I ask, therefore," he once wrote, "that you turn from everything usually reckoned religion, and fix your regard on the *inward emotions and dispositions,* as all utterances and acts of inspired men direct."[1] He later defined religion in terms of the feeling of being absolutely dependent on God.

So whereas the Enlightenment era had proved to be thorny ground for mysticism, Romanticism, with its higher regard for the inner emotional life and greater feeling for spirituality, was much more fertile. Yet the spirit of mysticism seems to have largely passed over the mainstream churches—even though there was a revival of Catholicism and a strengthening of the papacy in the nineteenth century—and settled on secular artists and writers. In Germany, for example, there was Novalis, the pen-name of Friedrich von Hardenberg (1772–1801), an early Romantic mystical writer who asserted that "the spirit world is in fact revealed to us; it is always open. Could we suddenly become as sensitive as is necessary, we should perceive ourselves to be in its midst."[2] His best-known works are his *Hymns to the Night*, a mystical rhapsody of death and night prompted by the death of his young fiancée, and *Heinrich von Ofterdingen*, in which the eponymous hero, a medieval poet, searches for a mysterious blue flower, representing spiritual truth.

In England, there was a great flowering of poets who covered the spectrum of Romantic ideals, from Lord Byron's heroic individualism to Keats's melancholic introspections and Shelley's flights of Platonism. Coleridge, the greatest thinker among them, explicitly acknowledged the debt he owed to the mystics of the past, men such as Jacob Boehme, George Fox, and William Law, who had helped him "keep alive the heart in the head" and showed him that "all the products of the mere reflective faculty partook of death."[3] But the two greatest English mystical poets were the early Romantic William Blake and William Wordsworth, the first an artist and visionary with a mystical view of the imagination, the second a subtle, reflective writer who was one of England's most expressive nature mystics.

William Blake

"A true mystic to whom the eternal was the natural and the human indistinguishable from the divine,"[4] William Blake saw visions from an early age. It is said that when he was four he screamed in shock at seeing the face of God at his bedroom window. Some years later, while walking in Peckham, he saw "a tree filled with angels, bright angelic wings bespangling every bough like stars." On another occasion, in summer, he was watching haymakers in the fields when he saw angels walking among them.[5] It is not surprising then that he was later influenced by mystical and unorthodox visionaries such as the alchemist Paracelsus (1493–1541); Jacob Boehme, whom Blake described as "a divinely inspired man"; and the Swede Emanuel Swedenborg (1688–1772). Like Swedenborg, Blake claimed to have constant access to a supramundane reality, communing with spirits and angels who directed his work ("I am under the direction of messengers from Heaven, daily and nightly"[6]).

The son of a hosier, Blake was born in 1757 in London, the city where he lived for almost his entire life. From the age of fourteen to twenty-one he was apprenticed to an engraver, a period when he developed a fascination for Gothic art. After his apprenticeship he studied art at the Royal Academy for a while before setting himself up as an engraver, the profession by which he supported himself for the rest of his life (his poems, nearly all of which he hand engraved and published himself, brought in little money). In 1782, at the age of twenty-five, he married Catherine Boucher, whom he taught to read and write and who would remain his lifelong companion, helper, and fellow pilgrim on his spiritual journey. In 1789 Blake engraved his *Songs of Innocence*, which, along with the *Songs of Experience*, completed five years later, are his best-known lyrical poems.

In 1800 Blake left London for Sussex to do illustration work for William Hayley at Felpham by the sea. His three-year sojourn there— his only departure from London during his life—was a mixed experience, the joys of nature to some extent compensating for the frustration that working for the domineering Hayley entailed. Four years later, back in the metropolis, Blake began to engrave his long prophetic works *Milton* and *Jerusalem*. These, in common with his other prophetic books, have an arcane, private symbolism and idiosyncratic style that continue to divide readers, although few have failed to be impressed by their scale and originality. For the rest of his life, Blake continued to engrave and write, unfolding his inner vision, while his outward life was seemingly uneventful. When he died in 1827 he was largely unknown except to a small band of admirers. His reputation has grown steadily, however, with W. B. Yeats among the forefront of modern poets who have recognized his genius.

Blake abhorred anything that fettered spiritual energy. Much of his invective was directed against organized religion, with its "Priests in black gowns . . . binding with briars my joys,"[7] and those he saw as the moving spirits of the Enlightenment's culture of reason and scientific materialism:

> *Mock on, mock on, Voltaire, Rousseau;*
> *Mock on, mock on; 'tis all in vain!*
> *You throw the sand against the wind,*
> *And the wind blows it back again.*
>
> *And every sand becomes a gem*
> *Reflected in the beams divine;*
> *Blown back they blind the mocking eye*
> *But still in Israel's paths they shine.*
>
> *The Atoms of Democritus*
> *And Newton's Particles of Light*
> *Are sands upon the Red Sea shore,*
> *Where Israel's tents do shine so bright.*[8]

Embodying one of Blake's central themes, the poem sets out, with the concision and sharpness Blake valued so much in art, two opposing worldviews, that of the skeptical rationalists and scientists and that of the Bible and "true" religion. The sand that in the first verse is used in the act of childish rejection of true religion (the "wind") becomes in the second verse a numinous, jewel-like reflection of God's creation, seeming to light the path of the tribes of Israel as they make their way across the wilderness toward the promised land of Canaan (the implication being that divinely created nature can lead the soul to its promised land, union with God). This contrast is again brought out in the last verse, in which the scientific—and for Blake reductionist—ideas of the Greek philosopher Democritus and Sir Isaac Newton regarding the nature of matter are set against the image of Israel's tents, suggesting stasis and peacefulness, even freedom, since the reference to the Red Sea indicates that the tribes have crossed the sea and escaped Pharaoh's chariots and bondage in Egypt. Again the suggestion is of the soul escaping the bondage of materialism.

For Blake, ever aware of a reality beyond the external world, nature, even in its minutest and seemingly inert form, was a portal to the timeless realm of God, as his best-known quatrain suggests:

> *To see a World in a grain of sand,*
> *And a Heaven in a wild flower,*
> *Hold Infinity in the palm of your hand,*
> *And Eternity in an hour.*[9]

The core of Blake's mysticism was his view of the imagination, which for him was not just a faculty of the mind but a divine reality. He also called it "vision" and compared it unfavorably to "fable" or "allegory."[10] Whereas allegory is the product of memory, imagination is "surrounded by the daughters of inspiration," who, in Blake's terminology, are collectively called "Jerusalem." That is not to say that allegory cannot have imagination or vision within it—and he cites John Bunyan's *The Pilgrim's Progress* as one such "fable" that contains visions. But essentially the two modes of expression are distinct.

Blake equates imagination with the infinite "world of eternity" into which mortals go after the death of the body; by contrast, the world of generation or, as he calls it, "vegetation," is finite and temporal. Imagination contains "the permanent realities of everything which we see are reflected in this vegetable glass of nature," in which respect it is similar to Plato's world of Forms, the imperfect copies of which can be found in our world. Blake then identifies this realm of imagination with the "divine body of the saviour, the true vine of eternity," rooting his visionary system in Christianity. In "To the Christians" in his book *Jerusalem*, he makes explicit this connection between the imagination and his own brand of the faith: "I know of no other Christianity and of no other Gospel than the liberty both of body and mind to exercise the divine arts of imagination. . . . The Apostles knew of no other Gospel."[11]

Blake claimed to be able to apprehend the divine through his visionary powers, and he believed that this gift was natural and open to humanity, but most people are unaware of it because of the habitual and limited way they think and behave: "If the doors of perception were cleansed everything would appear to man as it is, infinite. For man has closed himself up till he sees all things through narrow chinks of his cavern."[12] Blake recognized that people see different things according to their conditioning: to the miser a coin is more beautiful than the sun, a money bag more shapely than a vine full of grapes. One person may delight in a tree, while someone else may think it is just an impediment. Some people think nature is full of ugliness, others scarcely notice it, while to the person of imagination, "Nature is Imagination itself."[13]

Blake himself saw the world through a lens that pierced the ordinary appearances of everyday objects and revealed their inner sacred nature: "'What,' it will be questioned, 'when the sun rises, do you not see a round disc of fire somewhat like a guinea?' Oh! no, no! I see an innumerable company of the heavenly host, crying 'Holy, holy, holy.'"[14] The artistic task he set himself, therefore, was "to Restore what the Ancients call'd the Golden Age,"[15] or a state of spiritual harmony, and he saw it as his life's work to convey this vision to his fellow human beings, despite the incessant incomprehension and scorn he received from them. As he says in the first chapter of *Jerusalem*: "I rest not upon my great task / To open the Eternal Worlds, to open the immortal Eyes / Of Man inwards into the Worlds of Thought: into Eternity / Ever expanding in the Bosom of God, the Human Imagination."[16] To do this was a gargantuan task, and Blake's prophetic books show the barely subterranean tensions of the times—the oppressiveness of reason and materialism, revolutionary fervor, and increasing dehumanization brought about by the industrial revolution. Yet his unitary vision, often expressed by violent imagery, was always underpinned by his not entirely orthodox faith, and the central place in his life of Christ, his anchor and shepherd, whose relationship with us recalls the reciprocal indwelling described in John's Gospel:

> *Mutual in one another's love and wrath all renewing,*
> *We live as one man; for contracting our infinite senses,*
> *We behold multitude; or, expanding, we behold as one,*
> *As one man all the universal family; and that one man*
> *We call Jesus the Christ: and he in us, and we in him,*
> *Live in perfect harmony in Eden, the land of life,*
> *Giving, receiving, and forgiving each other's trespasses.*

He is the Good shepherd, he is the Lord and master;
He is the shepherd of Albion, he is all in all,
In Eden, in the garden of God, and in heavenly Jerusalem.[17]

William Wordsworth

For Blake, as we have seen, nature was a world of divine illumination and boundlessness for those who had exchanged their "vegetable eyes" for the eyes of cleansed perception. His fellow poet and younger contemporary William Wordsworth, arguably the greatest of the English Romantic poets, also found in nature a source of wonder, although the two men differed in their approach to it. Blake was critical of the way Wordsworth saw nature as a divine end in itself, whereas for him nature was a means to entering a further eternal world. Wordsworth's descriptions of nature are less obviously visionary than Blake's, but his early devotion toward creation, and the perceptiveness of his own feelings toward it, provide an eloquent record of what is generally known as nature mysticism.

The nature mystic is one who through an intimate contemplation of, and communion with, the natural world is able to experience the presence of a divine reality, which, for Christians, is the one God, creator of the universe. The modern German theologian Rudolf Otto wrote of the nature mystic's "sense of being immersed in the oneness of nature, so that man feels all the individuality, all the peculiarity of natural things in himself. He dances with the motes of dust and radiates with the sun; he rises with the dawn, surges with the wave, is fragrant with the rose."[18] It is this sort of identification between the self and natural object that makes nature mysticism tend toward pantheism, the idea that God is identical with the universe and cannot be found outside it. The position of Christian nature mystics, however, has been called "pan*en*theism," the belief that the universe and all its parts exist in God but that he is also a transcendent being existing beyond the created world.

Christians have long regarded nature with ambivalence. In the classical world, woods, streams, mountains, and the like were identified with pagan gods, whom Christians considered diabolical. On the other hand, nature was the creation of God, as set out in the first book of Genesis and echoed in other parts of the Bible. Psalms 65, for example, praises a world in which "The grasslands of the desert overflow; the hills are clothed with gladness. The meadows are covered with flocks and the valleys are mantled with corn; they shout for joy and sing." Although the Gospels do not celebrate nature in such terms, they do present a world in which Jesus is constantly communing with or referring to nature, for example vines, figs, cornfields, the Sea of Galilee, the desert places and mountains where he withdrew to pray, the lilies of the field, the birds of the air, flocks of sheep, fish, the wind, rain, storms, and so on.

In a later period the Christian tradition of celebrating the divine in nature found notable expression in the words of Francis of Assisi, for whom God's creatures were his brothers and sisters. But the idea of the "nature mystic," one who obtains a sense of God *primarily* through nature and not simply as a result of a unitive vision, seems to be a particular phenomenon of post-Reformation times. As the modern literary critic Basil Willey has written, "Ever since the Renaissance the Creation had been steadily gaining in prestige as the 'art of God.' . . . The emotion of the 'numinous,' formerly associated with super-nature, had become attached to Nature itself; and by the end of the 18th century the divinity, the sacredness of nature was, to those affected by this tradition, almost a first datum of consciousness."[19]

The vision of divine nature appealed especially to those whose religious instincts were not being satisfied by either the sometimes passionless established churches or the sometimes overemotional dissenting groups. In England, Blake, Wordsworth, Coleridge, Keats, and Shelley, and, later, Gerard Manley Hopkins, channeled in different degrees their religiosity through the lens of the created world, and it was Wordsworth—"In aloofness and loneliness of mind he is exceeded by no mystic of the cloister"[20]—who was the most persistent and convincing, with his evocations of nature and his own ecstatic feelings toward it.

For Wordsworth, at least in his youth, nature was animate, a living creature, a manifestation of God. In *The Excursion* (book 1), for example, he describes how a panoramic sweep of earth, sky, and ocean viewed from a headland imbued him with a sense of "unutterable love" and "sensation, soul, and form":

> *All melted into him; they swallowed up*
> *His animal being; in them did he live,*
> *And by them did he live; they were his life.*

He refers to the experience as "a visitation from the living God" and compares his rapt state of "still communion" favorably with the "imperfect offices of prayer and praise"—although later in his life he was to become a pillar of the Church of England.

The son of a lawyer, Wordsworth was born in Cumberland in northwest England in 1770. After graduating from Cambridge University, he traveled around France, where he had a love affair with a woman named Annette Vallon, by whom he had a daughter. After his return to England in 1792, initially enthusiastic about the French Revolution (before the onset of the carnage of "the Terror") and full of political idealism, he began to publish his first poems. In 1798 he and the poet Samuel Taylor Coleridge brought out their highly influential *Lyrical Ballads*, a joint book of poems that proclaimed a new literary aesthetic: the mannered, artificial diction and style typical of the eighteenth century was rejected in favor of what they claimed was a language spoken by ordinary people, especially the humble and uneducated, and an emphasis was placed on nature, introspection, and personal feelings.

In 1799 Wordsworth moved north with his beloved sister Dorothy to the Lake District, where he would reside for the rest of his life. Three years later he married a woman named Mary Hutchinson, by whom he had five children (two of whom died young), and settled down to a long and contented domestic life. In fact by about 1807 he was no longer the adventurous soul and daring original poet of a few years before. By this time he had more or less completed all the poems for which he would be famous, including his great autobiographical work, *The Prelude*, published after his death. From then on his poetic vitality began to wane. He continued to write throughout the rest of his life—indeed he was appointed poet laureate in 1843—but his later work seems more dutiful than inspired, reflecting the worthy sentiments of an establishment figure. He died in 1850.

The art of creating poetry, as Wordsworth describes it, is not so remote from the meditative exercises of Ignatius Loyola or Francis de Sales. Poetry is born from "emotion recollected in tranquillity," that is, it is re-created from primary experiences (for example, seeing a cascade of wild daffodils) by a sort of controlled meditation in which, during a state of calm, the emotion that was originally felt is allowed to rise to the surface. Yet unlike other Christian mystics, Wordsworth directed his religious gaze not directly at God or Christ but at God's creation. He found his spiritual center at the conjunction of nature—earth, air, light, darkness, sea, rushing streams, mysterious woods, wild mountain crags, which filled him "with joy exalted to beatitude"—and the inner workings of his mind and heart. Perhaps the best example of this nature mysticism can be seen in his poem "Lines Composed a Few Miles above Tintern Abbey" (a ruined monastery lying in a fold of the river Wye in southeast Wales).

Wordsworth's poem recalls the idyllic setting and his feelings toward it during a visit five years before, in 1793. Looking at the scene of woods, orchards, groves, copses, farms, and "wreaths of smoke / Sent up, in silence, from among the trees," he considers how these images have had in the intervening years a vitalizing, even physical, effect on him ("felt in the blood, and felt along the heart") and how the memory of them has helped to create an inner state of peacefulness. He describes such a mood as "serene and blessed" and goes on to say that the "affections," that is, our feelings, "gently lead us on,"

> *Until, the breath of this corporeal frame*
> *And even the motion of our human blood*
> *Almost suspended, we are laid asleep*
> *In body, and become a living soul:*
> *While with an eye made quiet by the power*
> *Of harmony, and the deep power of joy,*
> *We see into the life of things.*

His words are reminiscent of the medieval mystics' descriptions of "recollection," the gathering in of thoughts and feelings prior to contemplation proper. The lines convey the sense of the body dematerializing and of the spiritual faculties tuned in to a reality normally obfuscated by the excitation of the mind.

It was one of Wordsworth's gifts to be able to make subtle distinctions in the complexities of the inner life, and in the same poem he describes a shift in his attitude toward nature over the years. Whereas on his first trip the Wye valley affected him viscerally as "an appetite; a feeling and a love," now, five years later, older and more sophisticated, he experiences nature with less raw emotion but with a greater sense of spiritual uplift:

> . .   .   .   .   .
>
> *And I have felt*
> *A presence that disturbs me with the joy*
> *Of elevated thoughts; a sense sublime*
> *Of something far more deeply interfused,*
> *Whose dwelling is the light of setting suns,*
> *And the round ocean and the living air,*
> *And the blue sky, and in the mind of man;*
> *A motion and a spirit, that impels*
> *All thinking things, all objects of all thought,*
> *And rolls through all things. . . .*

For the youthful Wordsworth, this indwelling presence is what he calls in *The Excursion* (book 4) the "active principle," which informs all parts of creation, subsisting in "the stars of azure heaven" as well as clouds, trees, flowers, and stones: it is a unifying spirit or "the Soul of all the worlds." In *The Prelude* (book 1), he talks of his ineffable bliss when experiencing "the sentiment of Being spread / O'er all that moves and all that seemeth still." In short, nature gave him an entry into a sublime, spiritual world in which everything was infused with a sense of divine harmony and unity. In a journey through the Simplon Pass in the Alps in *The Prelude* (book 5), he likens the diversity of nature—the waterfalls, torrents, rocks, crags, and sky—to the "workings of one mind, the features / Of the same face, blossoms upon one tree." So potent and luminous do these natural features appear to him that he sees them as "The types and symbols of Eternity."

However, Wordsworth's ecstatic reaction to nature did not last.

Like mystics who experience the presence of God only to suffer after the withdrawal of his divine favor, Wordsworth records his own disenchantment with nature in his poem "Intimations of Immortality," in which he states poignantly: "The things which I have seen I now can see no more." The poem, completed in 1806, stands like a dismal arch through which he passed from poetic life to death.

17

THE MODERN AGE

*It was a light that was so bright that it had no
relation to any visible light and so profound
and so intimate that it seemed like a
neutralization of every lesser experience.*
—Thomas Merton

IT IS TEMPTING to characterize Christianity in the West during the last two centuries as a period when it suffered a relentlessly steady decline in churchgoing and, in the face of increasing seculariization, a falling away from, or at least a greater questioning of, the faith. But generalizations of this sort have to be modified by acknowledging all sorts of exceptions, such as the rise of Marian piety in nineteenth-century Europe (symbolized by Pope Pius IX proclaiming the doctrine of the Immaculate Conception in 1854), as well as, say, the rise of the vibrant African independent churches in the twentieth century. Nevertheless, the mainstream churches of the West have had to face up to a number of challenges, which to varying degrees have negatively impacted individuals' faith, church attendance, and general morale. For example, scientific advances, from astronomy to genetics, have served to demystify the universe and shift people's reliance on God to the intellectual capability of mankind, and the rise of the psychotherapeutic movement has generally had the effect of focusing interest on the human personality, often at the expense of the place of the transcendent. Other changes in modern times that have affected Christianity have been tentatively suggested by the church historian Owen Chadwick: the diminishing specter of mortality through improved medicine; population shifts from country to towns, removing people from the liturgical rhythm connected with the seasons; and growing toleration, making alternatives to Christianity increasingly available.[1]

The challenge to religious faith in the modern era is usually associated with the rise of scientific method in the seventeenth and eighteenth centuries, which gradually began to undermine the traditional authority of the churches and literalist readings of the Bible. In the nineteenth century, the book of Genesis, with its account of Adam and Eve and Noah's Ark, came in for particular attention when theories of evolution seemed to some to turn it from being the repository of sacred literal truth to just another Near Eastern creation myth. Discoveries of fossils of long-extinct animals shook the widespread belief that the earth was just a few thousand years old (James Ussher, the seventeenth-century archbishop of Armagh, had confidently assigned the first day of creation to October 23, 4004 B.C.).

Evolution had been in the air for some time before Charles Darwin. The German philosopher Johann Fichte (1762–1814), for example, had scoffed at the idea that an orangutan might be the ancestor of such distinguished thinkers as Leibniz and Kant.[2] But it was Darwin who, in *The Origin of Species* (1859) and *The Descent of Man* (1871) compellingly presented the idea that animal and plant species evolve through a process of natural selection. For many, descent from apes and not Adam and Eve not only contradicted Genesis but seemed risible (in a debate in Oxford in 1860 Bishop Samuel Wilberforce famously asked the Darwinist T. H. Huxley whether his ape ancestors came from his grandmother's or his grandfather's side of the family). But the evolutionist challenge to the Bible was there to stay.

The integrity of the Bible also came under pressure from the new science of biblical criticism. Protestant biblical scholars, such as the German theologian David Strauss, examined and analyzed it as if it were just any other ancient text. In his influential *Life of Jesus Critically Examined,* published in 1835, Strauss denied the historical basis for the miraculous happenings in the scriptures and searched for patterns of myth. The subsequent chorus of outrage led to his being dismissed from his teaching position at Tübingen.

The reactions to these new currents of science and scholarship that appeared to undermine the Bible and the church were various. Some Christians were able to accommodate them into their faith, some ignored them, and some launched a counteroffensive: in 1907 Pope Pius X issued his decree *Lamentabili,* officially condemning the modernist movement within the Catholic Church. Some, desiring encounters with the supernatural that their churches could not provide, turned to spiritualism, hoping to make contact with the dead through mediums (in Britain, the Society for Psychical Research was founded in 1882). And others, such as Darwin himself, slipped quietly into agnosticism (a word coined by T. H. Huxley) or atheism.

Yet although during the nineteenth century religious skepticism became more commonplace, the Christian faith was far from being a spent force. Indeed, Catholicism in France in the early years of the century experienced something of a new lease on life. There were also bursts of revivalism, such as those inspired by the Americans Dwight L. Moody and Ira D. Sankey in the nineteenth century and Billy Graham in the twentieth. And at a grassroots level, there were many instances of faith being kindled by new and reborn pilgrimages and devotions that have continued to the present. Many of them were founded on the mystical or visionary experiences of individuals, often children, occurring in places that have subsequently become world famous. They include Lourdes in southern France, Knock in the west of Ireland, Fátima in Portugal, Garabandal in northern Spain, and Medjugorje in Bosnia.

Although it is right to stress the continuity of popular piety, it remains true that Christian spirituality had, and has, never before encountered such competition from secular forces and rival faiths—especially those with strong mystical elements, such as Zen and other forms of Buddhism—as well as quasi-religious movements, such as Transcendental Meditation. Yet despite the odds, the flame of the

Christian mystical tradition was kept burning through the twentieth century by a number of mystics, including Charles de Foucauld, Simone Weil, and particularly Pierre Teilhard de Chardin and Thomas Merton.

A dashing and somewhat dissolute French cavalry officer, de Foucauld (1858–1916) underwent a religious conversion in 1886 and later became a hermit in Palestine. He was ordained in 1901, and in the same year he settled among the Muslim Tuareg people in a remote region of Algeria, studying their language and gaining their admiration for his piety and ascetical living. He was eventually killed by a Tuareg in 1916—the reason is not clear, but it may have been due to anti-French feeling current at the time. During his years in the desert, de Foucauld conceived the idea of writing a rule for communities of "Little Brothers" and "Little Sisters" that would be based on a life of contemplative prayer and an emphasis on living simply among the poor of a region, sharing their lives and burdens, and giving generously to everyone in need, regardless of their religion. Although his vision did not materialize during his lifetime, the Little Brothers of Jesus and the Little Sisters of Jesus came into being during the 1930s, inspired by the example of his life.

Like de Foucauld—and Teilhard de Chardin—Simeon Weil (1909–1943) was another unorthodox French mystic. Jewish by birth, Weil became renowned as a philosopher and later committed herself to Catholicism (although she never formally converted and she avoided churches). She was deeply concerned with the plight of the poor and oppressed—she once did a stint in a car factory to show her solidarity with the workers—and she joined the Republican side as a cook during the Spanish Civil War. Her passionate interest in Catholicism stemmed from a mystical experience she had in 1938 while she was staying in a Benedictine abbey in France: reciting to herself a poem called "Love" by the seventeenth-century English poet George Herbert, she felt Christ come down and possess her. During the Second World War she left France and eventually made her way to England. There she fell ill, and refusing to eat sufficient food out of solidarity with her fellow French citizens under German occupation, she died in 1943. Weil's thoughts on spirituality were published after her death in books such as *Waiting for God* and *Gravity and Grace*. These works, which are models of clarity and lucid thinking, reflect not only her interest in Christian mysticism but also her love of ancient Greek thought and Hinduism. One of her important themes is the spiritual benefits that suffering can bring, along with her idea of "waiting in patience" for God in the spiritually impoverished times of the contemporary world.

Weil's life and works reflect the turbulent spirit of her time, and the same can be said of probably the two most important mystics of the twentieth century, the French Jesuit and scientist Pierre Teilhard de Chardin and the American monk Thomas Merton. Teilhard's works explore the idea of spiritual evolution and the noosphere, a sort of global consciousness that has reminded some of the Internet, while Merton's interest in Eastern religions and his commitment to social and political justice mirrored the prevailing atmosphere in America and the West in the 1950s and 1960s.

Pierre Teilhard de Chardin

Like William Wordsworth, Pierre Teilhard de Chardin was fascinated by nature and regarded it with religious awe, but at a much more fundamental level than the poet. For Teilhard it was the rocks, soil, minerals, and metals, the very substance of the earth, that were tangibly holy—he once wrote of the world's gradually appearing to him as "fire and light," eventually enveloping him "in one mass of luminosity, glowing from within."[3] As a geologist and paleontologist as well as a priest, he straddled two worlds, and throughout his life he tried to reconcile them, seeing theology and science as complementary partners rather than as warring neighbors. The keystone of his mystical vision was the concept of evolution, which he saw as spiritually purposeful and end directed.

Teilhard believed that nature was evolving into higher and more complex forms of life, culminating in human beings, with their capacity for self-reflection. Not only that, he thought that humans had the power actually to participate in and influence evolution as it progressed toward a focal terminus that he termed the Omega point and identified with Christ, whom he describes as "a center of radiation for the energies which lead the universe back to God through his humanity."[4] Yet despite his elevated and cosmic mystical vision, Teilhard was ever conscious of its roots in Christian scriptures: "However far we may be drawn into the divine spaces opened up to us by Christian mysticism, we never depart from Jesus of the Gospels. On the contrary, we feel a growing need to enfold ourselves ever more firmly within his human truth."[5]

Pierre Teilhard de Chardin was born in 1881 near Clermont in the Auvergne in central France. One of eleven children, he developed a love of nature from his father and the wild, rugged scenery of the local countryside, and he became an avid collector of rocks and stones, the beginnings of his love affair with geology. In 1899, at the age of eighteen, he entered the novitiate of the Jesuit order in Aix-en-Provence, later continuing his teacher training and studies—which included natural sciences—in Egypt and England. In 1911 he was ordained a priest, but he continued to pursue his scientific studies in Paris. This came to a halt after the outbreak of the First World War in 1914. Teilhard served as a stretcher bearer and emerged from the experience unshaken in his religious faith and decorated twice for bravery. It was during this difficult period that he experienced a powerful mystical vision while looking at a picture of Christ in a church close to the battlefront. The image seemed to vibrate, blur, dissolve, and take on a life of its own, and the space around the figure of Christ seemed to radiate "outwards to infinity" and was punctuated by "trails of phosphorescence" which he compared to a sort of "nervous system running through the totality of life."[6]

After the war Teilhard again concentrated on his scientific studies, and in 1922 he gained a doctorate from the Sorbonne and became a geology teacher in the Catholic Institute in Paris. In the following year he embarked on a paleontology trip to China, a country he would spend many years working in and where he would further his professional reputation (he was part of the team that discovered the famous Peking man, or *Sinanthropus*, in 1929). But his success as a paleontologist was balanced by his difficulties as a Catholic priest. His Jesuit superiors became aware of his views on evolution and its challenge to the orthodox teaching on original sin, and they censured him, preventing him from teaching. The Jesuits also refused to give him their approval to publish his theological and philosophical books, which reached the general public only after his death.

However, these restrictions did not affect Teilhard's scientific work, and toward the end of his life he received recognition from academic institutes in France and also America, where he was to die in New York in 1955 shortly before his seventy-fourth birthday. After his death, books such as *The Phenomenon of Man* and *Le Milieu Divin*, written in expressive, often poetic, and sometimes difficult prose, became widely known for their optimistic vision of a world evolving ever more spiritually. They brought him the fame and recognition as a religious thinker that had largely evaded him during his life.

Teilhard stands out in Christian spirituality for his mystical vision of the sacredness of matter and its fundamental place in creation: he talks of "the world [manifesting] itself to the Christian mystic as bathed in an inward light,"[7] and of God penetrating and shaping us through his creation.[8] He recognizes the scientific view of matter, but he expands it, attributing to matter an energy that is spiritual. In other words it is not an inert substance waiting to be manipulated but an aspect of life itself, and so should be given reverence. He also describes matter theologically as something that not only causes us physical suffering—making us "heavy, paralyzed, vulnerable, guilty"—but also as a principle of growth and renewal.[9] Nor does Teilhard maintain an opposition between matter and spirit but sees them as complementary forces together forming a continuum of cosmic energy.[10] He also describes how he experienced God continuously interacting with the world in such a way as to produce "a sudden blaze of such intense brilliance that all the depths of the world were lit up for me."[11]

Allied with Teilhard's vision of matter is his spiritual vision of evolution. He suggests that there are three main stages in the evolutionary process: chemical, organic, and psychosocial. These relate respectively to the formation of the earth itself, the emergence of organic life, and the rise of human beings and their capacity for self-reflection. He also posits the idea of the noosphere (a word he coined from the Greek for "mind"): in the same way that there is the geosphere (the nonliving world) or the lithosphere (the outer layer of the earth) or the biosphere (the realm of living organisms), Teilhard suggests that there will evolve a noosphere, which he describes as a layer of thought enveloping the world and linking human beings to each other (for many people the noosphere has seemed to be prophetic of the Internet, itself a global, interconnecting sphere of "thought").

For Teilhard, the idea that life has evolved to the point of human consciousness only to stop seems implausible. The biosphere is characterized by "a network of divergent lines," but through the agency of reflective thought these lines converge and the noosphere becomes "a single closed system in which each element sees, feels, desires and suffers for itself the same things as all the others at the same time."[12] The noosphere itself is not the final phase of evolution. Teilhard envisages a future when people will develop their human potential fully and will individually and collectively converge toward a point that he calls Omega and identifies with Christ,[13] who is therefore the evolutionary terminus. Alongside this sense of convergence is the Christian ideal that to love Christ is to love one another, and to love one another is to draw closer to Christ.[14]

Teilhard had a holistic vision of the world in which everyone has a part to play, no matter how lowly his or her work or station—God is "at the point of my pen, my pick, my paint-brush, my needle."[15] He balances the traditional strand of Christian teaching that emphasized detachment and avoidance of the world—the ascetic's search for isolation and purity—with the idea that the whole of human life is holy and that we must embrace it, with all of its joys and sufferings. Teilhard, for all his general optimism, fully recognized the reality of suffering, sin, and evil, but he insisted that for those who trust him lovingly, God uses evil as an occasion for a higher good, just as a sculptor will create beauty out of some flaw he might detect in the stone he is working on.[16] Death itself, which from a human perspective is the ultimate "diminishment," is simply the natural and necessary way of preparing the individual for God to enter him or her fully with his divine fire.

Thomas Merton

Like Pierre Teilhard de Chardin, the American monk and writer Thomas Merton was a mystic for the troubled times he lived in. He was born during the First World War, celebrated his twenty-fifth birthday during the Second World War, and died during the height of the Vietnam War. A complex, questing soul, he sought solitude, silence, and detachment from the world in a Trappist monastery. Yet, especially toward the end of his life, he became more involved in social and political issues, including the antiwar movement. A devout Catholic, he explored Eastern religions, especially Zen Buddhism, and he always sought to emphasize the agreements rather than the differences between his and other faiths. His most obvious personal gift was his ability to write—with clarity, honesty, and vitality. He authored some fifty books, including poetry, journals, essays, and works on church history, the Bible, theology, and mysticism. His best-known book, the autobiographical *Seven Storey Mountain*, became an international best-seller: the warts-and-all story of his groping toward his spiritual vocation is a compelling one, and it touched a nerve with readers in America and other countries who were seeking some sort of meaning in life after the traumas of the Second World War.

With Merton we enter a world in which psychology and the psychoanalytic movement have made their mark. He is at home with Freudian terms such as *ego* and *id*, and his distinction between a false self and a true self recalls C. G. Jung's distinction between the persona and the Self. At the heart of Merton's spirituality lies the practice of contemplation. He stressed that contemplation is not synonymous with visions, trances, locutions, raptures, and the like, although they may accompany it. Rather, contemplation is "the union of the simple light of God with the simple light of our spirit, in love."[17]

Thomas Merton was born in Prades in the south of France in 1915. His father was from New Zealand and his mother was American. He suffered the loss of his mother when he was six, and his childhood was constantly disrupted by his artist father's moving from place to place in search of congenial locations in which to live and paint. Merton was educated at boarding schools in France and in England, where he later went to Cambridge University to study modern languages. His time at university turned out to be short and miserable. By this time his father had died of cancer and his only brother, John Paul, and his maternal grandparents lived thousands of miles away in America. Rootless and confused, Merton threw himself into a wild social life, to the neglect of his studies and the icy reproach of his English godfather and guardian. The final straw occurred when he seems to have gotten a girl-friend pregnant: he left Cambridge after a year's study and settled in America for good.

Merton continued his studies at Columbia University, where he blossomed and made strong friendships. In 1938 his unfulfilled and nagging religious instinct led him to become baptized as a Catholic and to aspire to enter a religious order. Three years later, having taught for a while in a Franciscan college in New York, he finally entered the Order of Cistercians of the Strict Observance, commonly known as the Trappists, at the monastery of Gethsemani near Louisville, Kentucky, where he would remain until his death.

The Trappist way of life was severe, a daily routine of prayer, meditation, reading, and manual work, with communication between the brothers conducted in sign language to preserve the silence. Gethsemani's abbot, however, recognized the gift Merton—or Brother Louis, as he was known—had for words, and he allowed him to continue his writing. In 1948 *The Seven Storey Mountain* was published to great acclaim, bringing Merton into the public eye. Further books on Christian spirituality added to his growing reputation; then in the 1950s his interests broadened to include Eastern religions and social and political issues. This change of direction inevitably alienated some of his earlier readers, but it also brought him a new following, especially in the 1960s during the Vietnam War, when many peace campaigners found inspiration in his writings.

Since his arrival at Gethsemani in 1941, Merton had not ventured from his monastery apart from occasional trips to Louisville for medical reasons. But in 1968, the last year of his life, his abbot allowed him to attend interfaith conferences in India and Thailand. Rejoining the world again, Merton savored the new sights and sounds and engaging with minds of other spiritual persuasions. On December 10, however, after giving a talk in Bangkok, he returned to his room and was later found dead, lying on the floor, having been electrocuted, it seems, by a faulty electric fan.

During his life, Merton had at least two spiritual experiences that affected him profoundly. The first occurred while he was visiting Rome when he was eighteen. One night, in his *pensione* room, he suddenly felt the presence of his dead father "as vivid and as real and as startling as if he had touched my arm or spoken to me." In that moment he saw into the darkness of his own soul and was filled with revulsion and an intense desire to be liberated from his "misery and corruption." For the first time in his life he prayed to God with his whole being. The experience later seemed to him to be "a grace, and a great grace." It did not save him from his misspent time at Cambridge, but it was nevertheless a memorable landmark on the path toward his spiritual vocation.[18]

The second experience happened in 1940 during a visit to Cuba. One Sunday, while attending Mass in Havana, he heard a group of children at the front of the church cry out the creed in joyful unison and was struck by a sudden awareness of God's presence: "It was a light that was so bright that it had no relation to any visible light and so profound and so intimate that it seemed like a neutralization of every lesser experience." He was sure he had received a divine illumination, and the first articulate thought he had was, "Heaven is right here in front of me: Heaven, Heaven!"[19] Yet in the midst of what appeared to be an extraordinary experience, Merton was also struck by the thought that the light was in fact "ordinary" and open to anybody.

Indeed, it was one of Merton's beliefs that contemplation was not something that only monks and other religious should practice. All Christians, whether they be monks, teachers, or nurses, single or married, are called to deepen their inner lives, to become "fused into one spirit with Christ in the furnace of contemplation," then benefit others with the fruits of their spirituality.[20]

Merton's thoughts on mysticism and contemplation are scattered throughout his works, including *The Ascent to Truth* and, especially, *New Seeds of Contemplation*. Merton approaches contemplation in different ways, trying to define it and to explain what it is *not* as much as what it is, as well as describing the necessary preparation for it. He says that contemplation is a type of spiritual vision but that it sees "without seeing" and knows "without knowing."[21] Elsewhere he refers to the "ignorance" of the "true mystic" being not "unintelligence but superintelligence" and says that although "contemplation seems to be a denial of speculative thought, it is really its fulfillment."[22] Contemplation involves dying to our old way of living and uniting our minds and wills with God "in an act of pure love that brings us into obscure contact with him as he really is."[23] Through union with God by love, the soul receives the "hidden" or "secret" knowledge of God.[24]

Fundamental to the practice of contemplation is the destruction of the false self and the emergence of the true self, which participates in God through Christ. The false self is the "I," or the ego, which deals with the outside world, with everyday life, and with which the individual usually identifies himself or herself to the exclusion of the true self. It is my "I" that dominates my life: insofar as I do things—wanting, loving, hating, eating, resting, thinking, and so on—it is my "I" that is in control, experiencing, evaluating, comparing. But in doing so the "I" is strengthened, dominating the personality, leaving no room for the true self, the real spiritual center, to develop and for contemplation to blossom: "As long as there is an 'I' that is the definite subject of a contemplative experience, . . . we remain in the realm of multiplicity, activity, incompleteness, stirring and desire."[25]

The key to destroying the false self is humility, which, with faith, is the foundation of the contemplative life. It is pride that bolsters the ego, and it is humility that erodes this sense of self, allowing the divine to shine through. The more we abase ourselves—not through a deliberate process, which can lead to a false humility, but by a genuine abandonment of any sort of self-aggrandizement—the more likely we are to be filled with the happiness that comes with encountering God: "for the only way to enter joy is to dwindle down to a vanishing point and become absorbed in God through the center of your own nothingness."[26]

Merton did not underestimate traditional attitudes toward, and preparations for, contemplation. Like the mystics of old, he stressed the importance of detachment, not just from material things, but also from more "virtuous" desires, such as for serenity and enlightenment. He also acknowledged to some extent the need for solitude and quiet, but he emphasized that they were strictly a means to an end: if solitude is regarded as a way of escaping the world and responsibilities, it cannot serve contemplation. True solitude is "an abyss opening up in the centre of your own soul." And the point of contemplation is that we share its fruits—the inner joy and peace—with others and not simply revel in them narcissistically in a remote cave or desert. Contemplation and the active life are complementary, but activities must be infused with the spiritual energy received in contemplation. Equally, contemplation must be nourished by the right kinds of activities, that is, those that fulfill God's will.[27]

Merton admits that the contemplative path can be long and testing, passing through a wilderness that has no vegetation, beauty, or water—for mysticism is all-demanding, embracing "the whole interior experience of the soul immersed in the Absolute."[28] Yet despite inevitably experiencing confusion and anxiety, the contemplative will sense that "peace lies in the heart of this darkness." Those that persevere will reach the promised land and "taste the peace and joy of union with God" and have "a habitual, comforting, obscure and mysterious awareness of . . . God, present and acting in all the events of your life."[29]

Epilogue

Who may ascend the hill of the Lord? Who may
stand in his holy place? He who has clean hands
and a pure heart, who does not lift up his soul
to an idol or swear by what is false.
— Psalms 24:3–4

A T THE END of this survey of mystics of the past, it remains to consider briefly what the future holds for Christian contemplation at the start of the twenty-first century. Since the 1960s there has been a considerable growth in the West of a variety of movements involving personal spiritual growth, which might suggest a need for Christian contemplation. Yet it is also clear that the churches have not been automatic beneficiaries of this growth. In 2003 a correspondent on religious affairs in the *Irish Times* wrote the following, and his words must surely resonate with other Christians throughout the west:

There probably isn't a shopping centre in Ireland that doesn't have a shop selling incense, candles and statuettes of money frogs. The superfluity of mystic merchandise and fortune-tellers highlights a problem within Christianity. One has to ask why people feel they need the services of mediums, fortune-tellers and card-readers in the 21st century.

As churches face dwindling memberships it seems strange that the thirst for matters spiritual is on the increase. In fact it is becoming obvious every day that these practices are replacing traditional religion in our society. The reason could lie in the fact that much of what is being preached by churches is *failing to satisfy the need for spiritual and mystical experience.*[1]

If this observation is true, how can the churches in the West nurture and satisfy the hunger for spiritual and mystical experience? In fact, in recent times there have been a number of Christian grassroots initiatives that have attempted to address the apparent need for a more engaging and participative spirituality. Many of these movements tap into the Christian mystical tradition, emphasizing the importance of prayer, meditation, and contemplation. Together they may be seen as raising the water table of Christian spirituality, providing a genuinely fertile soil for individuals to grow inwardly toward God.

One such movement is that associated with the Burgundian village of Taizé, where Brother Roger Schutz founded an ecumenical Christian community during the Second World War. Taizé has become one of the most successful spiritual movements in the West. Every year thousands of Christians from different denominations—from Roman Catholic to Eastern Orthodox—converge on Taizé to attend prayer meetings and talks, sing Taizé's distinctive simple and melodic songs, or meditate in silence. Visitors are then encouraged to return home and put Taizé's values, such as its emphasis on fruitful spiritual reflection and tolerance, into practice.

Similar to Taizé's values are those of the Christian community based on the island of Iona off the west coast of Scotland. In 1938, some fifteen hundred years after the Irish monk Columba established a monastic presence on the island, a Church of Scotland minister named George Macleod founded the Iona Community, restoring the dilapidated medieval abbey and making it a center for retreats and programs of spiritual renewal. The community itself has an ecumenical flavor and is dedicated to inner devotion as well as to justice and peace in the world.

The success and popularity of Iona, which now attracts thousands of pilgrims each year, may be partly due to the modern phenomenon of Celtic Christianity or spirituality, which has become increasingly popular since the 1980s. Advocates of Celtic Christianity emphasize what they see as a distinctive and ancient spiritual tradition, which includes stressing the importance of the awareness of the natural world as God's creation; an openness to prophetic or mystical experiences; forms of worship centered around creativity, such as dance and poetry; and loose, informal organizational structures with equality between the genders.

Skeptics of the Celtic Christian movement point to the fact that its supporters seem to have a longing for a "pure" form of pre-Catholic spirituality that owes as much to a nostalgia for a golden age as to a discontentment with the more institutionalized forms of the churches. Indeed, it is possible that the whole Celtic movement—in both its Christian and neopagan forms (both of which have spawned a plethora of beautifully produced books on prayer, "wisdom," spirituality, music, art, and much else)—may have a tendency to spin webs of spiritual fantasies rather than inculcate spiritual and moral values. Yet skeptics have to be reminded: Why did it spring up in the first place? What were the mainstream churches lacking that caused its popularity?

Another movement that places great emphasis on creativity is Creation Spirituality, founded by the American Matthew Fox, an Eckhart scholar who was once a Dominican monk and is now an Episcopalian priest after his expulsion from the order in 1993 for his allegedly unorthodox teachings. Creation Spirituality takes a holistic approach to spirituality. It seeks to interlace traditional Western spirituality with that from native cultures around the world while at the same time absorbing the latest scientific thinking in cosmology. It promotes an awareness of ecology and the idea that artistic creation is crucial to forming relationships between the individual and the other. The movement stresses that everyone is a mystic inasmuch as he or she is born with an innate sense of awe and wonder that can be recovered at any moment in life. It also believes that we all have the capacity to express or enact our spirituality through the creation of art, which in its meditative aspect can be seen as a form of prayer.

Perhaps the biggest-growing area of Christian spirituality in the West, however, is the retreat movement, where religious houses and organizations allow laypeople to spend a weekend or longer in peaceful surroundings to pray, read, and reflect on spiritual truths. There are now hundreds of retreat houses in America and Europe catering for different requirements. Some houses offer guided retreats, where a spiritual director will offer spiritual advice, or there are themed retreats, where an issue such as social justice forms the focus for discussion and reflection. Other houses allow participants simply to enjoy silence and the opportunity to read and pray. In some retreats, held in monasteries, visitors can sample the monastic lifestyle.

Apart from retreats, there are movements such as the Julian Gatherings and the Quiet Garden Trust that offer shorter but regular periods of time for spiritual reflection, particularly suitable for people who wish to take a brief time-out from their professional and domestic routines. The Julian Gatherings are an offshoot of the Order of Julian of Norwich, an Episcopalian contemplative order founded in the United States in the 1980s and now based in Wisconsin. The order is named after Julian of Norwich, whose writings form its inspirational core. The gatherings are informal groups that meet locally in a church or a house, perhaps monthly or weekly, to engage in silent prayer for half an hour or so, which is often followed by conversation and refreshments. The groups, which vary in size and in the frequency with which they gather, are flexible and informal, allowing people to discover silent prayer and the Christian mystical tradition at their own pace.

The Quiet Garden movement was the brainchild of an Anglican priest named Philip Roderick, who in 1992 realized his long-gestating vision of a simple and inexpensive ministry of prayer and hospitality through a network of private houses and gardens made available by the owners to those who wanted to withdraw from the world for a day or an afternoon every so often. The Quiet Garden Trust facilitates the provision of not only houses and gardens but also retreat centers, local churches, and areas in inner cities—anywhere, in other words, that can offer a peaceful, attractive setting, suitable for prayer, meditation, and reflection. Each Quiet Garden is affiliated with the trust but adapts itself to local conditions and needs. The first Quiet Garden opened in England in 1992, and by its tenth anniversary there were some 250 Quiet Gardens worldwide, with numbers increasing.

The spiritual movements and centers mentioned above are positive signs that Christianity is capable of renewing itself spiritually and that its long contemplative tradition still has relevance today—indeed some would say more relevance than ever. But it is noticeable that initiatives for stimulating interest in prayer and contemplation tend to be the result of one person's genius and dynamism and that they remain at the fringes of the churches, almost as if they were add-ons or extra-curricular activities.

Yet surely the Christian mystical tradition should not be an optional extra. The experiences and teachings and example of the mystics are crucial to the prosperity, and perhaps even the survival, of Christianity. The greatest mystics, as this book has tried to show, demonstrate what it is to be fully Christian—and therefore fully human. They are outstanding examples of individuals whose love of and devotion to God is synonymous with their love of and devotion to humanity. Also, from Saint Paul to Thomas Merton, they were almost without exception loyal members of the church, for whom the sacraments and liturgy were central. It behooves us to learn from their lives and wisdom.

So what in essence can the mystics teach us today? First of all that the spiritual and mystical way is holistic: it is a journey to ultimate reality that involves the whole person—mind, body, and soul, the feelings and the intellect. Mysticism is not simply a mental exercise or a series of physical exercises; nor is it a case of splitting ourselves off from the rest of humanity to find personal ecstasy in a cocoon of peacefulness. Periods of uninterrupted quiet may well be necessary to foster contemplative prayer, but the whole modus operandi of mysticism is engagement with both God and the world to the extent that they become synonymous. As Mechthild of Magdeburg said, taking care of natural, commonplace needs ranks as high in God's sight as the highest states of contemplation.[2]

The mystics also make it clear that ecstasy, the sense of engulfing peace and joy that comes with the awareness of the presence of God, plays a relatively small part in the totality of their spirituality. The crowning moments of rapture cannot be split off from what happens before and afterward in the mystic's life, which is essentially unitive: it cannot be a case of receiving divine illumination out of the blue and then carrying on as if nothing had happened. True mystical experiences are divine blessings that deepen compassion and give energy to the individual. They are transformatory points that help to sway a person's life from habitual egotism to selflessness, and they rarely happen ex nihilo, if at all. For they require a spiritual commitment and discipline based on humility and faith, which, as the mystics remind us, form the cornerstone of contemplation, and the result of contemplation is love, a love that makes no distinction between great and small, rich or poor, worthy or unworthy. As Teresa of Ávila wrote: "The Lord does not look so much at the magnitude of anything we do as at the love with which we do it."[3] She is echoed by Brother Lawrence, who said that "we ought not to be weary of doing little things for the love of God, Who regards not the greatness of the work, but the love with which it is performed."[4] The mystics teach us how to reach God not through clouds of joy and ecstasy and angelic choirs but through the deepening of love.

NOTES

FOREWORD

1. Evelyn Underhill, *The Mystics of the Church* (New York: Schocken Books, 1971), p. 17, quoted in Nuth, *God's Lovers* p. 13.

INTRODUCTION

1. S.v. "Moon" in *The New Encyclopedia Britannica*, 15th ed.
2. James Irwin, in *Der Heimatplanet* (Frankfurt: Zweitausendeins, 1989), caption to photos 46–47.
3. Quoted in Happold, *Mysticism* p. 38.
4. McGinn, *Foundations of Christian Mysticism*, p. xviii.
5. Nuth, *God's Lovers*, p. 15.
6. 2 Cor. 12:2–4; all biblical quotations are taken from the New International Version of the Bible.
7. McGinn, *Foundations of Christian Mysticism*, p. xv.
8. Rufus M. Jones, *Studies in Mystical Religion* (Macmillan 1909), p. 284.
9. Quoted in Mursell, ed., p. 237.

CHAPTER 1: NEW TESTAMENT TIMES

1. See Stace, *Teachings of the Mystics*, pp. 10–12.
2. McGinn, *Foundations of Christian Mysticism*, p. 74.
3. Law, *Spirit of Prayer* 1.2.8.
4. Evelyn Underhill, quoted in Wakefield, *Dictionary*, pp. 230–31.

CHAPTER 2: THE EARLY CHURCH

1. See Chadwick, *Early Church*, p. 56.
2. See McGinn, *Foundations of Christian Mysticism*, p. 97.
3. Clement of Alexandria, *Miscellanies* 5.12, in Roberts and Donaldson, *Ante-Nicene Fathers*, vol. 2.

4. Williams, *Wound of Knowledge*, p. 26.
5. Quoted in Inge, *Christian Mysticism*, pp. 86–87.
6. McGinn, *Foundations of Christian Mysticism*, p. 104.
7. Clement of Alexandria, *Miscellanies* 7.10.
8. Ibid.
9. See McGinn, *Foundations of Christian Mysticism*, pp. 108–30; Louth, *Christian Mystical Tradition*, pp. 52–74.
10. McGinn, Meyendorff, and Leclerq, *Christian Spirituality*, p. 39.
11. Origen, *On Prayer*, ch. 5.
12. Ibid., ch. 7.
13. Spencer, *Mysticism in World Religion*, p. 159.
14. Quoted in O'Meara, *Plotinus*, p. 6.
15. Plotinus, *Enneads* 1.6.9.
16. Ibid., 6.9.11.
17. Ibid.

CHAPTER 3: THE CHRISTIAN EMPIRE

1. Louth, *Christian Mystical Tradition*, p. 98.
2. Quoted in Williams, *Wound of Knowledge*, p. 94.
3. Gregory of Nyssa, *On Virginity*, ch. 11, in Schaff and Wace, *Nicene and Post-Nicene Fathers*, vol 5.
4. Ibid.
5. Louth, *Christian Mystical Tradition*, pp. 81–83.
6. Gregory of Nyssa, *Life of Moses* 2:162–64, cited in Louth, *Christian Mystical Tradition*, p. 87.
7. McGinn, *Foundations of Christian Mysticism*, p. 151.
8. Evagrius, *On Prayer* 2, in Palmer, Sherrard, and Ware, *Philokalia, vol 1*.
9. Ibid., aphorisms 11, 23.
10. McGinn, *Foundations of Christian Mysticism*, p. 155.
11. See ibid., p. 147ff.
12. See Louth, *Christian Mystical Tradition*, pp. 102–10.
13. Evagrius, *On Prayer* 71, in Palmer, Sherrard, and Ware, op. cit.
14. Augustine, *Confessions* 1.1, trans. Pine-Coffin.
15. See Augustine, *On the Trinity* 8, cited in McGinn, *Foundations of Christian Mysticism*, p. 245.
16. Augustine, *Confessions* 7.10.16, trans. Pusey.
17. See McGinn, *Foundations of Christian Mysticism*, pp. 233–34.
18. E. R. Dodds, cited in Wakefield, *Dictionary*, p. 34. Augustine of Hippo, St.
19. Augustine, *Confessions* 9.10.23–24, trans. Pusey (translation slightly modernized by author).
20. Louth, *Christian Mystical Tradition*, 136.

21. See ibid., p. 137; McGinn, *Foundations of Christian Mysticism,* p. 254.
22. Augustine, *Literal Commentary on Genesis* 12.26, quoted in Graeff, *Light and the Rainbow,* p. 203.
23. Frank Tobin, in Bartlett, *Vox Mystica,* p. 43.
24. See Butler, *Western Mysticism,* p. 103.
25. Ibid., pp. 81–83.

CHAPTER 4: THE DARK AGES
1. Brown, *World of Late Antiquity,* p. 120.
2. Dionysius the Areopagite, *Divine Names,* ch. 3.
3. Williams, *Wound of Knowledge,* p. 120 (his emphasis); and see McGinn, Meyendorff, and Leclerq, *Christian Spirituality,* p. 134.
4. Dionysius the Areopagite, *Mystical Theology,* ch. 2, trans. C. E. Rolt.
5. Ibid., ch. 1.
6. Ibid.
7. Ibid., ch. 5
8. Brown, *World of Late Antiquity,* p. 134.
9. Gregory the Great, *Dialogues,* i., preface, quoted in Butler, *Western Mysticism,* 130.
10. Gregory the Great, *Moralia on Job* 6.58, in Butler, *Western Mysticism.*
11. Gregory the Great, *Homilies on Ezekiel* 2.5.9, cited in McGinn, *Growth of Mysticism.*
12. Ibid., 2.2.13.
13. Ibid., 2.2.12.
14. Gregory the Great, *Dialogues* 2.35.
15. Gregory the Great, *Homilies on Ezekiel* 40.17.
16. Ibid., 2.2.12.
17. Gregory the Great, *Moralia on Job* 31.101.
18. Luscombe, *Medieval Thought,* p. 35.
19. McGinn, *Growth of Mysticism,* p. 116.
20. Leff, *Medieval Thought,* p. 69.

CHAPTER 5: THE AGE OF THE CRUSADES
1. Deanesly, *Medieval Church,* p. 119.
2. See Butler, *Western Mysticism,* pp. 154–80; McGinn, *Growth of Mysticism,* pp. 158–224.
3. Bernard of Clairvaux, *Sermons on the Song of Songs* 23.15, quoted in Graef, *Light and the Rainbow,* p. 222.
4. Bernard of Clairvaux, *Sermons on the Song of Songs,* 74.6, in *Selected Works.*
5. Ibid., 46.5.7; quoted in Butler, *Western Mysticism,* p. 158.

6. Sermons on the Songs of Songs, 57.8.
7. Bernard of Clairvaux, *On Loving God*, ch. 10; quoted in Butler, *Western Mysticism*, pp. 168–69.
8. Bernard of Clairvaux, *Sermons on the Song of Songs* 18.6; quoted in Butler, *Western Mysticism*, p. 179.
9. Bernard of Clairvaux, *On Loving God* 11:33, quoted in Williams, *Wound of Knowledge*, p. 114.
10. Richard of Saint-Victor, *Benjamin Minor*, 73, quoted in McGinn, *Growth of Mysticism*, p. 404.
11. Richard of Saint-Victor, *The Mystical Ark* 1.6, translated by Grover A. Zinn.
12. Ibid., 5.
13. McGinn, *Growth of Mysticism*, p. 413.
14. See abridgement in Happold, *Mysticism*, pp. 211–17, from Clare Kirchberger, trans., *Richard of St. Victor: Writings on Contemplation* (London: Faber and Faber, 1957).
15. Cited in Beer, *Women and Mystical Experience*, p. 28.
16. Hildegard of Bingen, preface to *Scivias*, p. 59.
17. Dronke, *Women Writers*, p. 203.
18. Quoted in Beer, *Women and Mystical Experience*, p. 28.
19. Dronke, *Women Writers*, p. 170.
20. Hildegard of Bingen, *Scivias*, bk. 2, quoted in Malone, *Women and Christianity*, p. 115.
21. See McGinn, *Growth of Mysticism*, pp. 333–36.

CHAPTER 6: FRANCISCANS
1. Southern, *Church in the Middle Ages*, p. 273.
2. Ibid., p. 285.
3. Francis of Assisi, *Life of St. Francis*, ch. 13 in *The Little Flowers*.
4. Regis J. Armstrong and Ignatius C. Brady, introduction to *Francis and Clare*, p. 5.
5. *Life of St. Francis*, ch. 12, in *The Little Flowers*.
6. Quoted in *Francis and Clare*, p. 19.
7. Francis of Assisi, "Canticle of the Sun," in *Francis and Clare*, p. 39.
8. Bonaventure, *Sentences* 35.1, quoted in Wakefield, *Dictionary*, p. 54.
9. Bonaventure, *Journey* 4.3.
10. *The Threefold Way* 1.17, quoted in Graeff, *Light and the Rainbow*, p. 236.
11. Bonaventure, *Journey* 5.1.
12. Ibid., 7.6.
13. Dronke, *Women Writers*, p. 216.
14. Angela of Foligno, *Complete Works*, p. 302.
15. Ibid., p. 236.

16. Ibid., pp. 252–53.
17. Quoted in Underhill, *Mysticism*, p. 252 (translation slightly adapted).
18. Angela of Foligno, *Complete Works*, pp. 151–52.
19. Ibid., pp. 181–83.
20. Quoted in Underhill, *Mysticism*, p. 351.
21. Quoted in McGinn, *Flowering of Mysticism*, p. 151.

CHAPTER 7: THE BEGUINES

1. Furlong, *Medieval Women Mystics*, p. 13.
2. Southern, *Church in the Middle Ages*, p. 314.
3. Ibid., p. 321.
4. Bowie, *Beguine Spirituality*, p. 19.
5. Matthew Paris, *Chronica Majora*, 4.278, quoted in Southern, *Church in the Middle Ages*, p. 319.
6. Quoted in Petroff, *Body and Soul*, p. 14.
7. Vision 7, cited in Malone, *Women and Christianity*, p. 147.
8. Letter 9, quoted in Petroff, *Body and Soul*, p. 61.
9. Letter 6 and Poems in Couplets 5 and 6, in Bowie, *Beguine Spirituality*, pp. 106, 98–99.
10. Letter 30, in ibid., p. 113.
11. Letter 6, in Malone, *Women and Christianity*, p. 146.
12. Letters 10 and 20, in Bowie, *Beguine Spirituality*, pp. 109, 112.
13. Letter 19, quoted in Petroff, *Body and Soul*, p. 61.
14. Poems in Couplets 13, in Bowie, *Beguine Spirituality*, p. 101.
15. Poems in Stanzas 17, in ibid., p. 120.
16. Mechthild of Magdeburg, *Flowing Light of the Godhead* 5.13, in ibid, p. 74.
17. Mechthild of Magdeburg, *Flowing Light* 5.32, in Malone, *Women and Christianity*, p. 168.
18. Mechthild of Magdeburg, *Flowing Light* 1.2, in Beer, *Women and Mystical Experience*, p. 80.
19. Malone, *Women and Christianity*, p. 166.
20. Mechthild of Magdeburg, *Flowing Light* 1.44, quoted in Beer, *Women and Mystical Experience*, p. 94.
21. Mechthild of Magdeburg, *Flowing Light* 5.30, in Bowie, *Beguine Spirituality*, p. 76. The following references are taken from Bowie, pp. 48–85, unless otherwise stated.
22. Mechthild of Magdeburg, *Flowing Light* 5.4.
23. Ibid., 1.26.
24. Ibid., 1.23.
25. Ibid., 1.13.
26. Ibid., 6.42.
27. Ibid., 3.7.

28. Ibid., 5.4.
29. Ibid., 1.35.
30. Mechthild of Magdeburg, *Flowing Light* 7.61, quoted in Beer, *Women and Mystical Experience*, p. 107.
31. Porete, *Mirror of Simple Souls*, ch. 118, trans. Colledge, Marler, and Grant, p. 140ff.
32. Ibid., ch. 51.
33. Ibid., ch. 13.
34. Ibid., ch. 121.
35. Ibid., ch. 68.
36. Ibid., ch. 29.
37. Ibid., ch. 6.
38. Porete, *Mirror of Simple Souls*, ch. 28, quoted in Dronke, *Women Writers*, p. 219.

CHAPTER 8: THE RHINELAND MYSTICS

1. Eckhart, Sermon 12, in *Selected Writings*, p. 179.
2. Eckhart, Sermon 22, quoted in Stace, *Teachings of the Mystics*, p. 156.
3. Eckhart, German Sermon 38, in *Selected Writings*, pp. 112–13.
4. Eckhart, German Sermon 2, pp. 216, 221.
5. Eckhart, German Sermon 48, pp. 135–36.
6. Eckhart, German Sermon 83, p. 239.
7. Eckhart, German Sermon 52, p. 204.
8. Eckhart, *The Talks of Instruction* 6, in *Selected Writings*, p. 9.
9. Tauler, Sermon 11, in Woods, *Mysticism and Prophecy*, p. 114.
10. Tauler, Sermon 76, in *Sermons*, quoted in Woods, *Mysticism and Prophecy*, p. 115.
11. Inge, *Christian Mysticism*, p. 186.
12. Ibid., p. 189.
13. Quoted in Ferguson, *Illustrated Encyclopedia of Mysticism*, p. 190.
14. Tauler, Sermon 35, in *Inner Way*.
15. Quoted in Ferguson, *Illustrated Encyclopedia of Mysticism*, p. 191.
16. Quoted in Underhill, *Mysticism*, p. 187.
17. Inge, *Christian Mysticism*, p. 175.
18. Quoted in Wakefield, *Dictionary*, p. 366.
19. Suso, *Life of the Servant*, in *The Exemplar*, p. 197, quoted in Woods, *Mysticism and Prophecy*, p. 113.
20. Suso, *Little Book of Truth*, p. 185, quoted in Zaehner, *Mysticism*, p. 21.
21. Quoted in Raitt, *Christian Spirituality*, p. 165.
22. Ruysbroeck, *Spiritual Marriage* 1.26.
23. Ibid., 2.65.

24. Ibid., 3.1.
25. Ibid., 3.4.

CHAPTER 9: ORTHODOX MYSTICISM AND HESYCHASM
1. Lossky, *Mystical Theology*, p. 218.
2. Ibid., p. 227.
3. Kallistos Ware, "Prayer of the Heart," in Wakefield, *Dictionary*, p. 315.
4. Ware, *The Orthodox Church*, p. 75.
5. Symeon the New Theologian, *Mystical Life*, vol. 2, p. 106.
6. Symeon the New Theologian, Homily 29.2, quoted in Lossky, *Mystical Theology*, p. 218.
7. Symeon the New Theologian, *Discourses*, pp. 364–65; Lossky, p. 226.
8. Quoted in Lossky, *Mystical Theology*, p. 181.
9. Lossky, *Mystical Theology*, p. 209.
10. Symeon the New Theologian, *Discourses*, p. 80.
11. Ibid., p. 292.
12. Ibid., pp. 187–88.
13. Symeon the New Theologian, *Mystical Life*, vol. 2, pp. 109–10.
14. Symeon the New Theologian, *Discourses*, pp. 219–20.
15. Symeon the New Theologian, Homily 19.2, quoted in Lossky, *Mystical Theology*, p. 219.
16. Lossky, *Mystical Theology*, p. 219.
17. Symeon the New Theologian, *Discourses*, p. 365.
18. Ibid., p. 236.
19. Gregory Palamas, quoted in Ware, *The Orthodox Church*, p. 77.
20. Quoted in Lossky, *Mystical Theology*, p. 72.
21. Quoted in Spencer, *Mysticism in World Religion*, p. 226.
22. Palamas, *Antirrhetic against Akindynos* 4.14.36, quoted in Raitt, *Christian Spirituality*, p. 213.
23. Palamas, Homily 16, quoted in Ware, *The Orthodox Church*, p. 77.
24. Palamas, *Triads* 1.3.47, quoted in Raitt, *Christian Spirituality*, p. 219.
25. French, *Way of a Pilgrim*, p. 56.

CHAPTER 10: THE ENGLISH FLOWERING
1. See Bernard McGinn, "The English Mystics," in Raitt, *Christian Spirituality*, p. 195.
2. Rolle, *Fire of Love*, trans. Walters, ch. 5.
3. Ibid., ch. 29.
4. Ibid., ch. 39.
5. Ibid., ch. 15.

6. Rolle, *Fire of Love*, trans. Misyn, ch. 28.
7. Underhill, *Cloud of Unknowing*, introduction, p. 5.
8. Ibid., ch. 53.
9. Ibid., ch. 3.
10. Ibid., ch. 5.
11. Ibid., ch. 9.
12. Ibid., ch. 37.
13. Ibid., ch. 4.
14. Ibid., ch. 20.
15. Hilton, *Ladder of Perfection* 1.4.
16. Ibid., 1.5.
17. Ibid., 1.8.
18. Ibid., 2.5.
19. Ibid., 2.32.
20. Ibid., 2.21.
21. Ibid., 2.24.
22. Julian of Norwich, *Revelation of Love*, ch. 27.
23. Ibid., ch. 4 and 7.
24. Ibid., ch. 37.
25. Ibid., ch. 29.
26. Quoted in Nuth, *Gos's Lovers*, p. 119.
27. Julian of Norwich, *Revelation of Love*, ch. 41.
28. Ibid., ch. 5.
29. Ibid., ch. 86.

CHAPTER 11: THE LATE MIDDLE AGES

1. Scott, *Medieval Europe*, p. 366.
2. Hay, *Medieval Centuries*, p. 138.
3. Quoted in Ferguson, *Illustrated Encyclopedia of Mysticism*, p. 37.
4. Underhill, *Mysticism*, p. 365.
5. Catherine of Siena, *Dialogue*, ch. 79, cited in ibid.
6. Catherine of Siena, *Dialogue*, ch. 4, in Graeff, *Light and the Rainbow*, p. 258.
7. Catherine of Siena, letters 189 and 226, cited in Woods, *Mysticism and Prophecy*, p. 103.
8. Catherine of Siena, *Dialogue*, ch. 63, trans. Suzanne Noffke.
9. Ibid., ch. 78, p. 145.
10. Underhill, *Mysticism*, p. 441.
11. Cited in Underhill, *Mysticism*, pp. 181–82.
12. Catherine of Genoa, *Purgation and Purgatory*, p. 81.
13. Catherine of Genoa, *Spiritual Dialogue*, p. 109.
14. Cited in Underhill, *Mysticism*, p. 441.
15. Catherine of Genoa, *Purgation and Purgatory*, p. 81.

16. Ibid., p. 72.
17. Ibid., p. 78.
18. Catherine of Genoa, *Spiritual Dialogue*, p. 109.

CHAPTER 12: PROTESTANT MYSTICISM

1. Diarmaid MacCulloch, in Harries and Mayr-Harting, *Christianity*, p. 143.
2. Quoted in Gascoigne, *Christians*, p. 228.
3. Quoted in Spencer, *Mysticism in World Religion*, p. 279.
4. Quoted in Inge, *Christian Mysticism*, p. 275.
5. Ibid., p. 278.
6. Weeks, *Boehme*, p. 40.
7. Ibid., p. 2.
8. Ibid., p. 218.
9. Boehme, *Of the Supersensual Life* I, pp. 233–34, in Boehme, *Signature*.
10. Ibid., p. 243.
11. *Of the Supersensual Life* II, p. 247 in Boehme, *Signature*.
12. Ibid., p. 253.
13. Ibid., pp. 255–56.
14. Fox, *Journal*, ch. 2.
15. Eamon Duffy, in Wakefield, *Dictionary*, p. 156, "Fox."
16. Fox, *Journal*, ch. 1.
17. Ibid.
18. Ibid.
19. Ibid., ch. 2
20. Ibid.
21. Ibid.

CHAPTER 13: THE GOLDEN AGE OF SPAIN

1. Teresa of Ávila, *Life of Saint Teresa*, ch. 20.
2. Ibid., ch. 11.
3. Ibid., ch. 14–15.
4. Ibid., ch. 16–17.
5. Ibid., ch. 18.
6. Teresa of Ávila, *Interior Castle*, 5.2, in *Complete Works*.
7. Ibid., 7.2.
8. John of the Cross, *Mystical Doctrine*, p. 130.
9. John of the Cross, *Ascent of Mount Carmel* 1.13, in *Complete Works*.
10. John of the Cross, *Mystical Doctrine*, pp. 144–45.
11. "Spiritual Canticle," stanza 14 (author's version).
12. John of the Cross, *Dark Night of the Soul*, 1.9.4, in *Complete Works*.
13. John of the Cross, *Mystical Doctrine*, p. 104.

14. Ibid., p. 118.
15. Ibid., pp. 127–28.
16. John of the Cross, *Living Flame of Love*, stanza 2, in *Complete Works*.

CHAPTER 14: FRENCH MYSTICS AND QUIETISM
1. Quoted in Ferguson, *Illustrated Encyclopedia of Mysticism*, p. 63.
2. See Michael J. Buckley, "Seventeenth-Century French Spirituality," in Dupré and Saliers, *Christian Spirituality*, p. 35.
3. Francis de Sales, *Devout Life* 1.1.
4. Ibid., 2.2.
5. Ibid., 2.5.
6. Ibid., 2.6.
7. Ibid., 2.7.
8. Francis de Sales, *Treatise on Love*, 6.3, from Mursell, *Christian Spirituality* p. 225
9. Francis de Sales, *Treatise on Love*, 6.9, quoted by Michael J. Buckley in Dupré and Saliers, *Christian Spirituality*, p. 41.
10. Lawrence, *Presence of God*.
11. Ibid., First Conversation.
12. Ibid., Fourth Conversation.
13. Daniel Didomizio, "French Spirituality," in Wakefield, *Dictionary*, p. 163.
14. Quoted in Inge, *Christian Mysticism*, p. 232.
15. Guyon, *Autobiography*, part 1, ch. 8.
16. See Louis Dupré, "Jansenism and Quietism," in Dupré and Saliers, *Christian Spirituality*, pp. 136–37.
17. Fénelon, *Maxims of the Saints*, article 30, quoted in Upham, *Madame Guyon's Life*.
18. Quoted in Wakefield, *Dictionary*, p. 150, "Fénelon."
19. Fénelon, *Maxims of the Saints*, article 5, from Upham, *Madame Guyon's Life*.
20. Ibid., article 36.
21. Ibid., article 35.

CHAPTER 15: THE AGE OF ENLIGHTENMENT
1. Jane Shaw, in Harries and Mayr-Harting, *Christianity*, p. 173.
2. Quoted in Bainton, *Penguin History of Christianity*, p. 218.
3. Quoted in Graeff, *Light and the Rainbow*, p. 382.
4. de Caussade, *Present Moment*, p. 31.
5. de Caussade, *Abandonment to Divine Providence*, VA (*De la Vertu d'Abandon*) 1.2.3.
6. Ibid., VA 1.2.7.

7. Ibid., VA 1.2.1.
8. Ibid., VA 1.2.8–10.
9. de Caussade, *Present Moment*, p. 25.
10. de Caussade, *Abandonment to Divine Providence*, EA (*De l'Etat d'Abandon*) 2.2.6.
11. Ibid., EA 2.2.2.
12. Sampson, *History of English Literature*, p. 409.
13. Law, *Spirit of Prayer* 1.2.8.
14. Law, *Spirit of Love* 2.3.33.
15. Law, *Spirit of Prayer* 1.2.10.
16. Ibid., 1.2.16.
17. Ibid.
18. Ibid., 1.2.52.
19. Law, *Spirit of Love* 2.3.37.
20. Ibid., 2.3.49–50.
21. Ibid., 2.3.46.
22. Parrinder, *Mysticism*, p. 158.
23. Quoted in McManners, *Oxford History of Christianity*, p. 303.
24. Wesley, *Journal*, May 25, 1738.
25. Quoted in Bainton, *Penguin History of Christianity*, pp. 219–20.

Chapter 16: Romantics and Nature Mysticism

1. Quoted in Mursell, *Christian Spirituality*, p. 189 (author's emphasis).
2. Quoted in Ferguson, *Illustrated Encyclopedia of Mysticism*, p. 134.
3. Coleridge, *Biographia Literaria*, ch. 9.
4. Sampson, *History of English Literature*, p. 490.
5. Ackroyd, *Blake*, p. 23.
6. Letter to Thomas Butts, January 10, 1802, in Blake, *Selected Poems*, p. 297.
7. Blake, "The Garden of Love," in *Selected Poems*, p. 65.
8. Blake, "Mock on, mock on, Voltaire, Rousseau," from Poems from the Rossetti Ms., in *Selected Poems*, p. 79.
9. Blake, opening to "Auguries of Innocence," in *Selected Poems*, p. 107.
10. See prose note to "A Vision of the Last Judgment" in Poems from the Rossetti Ms., in *The Complete Poetry and Prose of William Blake*, edited by David V. Erdman (New York: Doubleday, 1988), p. 554.
11. Blake, "To the Christians," from *Jerusalem*, in *Selected Poems*, p. 251.
12. Blake, "The Marriage of Heaven and Hell," in *Selected Poems*, p. 146.
13. Quoted in Underhill, *Mysticism*, p. 259.
14. From *Descriptive Catalogue*, in Blake, *Selected Poems*, p. x.

15. Quoted by Northrop Frye, in Abrams, *English Romantic Poets*, p. 60.
16. Blake, lines from *Jerusalem*, in *Poems of William Blake*, p. 56.
17. Blake, "A Vision of England," from *Jerusalem*, in *Selected Poems*, p. 232.
18. Quoted in Ferguson, *Illustrated Encyclopedia of Mysticism*, p. 130.
19. Basil Willey, "On Wordsworth and the Locke Tradition," in Abrams, *English Romantic Poets*, p. 93.
20. Inge, *Christian Mysticism*, p. 307.

CHAPTER 17: THE MODERN AGE
1. Owen Chadwick, "Science and Religion," in McManners, *Oxford History of Christianity*, pp. 352–53.
2. Hampson, *Enlightenment*, p. 278.
3. Teilhard de Chardin, *Le Milieu Divin*, p. 13.
4. Ibid., p. 123.
5. Ibid., p. 117.
6. From "Christ in the World of Matter," in Teilhard de Chardin, *Hymn of the Universe*, p. 41.
7. Teilhard de Chardin, Pensée 15, in *Hymn of the Universe*, p. 81.
8. Teilhard de Chardin, *Le Milieu Divin*, p. 112.
9. Ibid., pp. 106–7.
10. Ibid., pp. 21–22; Teilhard de Chardin, Pensée 13, in *Hymn of the Universe*, p. 80.
11. Teilhard de Chardin, *Le Milieu Divin*, p. 37.
12. Teilhard de Chardin, *Phenomenon of Man*, p. 251.
13. Teilhard de Chardin, *Le Milieu Divin*, p. 38.
14. Ibid., p. 144.
15. Teilhard de Chardin, Pensée 9, in *Hymn of the Universe*, p. 77.
16. Teilhard de Chardin, *Le Milieu Divin*, p. 86.
17. Merton, *New Seeds of Contemplation*, p. 189.
18. Merton, *Seven Storey Mountain*, pp. 138–39.
19. Ibid., pp. 341–42.
20. Ibid., p. 501.
21. Merton, *New Seeds of Contemplation*, p. 13.
22. Merton, *Ascent to Truth*, p. 44.
23. Merton, *New Seeds of Contemplation*, pp. 13, 144.
24. Merton, *Ascent to Truth*, p. 46.
25. Merton, *New Seeds of Contemplation*, p. 181.
26. Ibid., p. 125.
27. Ibid., pp. 130–31.
28. Merton, *Ascent to Truth*, p. 46.
29. Merton, *New Seeds of Contemplation*, pp. 156–58.

Epilogue

1. "Thinking Anew," *Irish Times*, October, 25, 2003 (author's emphasis).
2. Mechthild of Magdeburg, *Flowing Light* 1.27.
3. Teresa of Ávila, *Interior Castle* 7.4, quoted in Graeff, *Light and the Rainbow*, p. 331.
4. Lawrence, Fourth Conversation, in *Presence of God*, p. 21.

SELECTED BIBLIOGRAPHY

Abrams, M. H., ed. *English Romantic Poets: Modern Essays in Criticism.* New York: Oxford University Press, 1960.

Ackroyd, Peter. *Blake.* London: Minerva, 1996.

Angela of Foligno. *Angela of Foligno: Complete Works.* Translated by Paul Lachance. New York: Paulist Press, 1993.

Augustine. *The Confessions.* Translated by R. S. Pine-Coffin. Harmondsworth, UK: Penguin Books, 1961.

———. *The Confessions.* Translated by E. B. Pusey. New York: J. M. Dent and Sons, 1953.

Bainton, Roland., *The Penguin History of Christianity.* Harmondsworth, UK: Penguin Books, 1967.

Bartlett, Anne Clark, ed. *Vox Mystica: Essays on Medieval Mysticism.* Cambridge: D. S. Brewer, 1995.

Beer, Frances. *Women and Mystical Experience in the Middle Ages.* Woodbridge, UK: Boydell Press, 1992.

Bernard of Clairvaux. *Selected Works.* Translated by G. R. Evans. New York: Paulist Press, 1987.

Blake, William. *Selected Poems of William Blake.* Oxford: Oxford University Press, 1927.

———. *Poems of William Blake.* Selected and Introduced by Peter Ackroyd. London: Sinclair-Stevenson, 1995.

Boehme, Jacob. *The Signature of All Things and Other Writings.* Cambridge: James Clarke and Co., 1969.

Bonaventure. *The Mind's Road to God.* Translated by George Boas. New York: Library of Liberal Arts, 1953.

Bowie, Fiona, ed., *Beguine Spirituality.* Translated by Oliver Davies. London: SPCK, 1989.

Brown, Peter. *The World of Late Antiquity.* London: Thames and Hudson, 1971.

Butler, Cuthbert. *Western Mysticism.* 2nd ed. London: Arrow Books, 1960.

Catherine of Genoa. *Purgation and Purgatory, The Spiritual Dialogue.* Translated by Serge Hughes. New York: Paulist Press, 1979.

Catherine of Siena. *Catherine of Siena: The Dialogue.* Translated by Suzanne Noffke. New York: Paulist Press, 1980.

Chadwick, Henry. *The Early Church.* Rev. ed. London: Penguin Books, 1993.

Coleman, T. W. *English Mystics of the Fourteenth Century.* London: Epworth Press, 1938.

Coleridge, Samuel Taylor. *Biographia Literaria.* London: Dent, 1965.

Cox, Michael. *Mysticism: The Direct Experience of God.* Wellingborough, UK: Aquarian Press, 1983.

Deanesly, Margaret. *A History of the Medieval Church: 590–1500.* London: Methuen, 1973.

de Caussade, Jean Pierre. *Abandonment to Divine Providence.* Translated by E. J. Strickland. St. Louis, MO: B. Herder Book Co., 1921.

——. *The Sacrament of the Present Moment.* Translated by K. Muggeridge. London: Fount Paperbacks, 1981.

Dionysius the Areopagite. *The Divine Names and The Mystical Theology.* Translated by C. E. Rolt. London: SPCK, 1940.

Dronke, Peter. *Women Writers of the Middle Ages.* Cambridge: Cambridge University Press, 1984.

Dupré, Louis, and Don E. Saliers, eds. *Christian Spirituality III: Post-Reformation and Modern.* New York: Crossroad, 1989.

Eckhart, Meister. *Selected Writings.* Translated by Oliver Davies. London: Penguin Books, 1994.

Fanning, Steven. *Mystics of the Christian Tradition.* London: Routledge, 2001.

Ferguson, John. *An Illustrated Encyclopedia of Mysticism and the Mystery Religions.* London: Thames and Hudson, 1976.

Forman, Robert K. C. *Meister Eckhart: Mystic as Theologian.* Shaftesbury, UK: Element, 1991.

Fox, George. *Journal.* Edited by Rufus M. Jones. New York: Capricorn Books, 1963.

Francis de Sales. *Introduction to the Devout Life.* Translated by John K. Ryan. New York: Image Books, 1972.

Francis of Assisi. *Francis and Clare: The Complete Works.* Translated by Regis J. Armstrong and Ignatius C. Brady. New York: Paulist Press, 1982.

———. *The Little Flowers of St. Francis, The Mirror of Reflection, The Life of St. Francis.* London: J. M. Dent, 1910.

French, R. M., trans. *The Way of a Pilgrim.* London: SPCK, 1941.

Furlong, Monica. *Medieval Women Mystics.* London: Mowbray, 1966.

Gascoigne, Bamber. *The Christians.* London: Granada, 1978.

Glasscoe, Marion. *English Medieval Mystics: Games of Faith.* Harlow: Longman, 1993.

Graeff, Hilda. *The Light and the Rainbow.* London: Longmans, Green and Co., 1959.

Guyon, Madame. *Autobiography of Madame Guyon.* Chicago: Moody Press, 1985.

Harries, Richard, and Henry Mayr-Harting, eds. *Christianity: Two Thousand Years.* Oxford: Oxford University Press, 2001.

Hampson, Norman. *The Enlightenment.* London: Penguin Books, 1982.

Happold, F. C. *Mysticism.* Harmondsworth, UK: Penguin Books, 1963.

Hay, Denys. *The Medieval Centuries.* London: Methuen, 1964.

Hildegard of Bingen, *Hildegard of Bingen: Scivias.* Translated by Columba Hart and Jane Bishop. New York: Paulist Press, 1990.

Hilton, Walter. *The Ladder of Perfection.* Translated by Leo Sherley-Price. Harmondsworth, UK: Penguin Books, 1957.

Inge, W. R. *Christian Mysticism.* London: Methuen, 1899.

———. *Light, Life, and Love: Selections from the German Mystics of the Middle Ages.* London: Methuen, 1904.

John of the Cross. *Complete Works.* Translated and edited by E. Allison Peers. London: Burns Oates, 1934.

———. *The Mystical Doctrine of St. John of the Cross.* Translated by David Lewis, revised by Benedict Zimmerman. London: Sheed and Ward, 1934.

———. *Poems.* Translated by Roy Campbell. Harmondsworth, UK: Penguin Books, 1960.

Johnson, Paul. *A History of Christianity.* London: Penguin Books, 1976.

Julian of Norwich. *A Revelation of Love.* Edited by Marion Glasscoe. Exeter, UK: University of Exeter Press, 1986.

———. *Revelations of Divine Love.* Edited by Grace Warrack. London: Methuen and Co., 1901.

Law, William. *Spirit of Love.* London: G. Robinson and J. Roberts, 1752.

———. *Spirit of Prayer.* 4th ed. London: J. Richardson, 1758.

Lawrence, Brother. *The Practice of the Presence of God*. Translated by Donald Attwater. Oxford: Oneworld, 1993.

Leff, Gordon. *Medieval Thought: St Augustine to Ockham*. Harmondsworth, UK: Penguin Books, 1958.

Lossky, Vladimir. *The Mystical Theology of the Eastern Church*. Cambridge, UK: James Clarke and Co., 1991.

Louth, Andrew. *The Origins of the Christian Mystical Tradition*. Oxford: Clarendon Press, 1981.

Luscombe, David. *Medieval Thought*. Oxford: Oxford University Press, 1997.

Maddocks, Fiona. *Hildegard of Bingen: The Woman of Her Age*. London: Headline, 2001.

Malone, Mary T. *Women and Christianity*. Vol. 2, *The Medieval Period, AD 1000–1500*. Dublin: Columba Press, 2001.

McGinn, Bernard. *The Flowering of Mysticism*. New York: Crossroad, 1998.

———. *The Foundations of Christian Mysticism*. New York: Crossroad, 1992.

———. *The Growth of Mysticism*. New York: Crossroad, 1994.

———, ed. *Meister Eckhart and the Beguine Mystics*. New York: Continuum, 1997.

McGinn, Bernard, John Meyendorff, and Jean Leclerq, eds. *Christian Spirituality I: Origins to the Twelfth Century*. New York: Crossroad, 1985.

McManners, John, ed. *The Oxford History of Christianity*. Oxford: Oxford University Press, 1993.

Mechthild of Magdeburg. *The Revelations of Mechthild of Magdeburg, or The Flowing Light of the Godhead*. Translated by Lucy Menzies. London: Longmans, Green and Co., 1953.

Merton, Thomas. *The Ascent to Truth*. London: Hollis and Carter, 1951.

———. *New Seeds of Contemplation*. London: Burns and Oates, 1962.

———. *The Seven Storey Mountain*. New York: Signet Books, 1952.

Mursell, Gordon, ed.*The Story of Christian Spirituality: Two Thousand Years from East to West*. Oxford: Lion Publishing, 2001.

Nuth, Joan M. *God's Lovers in an Age of Anxiety*. London: Darton, Longman and Todd, 2001.

O'Brien, Kate. *Teresa of Avila*. Cork: Mercier Press, 1951.

O'Meara, Dominic J. *Plotinus: An Introduction to the Enneads*. Oxford: Clarendon Press, 1995.

Origen. *On Prayer*. Translated by William A. Curtis. Published online by Nottingham Publishing, http://tedn.hypermart.net/origen.htm.

Palmer, G. E. H., Philip Sherrard, and Kallistos Ware, trans. and eds. *The Philokalia: The Complete Text.* Vols. 1 and 2. London: Faber and Faber, 1979 and 1981.

Parrinder, Geoffrey. *Mysticism in the World's Religions.* London: Sheldon Press, 1976.

Petroff, Elizabeth Alvilda. *Body and Soul: Essays on Medieval Women and Mysticism.* Oxford: Oxford University Press, 1994.

Plotinus, *The Enneads.* Translated by Stephen MacKenna. London: Penguin Books, 1991.

Pollard, William F., and Robert Boenig. *Mysticism and Spirituality in Medieval England.* Cambridge: D. S. Brewer, 1997.

Porete, Marguerite. *The Mirror of Simple Souls.* Translated by Edmund Colledge, J. C. Marler, and Judith Grant. Notre Dame, IN: University of Notre Dame Press, 1999.

———. *The Mirror of Simple Souls.* Translated by Ellen L. Babinsky. Mahwah, NJ: Paulist Press, 1993.

Raitt, Jill, ed. *Christian Spirituality II: High Middle Ages and Reformation.* New York: Crossroad, 1988.

Richard of St. Victor, *Richard of St. Victor: The Twelve Patriarchs, The Mystical Ark, Book Three of the Trinity.* Translated by Grover A. Zinn. New York: Paulist Press, 1979.

Roberts, Alexander, and James Donaldson, eds. *The Ante-Nicene Fathers: The Writings of the Fathers Down to AD 325.* 10 vols. Grand Rapids, MI: William B. Eerdmans Publishing (various reprints).

Rolle, Richard. *The Fire of Love.* Translated by Richard Misyn. 2nd ed. London: Methuen and Co., 1920.

———. *The Fire of Love.* Translated by Clifton Wolters. Harmondsworth, UK: Penguin Books, 1972.

Rousseau, Philip. *Ascetics, Authority, and the Church in the Age of Jerome and Cassian.* Oxford: Oxford University Press, 1978.

Ruysbroeck, Jan van. *The Adornment of the Spiritual Marriage.* Translated by C. A. Wynschenck. London: J. M. Dent and Sons, 1916.

Sampson, George. *The Concise Cambridge History of English Literature.* Cambridge: Cambridge University Press, 1970.

Schaff, P., and H. Wace, eds. *A Select Library of the Nicene and Post-Nicene Fathers of the Christian Church.* Vols. 1–14. Second Series. Grand Rapids, MI: William B. Eerdmans Publishing (various reprints).

Scott, Martin. *Medieval Europe.* London: Longmans, Green and Co., 1964.

Southern, R.W. *Western Society and the Church in the Middle Ages.* Harmondsworth, UK: Penguin Books, 1970.

Spencer, Sidney. *Mysticism in World Religion.* Harmondsworth, UK: Penguin Books, 1963.

Stace, Walter T. *The Teachings of the Mystics.* New York: Mentor Books, 1960.

Suso, Henry. *The Exemplar, with Two German Sermons.* Edited by Frank Tobin, New York: Paulist Press, 1989.

———. *Henry Suso: Little Book of Eternal Wisdom and Little Book of Truth.* Translated and edited by James M. Clark. London: Faber and Faber, 1953.

Symeon the New Theologian. *The Discourses.* Translated by C. J. de Catanzaro. New York: Paulist Press, 1980.

———. *On the Mystical Life: The Ethical Discourses.* Vol. 2: *On Virtue and Christian Life.* Translated by Alexander Golitzin. Crestwood, NY: St. Vladimir's Seminary Press, 1996.

Tauler, John. *The Inner Way: 36 Sermons for Festivals.* 2nd ed. Translated by Arthur Wollaston Hutton. London: Methuen and Co., 1909.

———. *Johannes Tauler: Sermons.* Translated by Maria Shrady. New York: Paulist Press, 1985.

Teilhard de Chardin, Pierre. *Hymn of the Universe.* Translated by Gerald Vann. London: Fontana, 1970.

———. *Le Milieu Divin.* Edited by Bernard Wall, et al.

———. *The Phenomenon of Man.* Translated by Bernard Wall. London: Collins, 1961.

Teresa of Ávila. *Complete Works.* Translated and edited by E. Allison Peers. New York: Sheed and Ward, 1946.

———. *The Life of Saint Teresa of Ávila by Herself.* Translated by J. M. Cohen. Harmondsworth, UK: Penguin Books, 1957.

Underhill, Evelyn, ed. *The Cloud of Unknowing.* 2nd ed. London: John M. Watkins, 1922.

———. *Mysticism.* Oxford: Oneworld, 1991.

Upham, T. C. *The Story of Madame Guyon's Life.* Atlanta, GA: Christian Books, 1984.

Vryonis, Speros. *Byzantium and Europe.* London: Thames and Hudson, 1967.

Wakefield, Gordon S., ed. *A Dictionary of Christian Spirituality.* London: SCM Press, 1983.

Ware, Timothy. *The Orthodox Church.* Harmondsworth, UK: Penguin Books, 1963.

Weeks, Andrew. *Boehme: An Intellectual Biography of the Seventeenth-Century Philosopher and Mystic.* Albany: State University of New York Press, 1991.

Wesley, John. *The Journal of John Wesley.* Edited by Percy Livingstone Parker. Chicago: Moody Press, 1951.

Williams, Rowan. *The Wound of Knowledge.* London: Darton, Longman and Todd, 1979.

Wolters, Clifton, trans. *The Cloud of Unknowing.* Harmondsworth, UK: Penguin Books, 1961.

Woods, Richard. *Mysticism and Prophecy: The Dominican Tradition.* London: Darton, Longman and Todd, 1998.

——, ed. *Understanding Mysticism.* London: Athlone Press, 1981.

Wordsworth, William. *The Poetical Works.* Oxford: Clarendon Press, 1947.

Zaehner, R. C. *Mysticism: Sacred and Profane.* Oxford University Press, Oxford: 1961.